A Tale of
Three Cities

CLASS AND CULTURE
A series edited by
Milton Cantor and Bruce Laurie

A Tale of Three Cities

Labor Organization
and Protest in Paterson,
Passaic, and Lawrence,
1916–1921

DAVID J. GOLDBERG

RUTGERS UNIVERSITY PRESS
New Brunswick and London

Library of Congress Cataloging-in-Publication Data

Goldberg, David J.
    A tale of three cities : labor organization and protest in
Paterson, Passaic, and Lawrence, 1916–1921 / David J. Goldberg.
        p.   cm.—(Class and culture)
    Bibliography: p.
    Includes index.
    ISBN 0–8135–1371–5   ISBN 0–8135–1372–3 (pbk.).
    1. Amalgamated Textile Workers of America—History.   2. Trade-
unions—Textile workers–New Jersey—Paterson—History—20th
century.   3. Trade-unions—Textile workers–New Jersey—Passaic—
History—20th century.   4. Trade-unions—Textile workers—
Massachusetts—Lawrence—History—20th century.   I. Title.
II. Series.
HD6515.T42A454   1989
331.88'177'00974—dc 19   88–15812
                                                                                          CIP

British Cataloging-in-Publication information available

Copyright © 1989 by Rutgers, The State University
All Rights Reserved
Manufactured in the United States of America

In memory of my parents,
Jerry and Sophie Goldberg,
who taught me how to live

Contents

List of Tables

Preface

This work originated out of my interest in the Lawrence textile strike of 1919 and my desire to learn how A. J. Muste had come to play a leadership role in that walkout. While engaged in this research, I became aware of similar upsurges in Paterson and Passaic and the efforts of labor organizers in all three cities to create a new union, the Amalgamated Textile Workers of America. As I embarked on a history of the organization's three key locals, I realized that only by exploring the inner workings of the labor movement in each city could I understand the union's fate. This led me to make numerous trips to Paterson, Passaic, and Lawrence to do research in local libraries, to talk to local residents, and simply to walk the streets of each city. This has proven valuable both in a research sense and in an educational sense as I have become acquainted with people who have fought for survival in the face of capital flight and deindustrialization.

During the time that I have been working on this project I have received the assistance of a number of academics, librarians, and residents of Paterson, Passaic, and Lawrence. I would especially like to thank Jim Borchert, Ciele Bucki, Elizabeth Chadis, Eartha Dengler, Daniel Downey, Eric Foner, Kenneth Fones-Wolf, Gary Gerstle, Mollie Pluhar, Julianna Puskás, Phillip Scranton, Tom Shear, Claire Sheridan, Jonas Stundza, and Daniel Tanzone. Dorothy Fennell and Joe Mesar proved faithful friends and helped me find employment that sustained the research. My sister Judith Hayman and Bob Harris, Lisel Burns, Janet Traynor, Mark Joy, and Jean Niccolazzo made my stays in New York and Washington enjoyable and economical. Lue-Venia Richardson has done a superb job in preparing the manuscript and Marlie Wasserman has been an extremely supportive editor. Financial aid from the Museum of American Textile History and the New Jersey Historical Society has also been of great assistance.

When I was an undergraduate at the University of Wisconsin, the late Harvey Goldberg first gave me a vision of the way I would like to approach the teaching and writing of history. Jim Shenton warmly welcomed me back to graduate school and has been a friend as well as an adviser. David Montgomery provided me with invaluable advice, encouragement, and criticism when this project was at the dissertation stage and Bruce Laurie and Milton Cantor have given me guidance on how to approach making the final revisions. To all of them I am deeply grateful.

Susan Hunt has aided this undertaking in her own very special ways. Without her support, interest, and good humor it would have been far more difficult to complete this project.

Abbreviations Used in Text

ACLU   American Civil Liberties Union
ACWA   Amalgamated Clothing Workers of America
AFL   American Federation of Labor
AFTO   American Federation of Textile Operatives
ASW   Associated Silk Workers
ATWA   Amalgamated Textile Workers of America
CLU   Central Labor Union
IWW   Industrial Workers of the World
NIUTW National Industrial Union of Textile Workers
NWLB   National War Labor Board
OBU   One Big Union
PTLC   Passaic Trades and Labor Council
SLP   Socialist Labor Party
SP   Socialist Party

Abbreviations Used in Text

UGW	United Garment Workers
UTW	United Textile Workers
WCU	Workers' Cooperative Union
WIIU	Workers' International Industrial Union
YPIL	Young Peoples International League

A Tale of
Three Cities

Chapter One

INTRODUCTION

In 1928, J.B.S. Hardmann looked back on the strike wave of 1919 and mused: "The language that we used then no longer sounds familiar to our ears. The emotions that overwhelmed people in those momentous days fails to excite us today."[1] Indeed, it must have been painful for workers as well as for labor activists to recall the disappointments of the postwar period. For in 1919, American workers staged a series of uprisings that momentarily challenged employers' control of the workplace, while by 1923, the labor movement had practically given up all thought of conducting offensive struggles.

The textile strikes that erupted simultaneously in Paterson and Passaic, New Jersey, and Lawrence, Massachusetts, on 3 February 1919, along with the Seattle, Washington, general strike and the revolt of the Butte, Montana, copper miners, set the stage for much of the labor activity of that year. In the case of the textile workers, the three strikes led directly to the formation of a new union, the Amalgamated Textile Workers of America (ATWA), which was headed by A. J. Muste, who had only recently left the ministry, and was sponsored by the Amalgamated

Clothing Workers of America (ACWA). The ACWA itself was only five years old. It had been established in 1914 by Sidney Hillman and other members of the United Garment Workers (UGW) who bolted from that union out of dissatisfaction with its craft structure and lack of interest in organizing immigrant workers. As one of the leading exponents of the "new unionism," the ACWA anticipated duplicating its success in the clothing field in the textile industry, which included cotton, woolen, silk, and a number of other specialty branches.[2]

For the most part, historians have paid little attention to the textile strikes or to the ATWA's efforts to organize the textile industry.[3] One reason for this neglect is that historians have treated the 1912–1913 strikes that were led by the Industrial Workers of the World (IWW) as an end rather than as a beginning point.[4] This emphasis on the Wobbly era can be misleading as these years represented only the early phase of an immigrant labor revolt that stretched from 1909 through 1922.[5] More particularly, the World War I era (1916–1921) constitutes a distinct epoch in the history of textile and other working-class communities. In a mere five-year span, workers rebounded from the 1913–1915 depression and once again challenged employers (1916), accumulated grievances during the period of United States involvement in the war (1917–1918), participated in mass strikes and union organizing efforts in the immediate postwar era (1919), and saw their hopes dashed by a new employer offensive and by another depression (1920–1921). The economic downturn crushed the ATWA's hopes, but one must remember that the union's founders had no premonition of the disaster that would leave many northern textile towns in a permanent state of depression. Instead, they approached their task with the expectation that it would be possible to create a vibrant, socialist-oriented industrial union in the textile industry.

Of course, textiles like the steel, meat-packing, and other mass-production industries had proven extremely difficult to organize. The work force was largely composed of immigrants who, as participants in an international labor stream, often viewed their jobs as being merely temporary. These immigrants came from diverse backgrounds and shared neither a common culture nor language. They were products of foreign environments, and the republican heritage that shaped much of the ideology of American workers in the nineteenth century meant little or nothing to them. Women composed approximately one-half of the work force and moved in and out of the mills depending on their family situation. Of most consequence, textiles as the advance guard of the industrial revolution had been the first industry in which the adoption of power-driven machinery had enabled capitalists to break jobs down into repetitive and routinized tasks performed by semiskilled operatives who required only a short period of training to learn their jobs. As a result, textile workers had been subjected to rigid work discipline and had proven relatively easy to replace during and after labor disputes.

Two national unions, the United Textile Workers (UTW) and the IWW had made efforts to organize the textile industry. The UTW was founded in 1901 when a number of craft unions joined together and received a charter from the American Federation of Labor (AFL). The AFL granted the UTW jurisdiction over the entire textile industry and the union's structure is most appropriately termed craft/industrial though in practice it remained essentially a federation of skilled crafts. Dominated by workers of British and Irish origin, it had enrolled large numbers of cotton and silk workers but had hardly made a dent in the woolen and worsted sectors.[6] Its leadership was extremely conservative and the UTW's president, John B. Golden, also served on the board of directors of the militantly antisocialist, Catholic workers association, the Militia of Christ.[7]

The IWW had employed a diametrically opposite approach as its belief in the need for "one big union" stemmed from its conviction that the capitalist mode of production had rendered craft distinctions meaningless.[8] During the Wobblies' eastern foray between 1909 and 1913, textile workers responded with more enthusiasm than any other group of employees to the IWW's advocacy of revolutionary industrial unionism. Whether they won as in Lawrence or lost as in Paterson, these walkouts demonstrated that the wage struggles of textile workers, which were endemic in this era of inflation, could be used to give voice to far broader social and political goals. And it was not just in Lawrence and Paterson that Big Bill Haywood, Elizabeth Gurley Flynn, and Carlo Tresca received a tumultuous welcome since mill hands in other textile cities such as Passaic; Lowell, Massachusetts; and Little Falls, New York, also fought strikes under the IWW banner.[9]

Despite the positive reception, the Wobblies only built permanent locals in a few cities and by 1916, their textile branch, the National Industrial Union of Textile Workers (NIUTW) had been reduced to a paper organization. Lawrence demonstrated most vividly how quickly a union victory could turn to dust. During the 1912 walkout that came to be known as the Bread and Roses strike, workers used the setting provided by a small industrial city to their advantage. Workers' control of the streets prevented the manufacturers from bringing in strikebreakers and the constant round of rallies and demonstrations built the confidence of mill hands. But shortly after the strike's conclusion, city officials and church authorities led an anti-IWW campaign while manufacturers engaged in blacklisting and selective mill closings that destroyed the IWW local.

Those who founded the ATWA hoped to rectify what they perceived as the IWW's errors. Modeled on the ACWA, the ATWA resembled the clothing workers' union as it believed in signing contracts, hiring a well-paid staff, and having a strong central office. Brought together by the 1919 textile strikes, its leaders firmly believed that a different type of industrial union could succeed in organizing the textile industry.

Rather than write a history of the ATWA, which at its peak enrolled 50,000 workers in over thirty locals, I have chosen to concentrate on the three cities in which the union invested its greatest hopes. As medium-sized industrial cities, Paterson, Passaic, and Lawrence offered a good opportunity to explore the advantages and disadvantages of that particular setting for labor organization.[10] These cities also suited my purposes for a number of other reasons. For one, all had been centers of IWW activity and thus provided a means to evaluate the Wobbly legacy. Second, since a number of antiwar activists served on the staff of the three locals, I had a unique opportunity to measure the difficulties that pacifists encountered in the labor movement. Third, all three cities remained centers of militant labor activity in the 1920s as long strikes occurred in 1922, 1924, and 1926 in Lawrence, Paterson, and Passaic respectively, so the union's failure could not be ascribed totally to the ability of the manufacturers and the state to quash labor activity. Last, I believe that it is only through an intensive examination of the local context that one can understand the extraordinarily complicated dynamics that make the American working class both so fascinating and frustrating to study.

My goal is to understand the reasons why it was so difficult to organize industrial unions in the United States. I have analyzed a variety of external and internal factors, but also in each city I have had to confront the problems posed by the differing political and cultural traditions of ethnic groups. Although most labor historians would agree that it is not possible to study industrial workers in the early twentieth century without an understanding of ethnicity, they have for the most part avoided examining how the diverse orientations of ethnic groups aided or hindered the organization of industrial unions. The most systematic interpretation has been offered by the sociologist Gerald Rosenblum, who has argued that since most immigrants had only the most immediate of goals, their presence in America prevented a radical labor movement from developing.[11] This is a position that I find untenable as it lumps all immigrant groups together in a way that obscures differences between the Irish and the Germans, the Czechs and the Slovaks, to cite only a few examples. Or to put it another way, one needs to examine the experience of particular immigrant groups rather than make generalizations about immigrant workers.[12] At the same time he has deepened our under-standing of the lives of immigrant workers, John Bodnar has argued that they had a conservative impact because he believes that family concerns almost exclusively determined their outlooks.[13] Significantly, Bodnar has paid little attention to how the world war and the rising tide of national-ism affected various immigrant groups.[14] And from his account, one would hardly be aware of the fierce battles that often divided Slovaks and Magyars or Italians and South Slavs in the mill towns.

To borrow a phrase normally used in a different context, the Ameri-can working class had an uneven rate of development. For example, in Lawrence, the viewpoint of French Canadians clashed with that of Franco Belgians, and in Passaic, the perspective of Poles differed from that of Magyars. In making this argument, I have been influenced by the works of Bruce Laurie and Peter Friedlander, who have demonstrated how the different world views of traditionalists and cosmopolites could make it difficult to built a united labor movement.[15] Though Laurie and Friedlander wrote about labor in the early nineteenth century and the 1930s respectively, I believe this framework is particularly useful for understanding the late nineteenth and early twentieth centuries, an era when immigrants formed an extremely high percentage of the American working class.[16]

A word of explanation about the format of the book is in order. The second chapter analyzes the wartime developments in all three communi-ties that led directly to the 1919 labor revolt. In chapters three through five, an account of the industrial settings, the immigrant groups, and the labor traditions of all three cities precedes a narrative of the 1919 events. Considerable attention is devoted to background material in this section as the local context varied so much from city to city. Chapter six treats the ACWA's role in the union's founding and the ATWA leadership and program, and it concludes with a comparison of the labor movements in Passaic and Lawrence. Chapters seven through nine cover the history of the ATWA local in each city, and a concluding chapter analyzes the various internal forces that led to the union's demise.

Chapter Two

THE WAR
AND THE TEXTILE WORKER

Wartime Prosperity and the Mill Worker

For textile manufacturers as well as for much of American industry 1913 and 1914 had been lean years. But by January 1916, American mill owners began to enjoy a three-year stretch of record-breaking profits. Silk manufacturers benefited from the war because silk was used in the production of powder bags and airplane cloth and because wartime prosperity led to increased consumer purchases of silk goods. By March 1916, the Silk Association of America reported that the industry was in the midst of a "boom" and that "every conceivable branch" was "strained to its capacity to meet the sudden enormous demand." The boom lasted right up until the Armistice and if there were idle looms in Paterson, it was only because the silk mills could not secure sufficient help.[1]

The gains made by the woolen and worsted manufacturers were even more impressive. These firms also benefited from the renewed prosperity in 1916, and once the United States entered the war in April 1917, they turned out vast quantities of cloth used in the manufacture of woolen blankets, trousers, overcoats, flannel shirts, and stockings. Over one-half of the machinery at the giant Pacific and Arlington mills in Lawrence and the Botany and Forstmann & Huffmann mills in Passaic was devoted to the production of goods required by the military. The greatest beneficiary of all was the largest firm in the entire textile industry, the American Woolen Company, which had extensive operations in Lawrence. Founded in 1899 in the midst of a merger wave that swept across much of American industry, this corporation had proven a disappointment to investors. But once the war began, it started aggressively to challenge British control of overseas markets. Of equal importance, what had been its greatest weakness—the overconcentration on the production of plain fabrics—became a strength, as these were precisely the types of goods required by the military. When the company's president, William M. Wood, declared that the war had "saved" American woolen mills, he was actually referring to his own firm, whose future had been very much in doubt before the firing began in Europe.[2]

Full-time operations were not a new phenomenon in Passaic, where the mills had operated on a fairly steady basis, but previously Passaic mill owners had always had a large pool of prospective employees to choose from whereas now they found it "almost impossible to replace vacancies" in low-paying or physically demanding jobs. In addition, since work was now plentiful in the Passaic area, mill employees could switch positions as soon as they became "uneasy" or "dissatisfied" with conditions in their particular rooms.[3] On the other hand, year-round employment was a new experience for many mill workers in Paterson and Lawrence. In Paterson, good years had been followed by lean years because the silk industry was more susceptible to changes in fashions than any other branch of the textile industry. In Lawrence, the American Woolen Company's erratic performance meant that many workers averaged only nine or ten months of employment in a normal year and suffered from massive layoffs during the 1907–1908 and 1913–1915 economic downturns.[4]

Even when fully employed, textile workers earned wages that were among the lowest received by all other industrial employees. In 1916, the average yearly earnings of New Jersey's woolen and worsted workers amounted to $575.73. Only workers in lamps and in cigars and tobacco (of twenty-five industries measured by the New Jersey Bureau of Industrial Statistics) made less. Even after receiving a considerable pay hike in August 1918, Paterson's 5,000 dyehouse employees still earned only $20 per week.[5] Prewar or wartime figures for Lawrence are not available, but at one large mill in March 1919 the male employees averaged $22 per week and the female employees $17.50 per week—this at a time when a family of five required a weekly income of $26.25 year-round to maintain a minimal standard of living.[6] Of course, textile workers commonly depended on a family wage so that in an optimal situation where a husband, wife, and children were employed, family income could be well above this amount. Money became scarce when a family member was sick or injured, when children were too young to work, or when dull times cut into family income. At moments such as these, a slim margin of existence could be reduced to a bare thread, which is why the Lawrence City Council had to vote special appropriations for soup kitchens to enable textile mill employees to survive the harsh depression winter of 1914–1915.[7] Slender earnings meant that before the war the concept of an American standard of living had little relevance for most textile workers.[8] Although ethnic historians are now locked in a debate as to whether immigrants from southern and eastern Europe came to America as part of a quest for social mobility or for security, in truth few textile workers had achieved either of these goals on the eve of the Great War.[9]

Once the economy picked up in early 1916, textile mill employees quickly recognized that the balance of power had shifted in their favor. Along with workers in many parts of the nation, mill hands in Paterson, Passaic and Lawrence, all won significant gains by striking or by merely threatening to strike in the spring of 1916.[10] In order to stem further unrest, mill owners in all three cities began to grant periodic "voluntary" wage increases. According to the American Woolen Company, its seven wartime wage increases advanced employees' pay 87 percent with a disproportionate share going to the unskilled, a standard practice of employers who for the first time had to worry about holding their lowest-paid employees.[11] The Arlington and the Pacific mills had been forced to follow the American Woolen Company's lead and mills in Passaic and Paterson had also announced wage hikes while stressing their "voluntary" aspect.[12] For two years, this strategy proved successful as workers in all three cities remained quiet between May 1916 and May 1918 before beginning a new round of strikes in the spring of 1918.

It is difficult to calculate the extent to which workers benefited from these increases since the cost of living soared between 1916 and 1918. Fortunately, there is relatively exact information available for Lawrence because the corporate-sponsored National Industrial Conference Board conducted a detailed examination of the rise in the cost of living that occurred in that city between November 1914 and November 1919. According to their findings, for a family trying to maintain a minimal standard of living prices had increased 84 percent although advances ranged from a low of 35 percent for shelter to a high of 120 percent for clothing.[13] The cost of food had increased 95 percent and Lawrence had the second highest prices for food of ninety-one cities surveyed by the U.S. Department of Labor.[14] And even these figures may underestimate the actual cost of provisions as immigrants normally shopped in ethnic food stores where prices were higher than in large groceries.[15] Paterson and Passaic workers also suffered from rising food costs, but workers in these two cities voiced far more concern over steep hikes in their rents. Paterson suffered a severe housing shortage as home building ceased while its population grew because the city had a number of munitions plants. Landlords, dubbed "rent sharks" by the local press, sharply increased their rents, which forced many families to double up.[16] In Passaic, where over 90 percent of all mill employees were tenants, building owners often raised rents immediately after pay hikes, leading one worker to wonder "what use we get more pay" as any increase was quickly swallowed up by landlords and grocers.[17]

While the increases in costs of food, rent, and other items make it unlikely that individual employees realized anything more than a 10 percent increase in real wages, the fact that entire families were steadily employed for three years allowed many immigrants to catch a glimpse of a better life for the first time since their arrival in America.[18] But the mills' great profits led many workers to wonder who had really gained the most from the war and many employees may have believed, as did those in Winnipeg, Canada, that "inflation was ruining their living standards and destroying their wage increases."[19]

Wartime Labor Unrest

On the shop floor, the war had a paradoxical effect as workers heard incessant cries to step up production while the favorable employment situation meant that many employees for the first time could risk defying their bosses. In Lawrence, for example, some employees "dared to 'speak' to their overseers at their work" without fear of being fired. Many workers also could risk taking a day off.[20] Some of these changes survived well into the postwar period. As late as 1921, an investigator hired by the Botany company noted that the war had "a decided influence for the worse" as it established "careless" work habits and led to work being done in a "superficial way."[21]

Due to the labor shortages, employees won unprecedented concessions from employers. In Passaic, as soon as the female menders and burlers at the Gera Mill expressed dissatisfaction with their pay, the foremen adjusted their rates to guarantee them a more equitable wage. On other occasions, the mill gave weavers samples to run in order to hold them (whereas previously they would have been told to take some time off) and hiked the wages of its unskilled help as soon as they talked about taking jobs at another plant.[22] Because it wished to reduce its high turnover rate, Forstmann & Huffmann became the first Passaic company to install an employee cafeteria, and all Passaic mills began to distribute items such as butter, flour, and sugar at wholesale cost.[23] In Lawrence, the American Woolen Company granted a 15 percent premium on the difficult-to-weave single yarn and the Arlington Mill, for the first time, hired a company nurse and a part-time physician.[24] And in Paterson, ribbon manufacturers faced with an extreme scarcity of labor, guaranteed all weavers a minimum weekly wage of $18—a demand that mill owners for a long time had strongly resisted.[25]

These gains need to be balanced against speedups that forced mill hands to work "like horses" with "no minute of rest" because government orders required "superhuman efforts."[26] According to one Lawrence worker, "every time they raised my pay they used to speed up my machine. They would say: 'You are being paid more; now you'll have to do more.' They wouldn't let me stop the machine when I cleaned it. I had to clean it at the risk of my hands."[27] Woolen and worsted employees suffered special annoyances because they had to work with the coarse wool that was used for army blankets. The sharpest contrast between peacetime and wartime goods came at the Forstmann & Huffmann company, which normally specialized in making some of the finest and lightest worsted products. Mollie Pluhar, the daughter of a Forstmann & Huffmann spinner, remembers that her father became "disgusted" with the heavy and "foul smelling wool" and resented the mills for making large profits through the sale of inferior products to the government.[28] These changes also bothered weavers since they could not make their "usual and proportionate pay" on the slow-running goods to which they were not accustomed.[29]

By the winter of 1917–1918, other vexations affected the lives of textile workers. Consumer items such as sugar became unavailable, solicitations for Liberty Loan and Red Cross drives reduced workers' earnings, wool and coal shortages forced mill closings, and the coal shortage meant that many families lacked coal during the coldest months of the year. As these hurts festered, workers wearied of calls for stepped-up production that accompanied newspaper reports of skyrocketing profits.[30] For these reasons, a new round of work stoppages broke out in all three cities during the spring and summer of 1918. These walkouts further demonstrated that workers had learned to use labor shortages to their advantage. On the other hand, strikers proved vulnerable to charges of disloyalty and of interfering with military production. Therefore, it remained difficult to carry out long strikes while the country was at war. And in Passaic, workers learned that mill officials could use threats of federal intervention in order to put a damper on strike activity.

The most successful of these work stoppages occurred in Lawrence where in July 1918, 1,800 American Woolen Company weavers struck in order to secure the abolishment of a premium system of pay. Anger at the "bonus" had figured prominently in the 1912 strike when it had been altered so that payment was calculated biweekly rather than monthly. Even with this modification, weavers could still lose a big chunk of their earnings if they became ill or had bad material or malfunctioning looms. Consequently, weavers demanded an end to the premium and a 55 percent increase over the base rate. William M. Wood reacted to the weavers' demands by threatening that the government would conscript the strikers and by charging that those of Italian and Belgian origin were undermining the cause of their compatriots overseas. For all of his bluster, Wood feared losing government orders. Thus, after his mills had been crippled for a week, Wood consented to intervention by Henry Endicott, an arbitrator for the Massachusetts Committee for Public Safety who had become known for his pro-labor decisions. And sure enough, Endicott granted weavers practically all of their demands; the hated premium was abolished, wages were readjusted 50 percent over the old scale, and no strike participants lost their jobs. In return, weavers pledged to submit all further grievances during the war to arbitration.[31]

In Paterson, dyehouse employees sparked the renewed labor militancy. In April 1918, 5,000 of these workers staged a walkout in order to win a pay hike from $16 to $20 per week. Their demands focused exclusively on wages as workers maintained that the sharp increase in the cost of living made it "practically impossible for them to exist."[32] As was often the case in wartime strikes, governmental and company officials portrayed the participants as disloyal and the dyehouse owners released a statement that told workers: "Your patriotism is now being put to the test. . . . Patriotism at this time should be above price. Our boys, your boys in the trenches have put patriotism above life itself. What are you going to do about it?"[33] At the same time, a U.S. Department of Labor representative criticized the strikers and pressed for a quick settlement. This intimidation proved effective and after remaining out for two weeks, dyehouse employees accepted a compromise offer of $18 per week. However, these workers remained dissatisfied and in August 1918, they staged a second strike and finally won the $20 per-week rate.[34]

Only in Passaic did renewed militancy fail to bring substantial changes. Strike activity here centered on the Forstmann & Huffmann company, whose weavers walked out when the firm refused to grant them ten hours' pay for nine hours' work as had been given at the Botany company.[35] The 400 weavers also demanded extra compensation for difficult weaves, reinstatement of leaders who had been discharged, and the recognition of shop committees. The federal government took an active interest in the dispute and the Department of Labor assigned Joseph Buchanan, one of its conciliators, to Passaic. Buchanan attended strike meetings and informed the mill hands that the need to fulfill government orders meant that the company could not grant the shorter hours. He also told workers that the strike leaders were Bolsheviks and that the Department of Justice would prosecute the "agitators" if the walkout did not end immediately. Strikers faced other difficulties in organizing their protest. Since the outbreak of the war, the Forstmann & Huffmann company had maintained "a confidential corps" throughout its plants "for the purpose of watching for anything that might be of a seditious character." These agents monitored labor activity and forwarded their information to Washington. City officials denied strikers use of local halls, raided meetings and, in the most disruptive action, arrested forty-one strike participants on the grounds they were draft evaders. Eventually, the company broke the strike and the firm's president, Julius Forstmann, with Buchanan's blessing, fired 250 of the weavers.[36]

The result in Passaic varied from that in Paterson and Lawrence because Forstmann was adept at dealing with labor disturbances and because many Passaic workers were classified as alien enemies by the federal government and thus especially vulnerable to accusations of disloyalty. But even in Paterson and Lawrence, the 1918 walkouts did not spread beyond the immediate workplace where they began. Clearly during wartime, limits existed and sometimes they were self-imposed by workers who wished to support the war effort as well as imposed from without. For these reasons, grievances that workers nursed during the war would not be fully voiced until the end of hostilities. At that time, workers having been tutored in the art of propaganda would call upon employers to make some "sacrifices."

Enforced Patriotism and Immigrant Nationalism

During the war, public and private officials sponsored a host of speeches, rallies, and parades in order to inculcate immigrants with a sense of Americanism. The most intense efforts at building support for the American cause came at the time of the Liberty Loan drives, which were designed to drum up support for the war as well as to raise needed funds. The mill owners eagerly cooperated in these campaigns as the patriotic emphasis dovetailed with their own push to increase output. According to Lawrence resident Annie Trina, you could not go anywhere in the mills without seeing a sign that implored you to "Buy a Bond" or "Be Patriotic." Those who refused to purchase bonds faced harassment or disciplinary action.[37] Appeals to contribute to the Red Cross and to other war-related agencies became so frequent that some Lawrence workers claimed that they had "never brought a full pay home" since the war began.[38] In Passaic, "bond slacker" committees checked up on mill employees and the head of the Liberty Loan campaign informed nonsubscribers that they would find the city "a very unpleasant place to live."[39]

Wartime fund-raising drives were often conducted on an ethnic basis as their organizers hoped to stimulate sales by pitting one nationality against another. But on at least one occasion in Passaic, such a strategy backfired as unwitting city officials praised the Magyar showing in a War Savings Stamp drive while addressing a Slovak audience.[40] Their remarks enraged many of Passaic's Slovak residents (and almost led to a riot) as Slovaks resented Magyar domination of their homeland and often portrayed the Magyars as unpatriotic in order to boost their own national cause.[41]

This incident highlights a basic point—the war affected immigrant groups in widely divergent ways. Magyars and Germans may not have said so publicly after April 1917 but they often remained sympathetic to the Central Powers and resented the muzzling of their ethnic press and the closing of ethnic halls.[42] The war had a far different impact upon groups whose national aspirations depended upon an Allied victory. Syrians looked forward to the breakup of the Ottoman Empire. Many

Jews anticipated that the Balfour Declaration of 1917 would contribute to the establishment of a Jewish national homeland in Palestine; many Italians supported the war because they expected that an Allied victory would aid Italy's irredentist claims; and after Woodrow Wilson's Fourteen Points Address of January 1918, many Slavic peoples grew confident that pledges of self-determination would result in the creation of independent states for the various subject nationalities in the Austro-Hungarian Empire.[43]

In particular, since the Fourteen Points contained a specific promise of Polish independence, Polish ethnic leaders could intertwine the Polish and American causes. At one patriotic rally in Passaic, a Polish priest told the audience that "as we look at the American flag, in its colors we behold the colors of Poland itself. Its red stripes are truly a representation of the Polish blood. All of us must love that flag and never can our love for it come in conflict with our beloved Poland."[44] On other occasions, Polish priests claimed that Polish soldiers fought behind two flags, that of Poland and of America and objected to any display of the Hungarian flag while proudly exhibiting their own national banners.[45]

The war enhanced the standing of the ethnic bourgeoisie as they were often the most ardent proponents of self-determination. This troubled many socialists who knew it would be suicidal to oppose their own national struggles, yet who questioned how much workers and peasants would gain if they merely exchanged one set of oppressors for another. After the Bolshevik Revolution, many of these leftists looked to Lenin rather than to Wilson for inspiration and began to combine calls for national independence with revolutionary appeals.

Much of the material in the following chapters will be concerned with how various immigrant groups responded to the competing pulls of revolutionary socialism and of ethnic nationalism. To a certain extent, the ATWA's hopes for building a permanent industrial union foundered because many workers distrusted its overly reformist approach while others hesitated to subjugate their own national causes to the larger trade union ideal. The task of balancing various ideological and national loyalties was never to be as difficult as during the World War I era when many immigrant workers experienced a new burst of national pride while others hoped that a Russian-style revolution would occur in their homelands or even in the United States.

The Impact of State Intervention

The war led the Wilson administration to grant unprecedented recognition to the rights of labor. During his first term, the president had made a number of concessions to labor, but it was the need to arrange a quick settlement of wartime work stoppages that led Wilson to establish the National War Labor Board (NWLB), which beginning in April 1918 had the responsibility for settling disputes between labor and capital. During its short life span, NWLB decisions often granted employees the eight-hour day and recognized workers' right to organize. While its edicts aimed at achieving a speedy resolution of walkouts and did not lead to union recognition, the board's pronouncements made it appear that the federal government had taken the workers' side in labor disputes.[46]

NWLB decisions also publicized the concept of a "living wage." Supporters of this idea maintained that every family in America should receive enough income to live at a minimal level of "health and comfort." Though estimates varied as to exactly how much a family of five needed to support themselves adequately, all proponents of this cause noted that large numbers of Americans earned far below the standard. Certainly this was true of textile workers who suffered from both low wages and chronic unemployment.[47]

While the federal government extended an olive branch to labor, local and federal officials took stern action to silence opponents of the war. After the United States entered the conflict, local authorities in all three cities banned street meetings, broke up antidraft rallies and required permits for all indoor gatherings.[48] In keeping with its goal of establishing itself as a "political police force," the Department of Justice's Bureau of Investigation blanketed Lawrence with its operatives while U.S. Military Intelligence reported that its agents, who monitored "suspicious or irregular activities," had Paterson and Passaic "well covered." As a result, workers in all three cities became fearful of attending meetings.[49] The most massive violation of civil liberties occurred during the September 1918 "slacker raids" when, as part of its search for draft evaders, federal officials with the aid of New Jersey state police seized over 2,000 Paterson and Passaic residents from mills, ethnic clubs, saloons, trolleys, and their own homes. Many of those taken in for questioning were held overnight in a dramatic display of the government's contempt for the Bill of Rights.[50]

During the war, the distinction between governmental and private authority became blurred as the military held draft physicals in the mills, mill foremen participated in the round up of suspected draft evaders, prominent businessmen headed the Liberty Loan drives, and organizations such as the American Protective League assumed quasi-public functions.[51] In Passaic, the separation of private and public authority lost all meaning when Charles F. H. Johnson took advantage of the conflict to elevate himself to a position of considerable power. Johnson, who headed the Passaic Board of Trade, had little textile or managerial experience, but the Botany Mill selected him for a high-ranking position because the company wished to fend off criticism of its German ownership. Johnson, for whom the description "opportunist" might be charitable, also became Passaic's leading "100% patriot" as he headed the city's four Liberty Loan drives, sat on the local draft board, and took "it upon himself to exercise the police authority in Passaic."[52]

To workers, it may not always have been clear when someone like Johnson was acting in a private or public capacity. In the postwar period, local businessmen still assumed the public mantle as they joined the anti-Bolshevik crusade, but by then their speeches appeared far more transparent. On the other hand, once the war concluded the Wilson administration became far more fearful of labor's power. And as class conflict intensified, the federal government ceased to play a genuine mediating role and instead sided with management during labor disputes.

The UTW and the Eight-Hour Drive

According to labor historian David Montgomery, "the second decade of the twentieth century was the decisive period in the battle for the 8-hour day." The greatest gains came between 1916 and 1918 when machinists, railroad employees, anthracite coal miners, and packinghouse employees all achieved this objective through federal legislation, strikes, and NWLB and arbitrators' decisions. During the war, textile workers also demonstrated an interest in winning shorter hours. In Lawrence, employees at the American Woolen Company staged a brief work stoppage in May 1917 for the eight-hour day. In Paterson, silk workers considered striking for this objective in May 1917, and the shorter-workday demand figured prominently in the June 1918 strike against the Forstmann & Huffmann company.[53] As part of its wartime organizing campaign, the UTW launched its own eight-hour movement in January 1917. But the union's president, John Golden, postponed this agitation once the United States entered the war on the grounds that he did not want to jeopardize military production.[54]

The UTW resumed its drive for shorter hours when the union's 1918 convention, which was convened in the wake of the Armistice, passed a resolution calling upon the textile mills to begin the eight-hour day on 3 February 1919. At this time, most northern mills operated on a fifty-four-hour-per-week schedule while many southern mill employees worked sixty hours per week. Golden called the convention's action "the most progressive step we have ever taken as an international union" and promised that the UTW would carry its fight to all sections of the country.[55] The union chose February 3 because it wished to seize the initiative from employers in the immediate postwar period and because textile strikes were often timed so as to coincide with the beginning of the busy spring season. The recent growth in its own membership and an increase in the organization's per capita tax bolstered the UTW's confidence that it could lead a prolonged battle.[56] Without a doubt, Golden's assessment was correct—the drive for the eight-hour day represented the boldest step ever taken by the UTW and demonstrated how even the most cautious of unions had been moved to action by labor's wartime gains.

Nevertheless, the UTW wished to avoid a repeat of the mass insurgency that accompanied the 1912–1913 IWW-led strikes. Despite the militant-sounding language of its eight-hour resolution, the UTW did not actually call for a strike and instead favored holding conferences with mill agents that it hoped would lead to the peaceful adoption of the eight-hour day. If this method failed, the UTW told workers that they should report to the mills as usual on February 3 but that they should go home after working eight hours. Employees would then report to work again on February 4 and if mill owners refused to admit them, the union would declare a lockout to be in effect. Such a strategy would avoid the calling of a nationwide strike that the union feared it could not fully control.[57]

The UTW's conservative approach became apparent in other ways. Though "Eight Hours, February third" served as the union's rallying cry, the UTW was willing to accept an eight-and-one-half-hour workday. This peculiar situation arose because the UTW actually sought a standard forty-eight-hour week and if workers were to keep their Saturday half-holiday, they would have to work over eight hours each weekday. More importantly, the union refused to inject any wage demands into the dispute and said it was content to accept a wage reduction for the present and leave wage adjustments to the future.[58] This had been the UTW's policy in the past even though it contravened normal trade union strategy, which was to fight for a wage increase to make up for the lost hours.[59] Above all, this stance demonstrated the UTW's insensitivity to the lowest-paid workers who were less able than the skilled workers to absorb a cut in their weekly pay.

The eight-hour campaign began at a time when textile workers were already on edge because the sudden end of the war had caused wholesale cancellations of orders and in both Passaic and Lawrence layoffs had already occurred. Many workers believed that the mills had made "immense profits" during the war and should be forced to give "everybody a chance to work" without cutting wages.[60] A Passaic worker best captured the prevailing mood in the three cities: "It's about time we got something. The manufacturers have gotten their share out of this war game and it's about time they gave us some of it."[61] The UTW's demand was merely the final ingredient in this cauldron of dissent. While the union led a number of bitterly fought strikes in the South and secured the forty-eight-hour week in the vast majority of northern textile centers, the forty-eight-hour campaign ignited a movement in Paterson, Passaic, and Lawrence that went far beyond the narrow goals of the AFL union.[62] Mill hands in these three cities thus joined a labor revolt that reached worldwide proportions in 1919. What follows is one chapter in the history of a remarkable era when workers sought to create a new order.

Chapter Three

PATERSON: IN THE SILK

The Silk Industry

The site of Alexander Hamilton's planned industrial community, Paterson, had long been a manufacturing center. Before the Civil War, locomotive and cotton factories dominated the city's industrial landscape, but beginning in the 1860's, the silk industry grew rapidly as the plentiful supply of water power provided by the Great Falls of the Passaic River and the proximity to New York City's selling houses made Paterson an ideal location for silk manufacturing. High tariffs and the nation's rapidly expanding market for silk dresses, handkerchiefs, underwear, hat bands, ribbons, and umbrellas further stimulated the industry's growth. By 1880, Paterson produced one-third of all silk manufactured in the United States and had already established itself as "Silk City" or the "Lyons of America."[1]

In the early years, silk manufacturing in Paterson resembled a cottage industry rather than a modern enterprise. Most of the city's hand-loom weavers in the 1860s and 1870s came from Macclesfield and Coventry,

England. These artisans came to America because the Cobden Treaty of 1860, which established free trade between England and France, wiped out the English silk industry. Often bringing their own looms with them, these weavers wanted to be their own masters and they recreated in Paterson "a system of outdoor weaving" that was rapidly disappearing in the English Midlands.[2]

Not all of those who arrived merely wished to perpetuate artisanal traditions and a number of former weavers such as Henry Doherty, James Wadsworth, and Catholina Lambert eventually became some of Paterson's leading manufacturers. The entrepreneurial ambitions of these men gave impetus to a series of technological changes that transformed silk from a handicraft to a machine-powered industry. Throwing, which involved turning raw silk into yarn, became the first segment in which manufacturers introduced modern technology. By 1880, spinning, doubling, and twisting had been combined into one continuous operation that was usually carried out by female and child employees in factories devoted exclusively to this process. Broad-silk (defined as any cloth wider than twelve inches) next fell in line as the power loom dominated that branch by the mid-1880s. The ribbon sector was the last branch to adopt the new technology. Here, the key development came in 1889 with the perfection of a high-speed ribbon loom that included a stop motion which halted the machine whenever a thread broke. After this date, the last bastion of hand-loom weaving quickly disappeared from Paterson.[3]

That former weavers could become manufacturers serves as a good indication that, unlike in woolen and cotton textiles, the mechanization of silk production did not result in the establishment of large, integrated mills. Since silk spinning only required a few steps, it had proven relatively simple to separate throwing from weaving. Even warping, which was an intermediate step between spinning and weaving, was often done on a commission basis for weaving mills. The fate of Catholina Lambert served as a warning to those who considered combining throwing, warping, and weaving in one plant. This Yorkshire-born mill owner had been one of Paterson's most successful manufacturers and his factory had even included its own dyehouse. At the height of his success, Lambert had erected a replica of an English castle on a large hill overlooking the city. But by 1914, Lambert had been forced to declare bankruptcy and to sell off his extensive art collection. Indeed, the failure rate for large mills had been so great that where there had been 151 employees per silk mill in 1891, the average had dropped to 58 by 1914.[4]

Since most throwing firms relocated to Pennsylvania, Paterson had a high concentration of weaving mills. By 1900, numerous three-to-five-story, red-brick mill buildings dotted the city's landscape as new sources of power had allowed manufacturers to locate away from the Passaic River. Small specialized mills predominated especially in the broad-silk sector, which produced goods such as georgette crepe, taffetas, satin lining, veilings, plushes, and velvets. As a result of this specialization, the silk business had remained intensely competitive. Most Paterson manufacturers belonged to either the local Broad-Silk or Ribbon manufacturers associations and to the Silk Association of America, but these trade groups exercised little effective control over the industry.[5]

Due to the war, competition actually intensified in the broad-silk sector. Between 1916 and 1918, many broad-silk manufacturers had been unable to fill all of their orders. Rather than lose these accounts, the large mills had contracted work out on a commission basis to weavers, practically all of whom were Jewish immigrants. In the postwar period, these weavers decided to stay in business for themselves since they could easily purchase a few looms on credit and peddle the goods on their own in New York City. Hence, part of the broad-silk sector began again to resemble a cottage industry. These tiny mills, which became known as cockroach shops, grew so rapidly that where there had been 210 broad-silk shops in Paterson in 1915, there were 385 such firms by 1918.[6]

Since cockroach shops had extremely poor working conditions, they posed a major threat to labor standards in Paterson. An even greater threat resulted from the movement of some Paterson firms to the anthracite coal region of Pennsylvania. Many of the runaway shops in the 1880s had been throwing mills, but by 1900, most of Paterson's larger broad-silk and even some ribbon manufacturers had opened branch plants in Pennsylvania. These mill owners moved part of their operations to the coal-mining communities so as to take advantage of the low-cost fuel, cheap rentals, low taxes, and the readily available supply of cheap labor. This last aspect was of prime importance as Paterson's manufacturers faced a constant round of shop strikes and disputes. Firms that wished to escape this labor turmoil expected that the wives and daughters of the region's miners would work for less and would put up less resistance to increased loom assignments than did male or female employees in Paterson.[7]

As early as 1886, Paterson's trade unionists had become concerned about the shift to low-wage areas and had begun to talk about the need to organize the Pennsylvania workers. The most concerted campaign came in 1907 when the UTW struck most of the plants in the Scranton district; this dispute was eventually resolved by an arbitrator's award that did little to narrow the wage differential between Paterson and Pennsylvania.[8] Again in 1912 and 1913, radical trade unionists sent organizers to Pennsylvania but they had no more success than the UTW.[9] By the First World War, whenever Paterson unionists sought improved conditions or wage increases, mill owners claimed that the need to compete with non-union Pennsylvania firms meant they could not grant the demands.[10] That the manufacturers had deliberately created this "unfair competition" only heightened the frustration of Paterson's workers over this turn of events.

As a result of the runaway shop, silk throwing, which required little skill, practically disappeared from Paterson. But since they depended on skilled labor, manufacturers of high-grade broad-silks and ribbons, despite their threats to do so, could not relocate. Paterson thus became a city that had an unusually high proportion of skilled textile workers. Although by 1910, Pennsylvania's silk production had exceeded New Jersey's, silk manufacturing (which was concentrated in Paterson and in nearby communities), remained the Garden State's leading industrial employer.[11] In fact, the war had actually led to an increase in the number of operating looms in Paterson (reversing a decline between 1909 and 1914) and in 1919, 23,661 of the city's 41,816 wage earners still worked in the silk mills and another 5,007 employees labored in the closely allied dyeing trade.[12] The "glory days" might have been over but the city's future remained very much bound up with this one product.[13]

The silk-dyeing industry must be discussed separately as it varied sharply with respect to the trends described above. Unlike in silk weaving, two large firms dominated this sector: the Weidmann Silk Dyeing Company and the National Silk Dyeing Company. The Weidmann firm had been founded by the Swiss-born Jacob Weidmann, who came from a family of master dyers. Weidmann arrived in Paterson in 1872 and by the 1880s, he had established himself as America's leading silk dyer. Weidmann's success led Paterson's silk manufacturers to give up all efforts to do their own dyeing as they could not match the firm's technical skill and scientific expertise. In 1895, Weidmann moved all of the company's operations to a plant in Paterson's Riverside District. And by 1919, 1,500 workers labored in this vast plant, which had been a steady money-maker for well over thirty years.

The National Silk Dyeing Company surpassed Weidmann in size. This company had been formed in 1908 as a result of a merger of five Paterson dyeing firms and one outside company. One of the largest dyeing operations in the world, National dyed silk both before and after weaving, unlike Weidmann, which specialized in dyeing in the skein (dyeing before weaving). National's Paterson operations employed over 2,500 workers, making it the city's largest employer.

Since the natural softness of Passaic River water was ideal for dyeing, neither of these firms had even considered leaving Paterson. Instead, large quantities of Pennsylvania silks were sent to the Paterson plants, which did over 80 percent of the country's silk dyeing. Although there were a number of smaller dye houses in the city, National and Weidmann had been able to standardize wages and to work in concert on labor matters. Thus, workers in the dyeing sector confronted a far more formidable set of opponents than those in the competitive and often chaotic silk sector.[14]

Sectorial Divisions and Labor Organization

The production of silk required far fewer steps than either cottons or woolens and six occupational categories dominated the trade: throwers, winders, warpers, loom fixers, twisters, and weavers.[15] After the silk had been spun, it had to be doubled, reeled, and quilled by winders. These workers also put the skeins on swifts and ran the silk onto the bobbins. The work was usually done by young female operatives who eventually moved on to other silk jobs or left the industry. Unions had rarely made efforts to organize these workers and they had not figured prominently in Paterson's labor disturbances.[16]

Next, warps had to be prepared for the looms. This work was highly skilled as the proper number of threads had to be fed onto the beam of the loom. Broad-silk warps, in particular, could be very heavy and most of Paterson's 400 to 500 warpers were men though some women performed this task as well. The horizontal warpers (the term for warpers in broad-silk) were highly organized and composed one of the UTW's strongest branches in Paterson.[17]

Twisters also did highly skilled work as they had to pass the ends of the thread through the eyes of the harness and reeds of the loom. And as in all sectors of the textile industry, the loom fixers were the most highly skilled and highly paid employees. These workers, all of whom were male, prepared the looms for operation and kept the machines in running order. Their skills and their freedom to move throughout the plant bred in them an air of arrogance that at times could be directed at mill owners or at other times at weavers who often resented delays in having their looms repaired.

The loom fixers and twisters comprised only 8 percent of Paterson's silk work force but they had an advantageous position as the manufacturers need for their services allowed them to win major concessions. Since they shared an ability to win high wages, the loom fixers and twisters belonged to a common association that in 1905, along with the Horizontal Warpers' Association, affiliated with the UTW. These crafts composed the core of the UTW's membership in Paterson and their members often refused to work with nonunion twisters, loom fixers, or warpers. But their solidarity extended only to fellow craftsmen and many weavers considered them to be "bosses' men" since the highly skilled workers rarely joined in the silk-mill strikes.[18]

Weavers comprised over one-half of the work force in silk but the nature of their work could vary greatly. Those who produced plain broad-silks for manufacturers such as Henry Doherty could be classified as semiskilled employees as it only took a few months to learn how to spot and to repair broken or knotted threads, which was their major task. On the other hand, Paterson's manufacturers produced much of the nation's fancy and high-grade broad-silks that required jacquard attachments on the loom. These mechanisms allowed a weaver to produce intricate patterns, including designs that had curved lines or pictures. Jacquard looms were extremely delicate instruments and weavers often had to make simple repairs and climb to the top of the loom to adjust the cards that determined patterns.[19] Due to the nature of this work, employers preferred to hire men for jacquard weaving while both men and women wove the plain goods on the regular box looms.[20]

Likewise, the ribbon sector had a number of divisions. Those ribbon weavers who operated the new, high-speed ribbon looms could also be considered semiskilled operatives. In this sector, manufacturers had made a concerted effort to replace male with female employees in order to reduce wage rates. But many of Paterson's ribbon weavers operated the German looms that took years to master and that produced fancy and complex patterns manufactured by firms such as Pelgram and Meyer. These ribbon weavers tended only one double-decked loom that could produce multiple ribbons simultaneously. This work was more arduous than broad-silk weaving as more shuttles had to be filled with quills, more harnesses adjusted, and more warp threads pieced together. Hat band weaving required even more skill and weavers in this branch of the ribbon trade earned wages only slightly below those of loomfixers, twisters, and horizontal warpers.[21]

Though Paterson's silk mills employed approximately 13,000 broad-silk weavers and only 3,000 ribbon weavers, the latter group played an extremely important role in the city's labor movement.[22] As veterans of the silk trade, ribbon weavers knew firsthand that they produced more than previously but did not receive proportionate increases in pay. Many of them believed that their working conditions had deteriorated since the 1890s when the operation of smaller and less stressful looms had left them with time to pursue "studies for self improvement and enjoyment." They partook of a shop culture resembling that of skilled clothing, cigar, and shoe workers and engaged in workplace struggles that aimed at preserving handicraft skills and traditional work customs.[23] Their preference for acting on their own irked outside IWW leaders such as Elizabeth Gurley Flynn and some historians picking up on her criticism of them have labeled the ribbon weavers as "conservative."[24] But ideological labels should not be attached to these shop-centered and independent-minded workers. After the unsuccessful 1913 walkout, they fought a bitter rear-guard battle throughout 1914, sparked the renewed labor militancy in 1916, and rebelled against the accommodating UTW leadership in 1919.

No matter what sector they labored in, ribbon and broad-silk weavers faced many of the same job-related hassles. Delays might occur because silk had not arrived from the dyehouses, because looms needed repairs, or because warps had not been prepared. Defective material could also lead to a loss in pay as practically all weavers worked on a piecework basis. Price lists based on the ligne (a fraction of an inch) could be unfathomable. The work could be extremely tedious and nerve-racking as the delicate threads often broke and the nervous strain suffered by weavers partly accounts for the frequency of shop disputes in Paterson.[25]

Indeed, strikes occurred so commonly in Paterson that one historian found that 137 walkouts took place between 1887 and 1900—a total that does not include the small disturbances that took place on a regular basis in the city.[26] Before the UTW came to Paterson, these walkouts had not led to the formation of permanent broad-silk or ribbon-weavers' unions though many efforts had been made at forming such organizations. This, however, did not mean weavers lacked power on the shop floor since "quickie" strikes conducted during the busy season could be highly effective. Some of the bigger battles became part of the city's folklore and in

1936 an investigator for the Works Progress Administration noted that "so conscious is the average worker of the city's labor history that the dates of marriages, trips, and other personal events are commonly fixed by the year of an important strike."[27]

The presence of the dyehouses complicated the task of building labor unity in Paterson as working conditions in these large plants differed markedly from that in the silk mills. Most jobs in this sector required little skill and were performed by dyers' helpers who worked under the supervision of boss dyers. The all-male work force had "the most laborious and disagreeable" job in the entire silk industry as they had to submerge and lift chemically treated silk out of the tubs that lined the plants.[28] In doing this, they inhaled noxious fumes and often contacted respiratory diseases from working in these wet and steamy places. Dyers' helpers also faced strict supervision as boss dyers carefully watched their work. Jacob Weidmann, in particular, had been known as "a stern task master" and workers had taken to rubbing their chins as a warning to fellow employees that this "easily aroused and very excitable" master dyer was present in the plant.[29]

Compared to employment in the silk mills, work in the dyehouses offered a few advantages. Since there was no machinery, dyers' helpers, who worked in teams, could converse with one another; piece-rate systems, a cause of much dissatisfaction to weavers, could not be applied to this type of work; although they earned less than broad-silk weavers, dyers' helpers suffered from fewer layoffs. But "quickie" strikes almost never occurred in this sector as dyers' helpers could not hope to carry on the type of shop struggles favored by weavers. Unions had never gained a foothold as the Weidmann and the other dyehouses had been able to maintain the open shop. As a result, when dyers' helpers struck, as they did in 1894, 1902, 1913, and 1919, they struck en masse and fought battles that became extremely violent and bitter.

Immigration and the the Paterson Working Class

When the U.S. Immigration Commission between 1907 and 1911 conducted its exhaustive study of the immigrant "problem" in America, it found that most of those immigrants employed in steel, meat-packing, and other mass-production industries had little prior industrial experience. Paterson's silk industry, along with the clothing industry, proved a notable exception to this pattern as a remarkably high total of 73.9

percent of all male and 76.1 percent of all female workers had been employed previously in textile manufacturing. This represented by far the highest rate of continuity in any industry examined by the commission.[30] Very often the victims of technological change in their homelands, these immigrants from European textile centers such as Macclesfield, England, Krefeld, Germany, Como and Biella, Italy, and Lodz, Poland, came to Paterson in order to preserve past work customs. In this sense, the city was a world apart from Passaic and Lawrence, whose immigrant work forces had little previous industrial experience.

Those who came from Macclesfield established the pattern of immigration that came to characterize the city. Most of the new arrivals initially worked as weavers and their residential district came to be known as Weavertown. They also sought to preserve social customs and met and drank together in English social clubs. As noted, a number of the English immigrants had entrepreneurial ambitions and came to own some of Paterson's largest mills. The majority, though, continued to work in weaving mills and by the eve of the First World War, their descendants had often become warpers, twisters, loom fixers, or ribbon weavers.[31]

Although a number of Dutch, French, and Swiss immigrants came to Paterson between 1870 and 1890, Germans who mainly hailed from the Rhine River textile city of Krefeld proved to be numerically the most important. By 1920, there were 14,313 residents of German origin in Paterson and they comprised about 10 percent of the city's population.[32] As was true of many of the immigrants who came to Paterson, they had a secular orientation and their social life centered around singing societies, benevolent associations and the *turnverein* (turner society).[33]

As in industrial communities throughout the nation, the Germans in Paterson contributed much to the building of the left between 1880 and 1914. They helped elect a Socialist Labor Party (SLP) member to the board of aldermen in 1894, gave strong support to the Socialist party after its formation in 1901 and most interestingly, helped found and nourish the Paterson IWW during its early years. Most of these German IWW leaders, such as Adolph Lessig, Ewald Koettgen, William Halbach, and Edward Zuerscher, had experience in the ribbon sector and large numbers of Germans appear to have been ribbon or hat-band weavers.[34] Though evidence is slim on this point, the IWW seems to have appealed to them because its emphasis on direct action comported with the shop culture of these workers.[35]

The arrival of approximately 6,000 northern Italians helped add the appellation "Red City" to Paterson's list of titles. These skilled weavers and dyers mainly came from Biella and Como, woolen and silk centers respectively. Most of them left Italy between 1890 and 1900 in order to escape the effects of deskilling as mechanization had begun to transform the silk industry in the Piedmont and Lombardy regions. In the 1870s and 1880s, they had participated in "spectaculatar" strikes that had been organized by groups known as the "Leagues of Resistance" and they became involved in walkouts almost immediately upon their arrival in Paterson.[36]

Besides being shop-floor militants, many of these northern Italians were anarchists and for awhile, Paterson "became the international center of Italian radicalism" as such luminaries of the movement as Errico Malatesta, Giuseppe Ciancabilla, Luigi Galleani, and Pedro Esteve (a Spaniard) settled in the city.[37] Even before the arrival of these leaders, the anarchists, who burned with rage at the injustices of the bosses, the church, and the state, gained influence in the Paterson labor movement as they participated in strikes of ribbon weavers and dyers' helpers in 1894 that had to be suppressed by New Jersey state troopers. At this time, Paterson's middle-class population remained unaware of the anarchist influence, but the anarchists' anonymity ended in 1900 when in a two-week space of time, a Paterson silk weaver, Gaetano Bresci, assassinated King Humbert I of Italy and another Paterson anarchist, Garriboni Sperandino, assassinated a foreman at the Weidmann dyehouse by the name of Guissepe Pessina. These actions shocked many local residents while anarchists celebrated them. Far more people turned out for Sperandino's funeral (he killed himself as he was about to be captured) than for Pessina's and for many years anarchists and sympathizers gathered to commemorate Bresci's act.

Only a small number of anarchists believed in relying solely on "propaganda by the deed" and those who belonged to an affinity group known as "The Group for the Right to Existance" and who published the newspaper *La Questione Sociale* remained active in the labor movement. The peak period of their influence came during an extremely violent 1902 dyers' helpers strike when workers engaged in "wholesale wrecking" of the dyehouses. The New Jersey militia had to be called to put down the uprising and some of Paterson's anarchists fled the city to avoid imprisonment. But truly widespread repression did not occur until 1908 when, using the powers granted him under a new city charter, Mayor Andrew F. McBride led a "Drive Them Out" campaign that forced many more anarchists to leave the city.[38]

Although this movement never regained its vigor in Paterson, these militants helped prepare the ground for the Wobblies. Many anarchists themselves eventually joined the IWW and beginning in 1906, the IWW logo appeared on *La Questione Sociale's* masthead.[39] Until 1920, when they became victims of a new wave of repression, the anarchists maintained their own clubrooms in the city.[40] And as we will see, they and the remaining IWW members in Paterson remained committed to direct action—a stance that led them to oppose vigorously the ATWA's organizing efforts in Paterson.

After 1900, thousands of southern Italians who came mainly from Calabria and from Sicily also immigrated to Paterson and by 1920, the city had over 22,000 residents who listed Italian as their mother tongue.[41] The arrival of the southerners meant that Paterson was one of the few American cities to have sizable colonies of northern and southern Italians. To a certain extent these two groups composed distinct nationalities as they spoke different dialects and did not necessarily recognize each other as compatriots.[42] Most importantly, few southerners had previous experience in the textile industry and consequently they clustered in the dyehouses where they, along with the northerners, composed about 80 percent of the work force by 1910. The residential patterns of the two groups also varied as southern Italians lived in the Riverside District in close proximity to the dyehouses.[43] In fact, this was the only part of the city that had the type of dense immigrant district that one associates with textile towns since the silk mills were scattered throughout the community and the most-skilled workers, in particular, lived on fairly pleasant tree-lined streets in Paterson or in the streetcar suburb of Haledon.[44]

The approximately 8,000 Polish Jews who came to Paterson between 1905 and 1913 further contributed to the city's ethnic diversity. Many of these new Jewish residents came from Warsaw and Bialystok but the vast majority came from Lodz, the "Polish Manchester," which was the most important textile city in Russian Poland. Although Lodz had a number of large, mechanized factories, most Jews had worked in small, handicraft shops located in a separate Jewish quarter known as "Balut." The owners of these shops often lived on the edge of poverty and perhaps for this reason, the bosses often exercised a tyrannical reign over the workers.[45]

Beginning in 1897, large numbers of Jewish hand-loom weavers in Lodz joined the Jewish Workers Federation of Poland, Russia and Lithuania that became known simply as the Bund. During its heyday between 1897 and 1905, the Bund helped forge a fighting Jewish working class as Jewish workers in Lodz and the rest of the Pale of Settlement (the area in the Russian Empire to which Jews were confined) engaged in countless strikes. The Bund also had political objectives and its adherents believed political and economic action needed to go hand in hand. But the Bund had other goals as well since it appealed to those Jewish workers who were abandoning orthodoxy and adopting a more secular world view. To meet the needs of these freethinkers, the Bund established Yiddish newspapers, schools, and theatre programs. Lastly, the Bund had nationalist goals and fought for the recognition of Jewish national rights in the Russian Empire as well as for socialism.[46]

Life for the Jewish textile workers became more difficult after 1900 as the small mills could not hope to compete against the large factories. The immediate impetus for large-scale emigration came as a result of a series of anti-Jewish outbursts that occurred in Lodz in 1905 and 1906. These pogroms came in the wake of both the aborted Russian Revolution of 1905 and an unsuccessful general strike.[47] Large numbers of Jews, who often became the victims of vengeful Polish workers, left Lodz after these events and much like those from other European textile centers, they came to Paterson because the city offered them an opportunity to perpetuate a familiar way of life.[48] The chain migration became so extensive that "in Lodz when one spoke of America, one referred to Paterson as America."[49] Perhaps no other Jewish community in the country was so bound up with one type of work as Paterson, which became "the largest and best known Jewish textile city" in the United States.[50]

The Jewish refugees of 1905, as did the Lithuanians and the Finns, contributed much to the American left. In an immediate sense, the Jewish silk workers occupied a world much like the one they had known in Lodz. Almost all Jewish weavers worked in broad-silk, the sector where the small shop predominated, and the social life of Paterson's Jewish proletariat centered around eight chapters of the Workmen's Circle. Founded by former Bundists, this organization carried forth the Bundist idea, and Jewish workers in Paterson shared in the blossoming of a secular, Jewish working-class culture known as *Yiddishkeit*.[51]

Whether members of English social clubs, the turnverein, anarchist study groups, or the Workmen's Circle, most of Paterson's immigrant workers structured their social life outside of the church and the synagogue. On the other hand, these organizations were male dominated and even when they welcomed female participation, women played a distinctly secondary role in them.[52] This aspect had implications for labor organization since approximately 40 percent of Paterson's labor force was female and unions could not succeed unless they attracted women members. Gender divisions were, of course, of no consequence in the dyehouses as they employed men exclusively. Judging from accounts of strikes compiled by the New Jersey Bureau of Industrial Statistics, male and female broad-silk weavers consistently struck side by side and little overt tension occurred in this sector.[53] The most significant division occurred in the ribbon and warping trades where manufacturers had openly boasted that they had hired women so as to reduce wage rates and weaken labor organization.[54] Male workers had not always responded in positive ways. Ribbon weavers had struck to prevent mills from hiring female weavers and the Horizontal Warpers' Association had long opposed the entry of women into their trade. When they finally reached out to these employees in 1916, the UTW chartered a separate Ladies Horizontal Warpers' Association rather than admitting the women on an equal basis to their organization.[55]

Work, ethnic, and gender divisions thus all contributed to the complexity of Paterson's labor relations. Building labor unity in Paterson meant convincing (to cite a few examples) an English loom fixer, a German male hat band weaver, a Jewish female broad-silk weaver, and an Italian dyers' helper that they should all work together. As we will see, these workers, who also had distinct ideological orientations, often defined their interests separately from one another, and consequently a plethora of unions competed for the loyalties of Paterson workers between 1908 and 1921.

The 1911–1913 Strikes and Their Aftermath

The UTW had been founded in 1901, but it did not establish a base in Paterson until 1905. The delay came about because Paterson's silk workers, fearful of being dominated by woolen and cotton-textile workers, had tried to get their own charter from the AFL. Only after being rebuffed, did the loom fixers and twisters affiliate with the UTW and in 1907 they were joined by the Horizontal Warpers' Association. These two locals, which had about 400 members apiece, had sufficient muscle to enforce a closed shop, restrict the number of apprentices, and establish a union scale of wages. Disdaining written contracts, their business agents, Thomas Morgan and James Starr, usually visited the shops to settle any disputes that might develop.[56]

In 1908, the UTW chartered a new branch of broad-silk weavers. The following year, this local signed the fateful agreement with the Henry Doherty Silk Company that permitted the mill to operate on a four-loom

31

rather that on a two-loom basis. The Doherty firm was hardly a typical Paterson plant as it employed close to 1,000 workers and specialized in making the plainest broad-silks. All of the employees worked in a large mill, located in an outlying district, that Doherty had erected in 1903. By installing the multiple-loom system, Doherty hoped to compete with Pennsylvania mills that for many years had operated on a four-loom-per-weaver basis. The UTW acquiesced to the increased loom assignment since it feared that otherwise the remaining plain broad-silk manufacturers would leave the city and because it sought to establish harmonious relations with Paterson's largest manufacturers.[57]

Both Doherty and the UTW believed that workers would agree to operate four looms since under the piecework systems of pay, they would earn more money. But to their surprise, the introduction of the four-loom system set off a wave of strikes that lasted for three years. While workers believed that the additional loom assignment would inevitably lead to a reduction in the work force, the intense reaction mainly stemmed from workers' belief that in the past only the manufacturers had gained from higher productivity rates.[58]

The protests began in 1911 when the angry Doherty weavers handed their union books over to the Detroit IWW.[59] This union had been formed in 1908 as a result of Daniel DeLeon's opposition to the IWW's de-emphasis of political action. Mainly composed of SLP members (the political party that DeLeon headed), the Detroit IWW had held its founding convention in Paterson and due to the efforts of Local 25 had attracted a mixture of seasoned Paterson unionists and Jewish immigrants. Though never having more than 12,000 members nationally, the Detroit IWW had gained a considerable following in Paterson as many workers there believed in the need for industrial unions and socialist political parties to work together.[60]

Having captured the UTW broad-silk local, the Detroit IWW organized an Anti-Four Loom Conference Committee and in November 1911, struck the Doherty company. During the ensuing six months, over 3,000 weavers walked out of many of Paterson's other broad-silk mills in an attempt to win higher wages. These work stoppages led many of the smaller mills to grant wage increases, but upon the conclusion of the February–March busy season, they reneged on their agreements. Of greatest consequence, the Doherty company refused to budge from its four-loom stance and all of the strikes ended in May 1912 with the Detroit IWW having suffered a major defeat.[61]

One reason that the 1911–1912 broad-silk strikes failed is that the

Paterson branch of the IWW did not support them. This local belonged to the IWW's National Industrial Union of Textile Workers, which also had held its founding convention in Paterson. Since 1908, it had attracted a small but steadily growing following. As one might expect, the Wobblies vigorously objected to the Detroit IWW's expropriation of its name. During the spring of 1912 broad-silk strikes, the IWW referred to ex-Wobbly Rudolph Katz as "Pubadolph Cats" and warned workers not to be "flim-flammed by the Katz-DeLeon crew masquerading in the name of the IWW."[62] The Detroit IWW, which could hurl invective with anyone, responded in kind. But of most significance, with the Detroit IWW's defeat, the IWW—its reputation enhanced by a tremendous victory in Lawrence—was in a perfect position to take over the leadership of the anti-four-loom struggle and the fight for the eight-hour day.[63]

The IWW's organizing work paid off in January 1913 when the Doherty weavers again struck against the four-loom system. They were soon joined by weavers in other broad-silk shops where owners had attempted to increase loom assignments. And much to the puzzlement of Paterson's fancy and high-grade broad-silk manufacturers, their weavers proceeded to walk out even though they continued to tend two looms. Next, the dyers' helpers abandoned their vats and, more remarkably still, the ribbon weavers during the first week of March joined the picket lines. These workers originally came out in sympathy with Paterson's other employees but they soon framed their own demands, including a call for a return to the 1894 price list and the abandonment of the two-loom system (a demand that applied only to those who tended the high-speed looms).[64]

Never before in Paterson's history had dyers' helpers, broad-silk weavers, and ribbon weavers struck together. In part, the unified response was due to the charismatic leadership provided by such Wobbly notables as Elizabeth Gurley Flynn, Big Bill Haywood, and Carlo Tresca. The unified response was also due partly to the appeal of the eight-hour demand as weavers complained strenuously of eyestrain caused by work done in artificial light and dyers' helpers still worked the twelve-hour day.[65] But this was a defensive as well as offensive struggle and the readiness of silk workers to battle the mill owners also resulted from years of accumulated anger over deteriorating shop conditions.

Despite the display of solidarity, after staying out for six months, workers began to drift back to the mills in July and August. Few workers won even the nine-hour day though the Doherty company did abandon its efforts to impose the four-loom system. A number of factors led to the disappointing outcome. City authorities adopted an extremely harsh stance, strike funds grew short, a Madison Square Garden pageant created jealousies, and old sectorial divisions reappeared. But the IWW's "all return or none" position also contributed to the defeat. This strategy made sense in a city such as Lawrence that had a few large mills, but applied to Paterson, it prevented workers from playing employers off against one another and actually served to unite the normally divided mill owners.[66]

To a historian trying to make sense of Paterson's complex labor history, the 1912 and 1913 strikes are important because they shed light on ethnically based ideological divisions that made it difficult to build a united left in the city. Many of Paterson's Jewish labor radicals had supported the Detroit IWW and the SLP because the emphasis these organizations placed on joint economic and political action, cultural advancement, and gradual rather than cataclysmic change appealed to those who had cut their political teeth in the Bund. As evidence of the prominent Jewish role in the Detroit IWW, many of the 1912 strike leaders were Jewish, the Workmen's Circle chapters gave strong support to the strike, and the series of walkouts only affected the broad-silk sector where most Jewish weavers worked.[67] So strong did the Jewish influence in the WIIU become that by 1918, its executive committee in Paterson was entirely Jewish and Paterson became one of only five cities where the SLP had enough members to establish a separate Jewish Federation.[68]

Although Jewish workers participated in great numbers in the 1913 walkout few of them in Paterson, or anywhere else for that matter, joined the IWW. By contrast, Italians in Paterson, Lawrence, and other mill towns often gave enthusiastic support to the Wobblies. Northerners backed them because of the affinity with their own anarchist traditions. In the case of the Southerners, their strikes had often resembled jacqueries and the Wobblies' preference for mass action and readiness to challenge legal authorities had great appeal to them.[69] And since neither northern nor southern Italians had displayed much interest in electoral politics, the Wobblies' attacks on the SLP and on the Socialist party did not disturb either group.

These differences are revealed by opposing strategies followed in the two strikes. During the 1912 walkout, the Detroit IWW bent over backwards to avoid violence and actually ordered a halt to picketing when three strikers were arrested on the first day of the work stoppage. Yiddish handbills distributed by strikers cautioned workers to "give no one the slightest pretext to call you disorderly; practice no physical force whatever upon your opponents."[70] While never failing to emphasize its revolutionary goals, the Detroit IWW warned workers that disorder would not be tolerated, and the strike proved to be one of the most peaceful in Paterson's history.[71] By contrast, the IWW in 1913 made full use of the same confrontational tactics that it had employed at Lawrence. Unlike the Detroit IWW, the Wobblies refused to obey police rules and regulations that it considered unjust and over 2,000 strikers were arrested because of their refusal to cease picketing and demonstrating.

The Detroit IWW expressed contempt for tactics of this sort and criticized the IWW for appealing to workers' instincts rather than to their reason. To the followers of DeLeon, the ballot represented a step on the road to "civilization" while sabotage was viewed as a "remnant of barbarism." In keeping with this perspective, the Detroit IWW often called Big Bill Haywood "a brute" and referred to the IWW as "the bummery."[72] The extent to which the different orientations of ethnic groups entered into these divisions was noted by a witness at the U.S. Commission on Industrial Relations hearings who said that many Paterson residents had considered the 1912 walkout to have been a "Jew strike" and the 1913 walkout to have been an "Italian strike."[73]

These divisions proved important as both the WIIU and the IWW remained active following the 1912–1913 walkouts. The WIIU's Local 25 retained at least some of the support that stemmed from its early opposition to the four-loom system, and in 1918, it claimed to have members in over 100 shops.[74] Between 1912 and 1918, the Paterson local was often entitled to the most delegates of any branch at the Detroit IWW/WIIU conventions and two of its most prominent Paterson leaders, H. J. Rubenstein and Joseph Yannarelli, also sat on the Detroit IWW/WIIU general executive board.[75]

Although further weakened by the loss of a series of ribbon strikes that it led in late 1913 and 1914, the IWW hung on in Paterson.[76] Ironically, the Wobblies had more success in establishing a permanent base in Paterson than in Lawrence, despite the victory in the latter city. The Wobblies maintained a foothold in Paterson because employers could not effectively blacklist workers from hundreds of small silk mills and because many Wobblies were skilled workers whom employers depended upon. By way of contrast, the Lawrence manufacturers had a far easier time excluding local labor organizers due to the ease with which they could replace semiskilled workers in large worsted mills.

Between 1915 and 1918, Wobbly activity came in spurts. For example, Elizabeth Gurley Flynn led a highly successful free-speech fight between

September 1915 and January 1916 that forced the city police to stop interfering with IWW meetings. In conjunction with this campaign, the IWW conducted a number of work stoppages in small broad-silk shops, and Adolph Lessig, the tireless workhorse of the local Wobblies, claimed that 300 new members had enrolled in Local 152.[77] Another IWW drive came in August–September 1916 when the UTW and WIIU submitted new price lists in order to take advantage of the war-induced prosperity. The Wobblies gained support by asking for slightly more pay per yard than the other unions. By the fall of 1916, the IWW said that fifty shops had adopted its wage scale and that twenty mills had IWW-controlled shop committees.[78] After the United States entered the war, the IWW continued to focus on shop issues, and federal agents reported that Local 152 had been "cagey" and "discreet" and less bold than the WIIU.[79] Such caution helped preserve the Paterson local at a time when the IWW throughout the nation faced severe repression.[80]

In 1918, the IWW still had 625 paid-up members.[81] But never again could the Wobblies capture the imaginations of thousands of silk workers as they had during the 1913 strike. Faced with the realization of this fact, the IWW began to direct its ire against other radical unions as well as against the manufacturers. Moreover, during the wartime boom, the UTW began to demonstrate a new vigor and actually regained much of the support it had lost at the time of the four-loom controversy.

The Nine-Hour Fight and the Resurgence of the UTW

When the workers returned to the mills in 1913, employers promised that once they disavowed the IWW, the nine-hour day would be granted to them. This proved a hollow promise since in January 1916, Paterson mills continued to operate on a fifty-five-hour-per-week schedule that had remained unchanged since the early 1900s. At the same time, great prosperity had come to the silk industry as a result of the war.

In order to take advantage of the favorable employment situation, the Passaic County Socialist Party (SP) in February 1916 convened a conference of all of Paterson's silk unions.[82] The Socialists had come close to winning the Paterson mayoralty in 1913 when workers, angered by the repressive policies followed by the city administration, had given its candidate great support. Its vote total had declined sharply, but the SP still won 10 percent of the vote in the November 1915 election, and the small, neighboring community of Haledon continued to have a Socialist party mayor. Though it had been feuding with the IWW, the Socialist party hoped that its status as a relatively neutral body could convince Paterson's warring labor unions to join together in the nine-hour fight.[83] Participants at the initial meeting included the UTW, IWW, WIIU, and Brotherhood of American Silk Workers (BASW). The last-named group had been founded in 1914 with the open support of the Paterson Manufacturers' Association and its stated purpose was to create harmony between labor and capital and to keep "outside agitators" from coming to Paterson.[84] Its head was Lewis Magnet, who had represented the ribbon weavers on the 1913 general strike committee. That Magnet defied easy description is indicated by Elizabeth Gurley Flynn's characterization of him as "conservative, Irish, Catholic, Socialist." In 1916, Magnet still belonged to the Socialist party though he dropped this affiliation shortly thereafter.[85] Most importantly, Magnet's attendance at this conference indicated that all factions of the Paterson labor movement supported the nine-hour drive.

In response to the nine-hour demand, manufacturers acknowledged that the time for shorter hours had arrived and asked only to delay its implementation until November 1. All four of the unions opposed any postponement and made plans for a strike. The initiative was then taken by the hat band weavers who set their own strike date of March 27. These workers, who formed part of the ribbon sector, had been the first to call for shorter hours and their militancy made it certain that a strike would occur if the nine-hour day was not granted immediately. The hat-band weavers forced the issue. When it became clear that the ribbon trade would be tied up by a strike, the Ribbon Manufacturers' Association convinced the broad-silk bosses to concede the shorter hours. All mill owners feared another strike when business was booming, so the nine-hour day and fifty-hour week finally took effect in Paterson on 3 April 1916. In return, the UTW promised to carry the nine-hour fight to the runaway shop sections of Pennsylvania and many workers pledged financial support for this effort.[86]

Although the participants in the silk-workers' conferences were reportedly "loath" to abandon them, the unity that marked the spring 1916 campaign did not last. Shortly after the nine-hour triumph, the WIIU charged that the BASW had followed a "peace at any price" policy and had tried to undermine the coalition's efforts. Shortly afterwards, both the UTW and the BASW withdrew from participation in the conferences altogether. As a sign of the deepening fissure, the radical organizations announced plans for a May Day jubilee while the UTW countered with plans for a Labor Day rally.[87] And even the radical groups resumed their bickering as the IWW was conspicuously absent from the May Day committee composed of members of the Socialist party, the WIIU, and a number of Jewish organizations. That a key purpose of the May Day rally was to call for the release from prison of Patrick Quinlan, a former Wobbly who had rejected the IWW and joined the Socialist party, most likely caused the renewed division.[88]

The UTW benefited the most from the radicals' squabbling. Immediately upon the conclusion of the nine-hour fight, it chartered new locals for broad-silk and ribbon weavers and in the wake of the spring 1918 walkout of the dyers helpers, for the first time it chartered a branch for that group of employees. By January 1919, the UTW claimed to have 8,000 members in Paterson, including all of the city's loom fixers, twisters, and warpers, most of the ribbon weavers and 3,000 broad-silk weavers—a dramatic turnabout for a union that had been viewed by many workers as a "strikebreaker" during the 1913 walkout.[89]

The UTW received renewed support because its leaders reversed their previous position and now strongly opposed the four-loom system and because craft unionism appealed to many silk workers who took pride in their skills and who identified with a specific sector of the industry.[90] Also, many of Paterson's manufacturers actually began to encourage their employees to enroll in the UTW and in some cases, they refused to hire those who did not join the AFL union.[91] The silk-mill owners adopted this policy because they hoped the UTW could bring a halt to the shop disputes that constantly occurred in Paterson. The UTW appeared to be an ideal vehicle for accomplishing this purpose since its constitution forbade strikes that lacked the authorization of the national office and the union had been known to discipline members and even entire locals that disobeyed its orders.[92]

The BASW's dissolution in the fall of 1916 further bolstered the UTW's position. Evidently, the manufacturers had realized that more could be gained by working with the UTW than with the BASW, whose relationship with the manufacturers was far too cozy for it ever to win the support of workers. Interestingly, Lewis Magnet, despite his experience in the ribbon sector, was named business agent for the broad-silk local.[93] Thus, on the eve of the eight-hour fight, the radical unions remained divided and the UTW was at the peak of its strength.

The Rival Eight-Hour Organizations and NWLB Intervention

With the end of the war in sight, the WIIU convened a meeting that established the Eight Hour Workday Conference.[94] The coalition's participants give a good indication of the breadth of support that the Paterson left could muster since, besides the WIIU, it included the Passaic County Socialist Party, Polish, Russian and Jewish branches of the Socialist party, the Passaic County Socialist Labor Party, Paole Zion, the Sons of Italy, and the IWW.[95] Paole Zion was a socialist Zionist organization that had a considerable following in Paterson. The Sons of Italy promoted both Americanization and Italian national pride. While often thought of as an organization of small businessmen and professionals, in cities such as Paterson and Lawrence it attracted many leftists who hoped to overcome the regional differences in the Italian community. This was not the first time that the Sons of Italy had backed a radical cause since its nine Paterson lodges had given considerable financial and moral support to the 1913 walkout.[96] The IWW's participation was also quite notable because for the past two years it had boycotted such gatherings, but by November 1918 the Wobblies had once again consented to work with other left-wing groups.[97]

Shortly after the radical conference met, the UTW, as part of the national campaign the union had launched, established its own Eight-Hour Workday Committee and began to plan for a February 3 strike. The radical grouping also set the first Monday in February as its strike date although it pointedly reminded workers that it sought "the real eight-hour day"—meaning eight hours on weekdays and four-hours on Saturday.[98]

During January 1919, both organizations flooded Paterson with eight-hour buttons, leaflets, and posters. The eight-hour demand had, of course, figured prominently in the 1913 strike and many workers had never stopped pushing this cause. During the war, both the WIIU and the IWW had initiated eight-hour drives that had stalled because of the lack of UTW support.[99] With the end of the war, silk workers showed a renewed determination to win shorter hours. To many employees, the issue had both symbolic and tangible importance. In concrete terms, it meant less eye strain, less physical exhaustion, fewer layoffs, and more leisure time. On another level, it signified that the "war for democracy" would have meaningful results at home. One of the radicals' eight-hour bulletins contrasted workers' definition of democracy with that of the mill owners:

. . . to you the term Democracy may have been only a cynical rallying cry, for you seem quite incapable of comprehending anything bigger than your profits. But to the producing classes Democracy meant during the war and means now something concrete—something that can be touched and felt.

To us Democracy means a more decent standard of living, less slavery to the machine, more leisure, more culture and—make no mistake about it—something to say about the conduct of the industries which our labor makes possible and by which we gain our living.[100]

And to make the connection with the wartime events clearer, a statement by President Wilson endorsing the eight-hour day adorned the top of each bulletin.[101]

Mill owners opposed any reduction in hours as they claimed a cut could not be made to apply "to all sections of the country alike."[102] Nevertheless, they agreed to discuss the issue with the UTW at a conference arranged by the Paterson Chamber of Commerce. Before this meeting convened, Paterson's Textile Council (composed of all of the UTW locals) made the surprise announcement that it was willing to accept a forty-seven-hour week. Sprung on the local membership without prior consultation, this declaration reversed the Paterson UTW's prior claim that "local autonomy" gave it the right to demand fewer hours than requested by the national union.[103] Although one can only surmise this point, the UTW's national president John Golden most likely ordered the Paterson UTW to change its stand so that it would more closely conform to the national union's goal.[104]

The UTW's last-minute switch meant that the strike began under the most bizarre circumstances as rival groups walked out for forty-seven and forty-four hours on February 3. While both factions wore eight-hour buttons, one was colored red, white, and blue and the other bright red. No effort was made to bridge the gap between the rival groups, which even sponsored separate picket lines. Workers struck in a city tense with memories of 1913 and police officers and private detectives patrolled the mill districts. Fears of violence though were eased after the first day of the walkout when the dyers' helpers resumed work after the National and the Weidmann Companies promised to grant their employees any concesessions won by the silk workers.[105] Neither the UTW nor the IWW had many members among this group of employees but their defection hurt the left-wing unions the most as they usually counted on their support during strikes.

The broad-silk and ribbon manufacturers still faced an extensive strike (called a lockout by the UTW) and the Chamber of Commerce as well as a representative of the Department of Labor's Mediation and Conciliation Service continued to sponsor meetings attended by representatives of the mill owners and the UTW. At one of these gatherings, the manufacturers suggested that the NWLB be called upon to settle the dispute. This agency still heard cases but since the end of the war, its decisions had become decidedly promanagement.[106] And, since the board had never granted less than forty-eight hours, manufacturers had no reason to fear that it would mandate a forty-four- (or even a forty-seven-) hour week. Thus the manufacturers had good reason to expect a favorable settlement from the NWLB. The broad-silk manufacturers, in particular, had another motivation for turning to the board as they hoped that the federal agency could somehow standardize hours for the entire silk industry. The idea of using a federal board for this purpose had first been broached in 1914 by Henry Doherty, the largest broad-silk manufacturer in the city. And quite notably, in 1919 Henry Doherty proved to be one of the strongest advocates of using the NWLB to end the unfair competitive advantage enjoyed by the Pennsylvania manufacturers.[107]

At first, the UTW balked at the idea of taking the dispute to the NWLB but the union relented on one condition—that the NWLB issue a temporary "short hours" ruling prior to its final decision. The UTW made this proposal at a time when a rebellion appeared to be brewing in its own ranks. The ever-militant hat-band weavers had just voted to back the forty-four-hour cause and the UTW's ribbon weavers' local had decided to send delegates to the radicals' meetings though holding off on whether to endorse the forty-four-hour demand.[108] To put a damper on this unrest, the UTW needed to arrange a settlement to the strike without appearing to cave in to management and the union hoped that a "short hours" ruling would accomplish this objective.

Since management anticipated slack times during the postwar readjustment period, it had no particular objection to a temporary period of "short hours." With both parties in agreement, then, the NWLB held a preliminary hearing on February 13. At this session, the UTW representatives made no effort to disguise their motivations and asked the board to give them a "short hours" ruling "in order to kill off the element that created so much trouble in 1913." Upon hearing the presentation of the UTW and of the manufacturers, Frederick N. Judson, the vice-chairman of the NWLB, questioned if the agency was not being asked "to be a party to a bit of camouflage for the sake of getting workers to come back to work" and other NWLB members expressed concern that they were being asked to give their stamp of approval to something that had been decided beforehand. After hearing these objections, both the manufacturers' and the UTW's representatives said they were agreeable to having the board itself set the temporary "short hour" week but they only requested that the NWLB act immediately as it appeared that the dyers' helpers were about to join "the forty-four hour side" and the situation in Paterson was "growing worse."[109]

Despite harsh questioning, the NWLB gave the manufacturers and the UTW what they wanted. Although the federal Mediation and Conciliation Division suggested a forty-hour ruling, the board decided that a temporary work-week of forty-two and one-half hours should begin on 17 February 1919. The NWLB's announcement constituted no more than a recommendation but the board worded it in such a way that it appeared to be an order.[110]

Upon hearing of the board's "decision," the Paterson UTW called the NWLB recommendation "the greatest achievement" in the history of Paterson's silk strikes even though the union knew for certain that the final determination would be for more than forty-two and one-half hours. The local press, mill owners, and city officials also welcomed the announcement and in order to further "awe the workers into submission" Paterson's police chief declared that until the final NWLB ruling, there could be "no strike in this city" and ordered the arrest of all pickets.[111]

None of this maneuvering fooled the radical forces who had opposed NWLB intervention from the beginning and who now warned that the agency's "ruling" was a "trick" to "smuggle in the 47 hour week through the back door."[112] The UTW's ribbon weavers local joined in these protests but when February 17 arrived, the vast majority of Paterson's silk workers returned to their shops as Lessig, Yannarelli, Rubinstein, and other radical leaders had little success in convincing employees to remain on strike. By the end of the week, the IWW and the WIIU had little choice but to instruct their members to return to work.[113]

Since Paterson workers were not easily "awed," their willingness to return to the mills requires explanation. First, many workers believed that the final NWLB decision would standardize hours in the silk industry as they anticipated that a number of Pennsylvania silk mills would sign the joint submission statement to the NWLB.[114] Second, without absolute proof that the final NWLB decision would not be for forty-two and one-half hours, the radicals, by telling workers to remain out for forty-four hours, actually appeared to be arguing in favor of a *longer* work-week. Third, the loss of the 1913 strike meant workers in Paterson, unlike those in Lawrence, had little taste for confrontations with police that would inevitably lead to mass arrests.[115]

Above all, a recrudescence of Paterson's sectarian divisions doomed all attempts to prolong the strike. Soon after the walkout began, the IWW managed to change the basis of representation on the Eight Hour Workday Conference so that delegates from specific shops rather than representatives of Jewish and Socialist groups would have the upper hand. This shift had given the Wobblies control of the strike.[116] In response to the IWW's actions, a committee of twenty Paterson workers, chiefly composed of WIIU members, journeyed to New York City to seek the support of the ACWA. This union had just won a strike for the forty-four-hour week in the New York City men's clothing industry and, as was to be true in the Passaic and Lawrence situations as well, responded enthusiastically to the request for help. Almost immediately, the ACWA dispatched three organizers to Paterson, who upon their arrival in the city announced that they had come "to assist workers in organizing and securing" the forty-four-hour week.[117]

The ACWA's entry into the strike angered the IWW, which had not been informed of the invitation's having been extended to the clothing workers' union. The Wobblies would have opposed the ACWA's participation in any case as these two unions had been rivals ever since the ACWA's founding in 1914.[118] According to the Wobblies, the ACWA's intervention was merely a "disguised" effort by the WIIU to regain control of the walkout, and the IWW moved forcefully to prevent the ACWA from playing a role in the strike. The ACWA also met strong opposition from the Paterson Police Department which, consistent with a ban on outside speakers imposed since the beginning of the walkout, physically forced the three ACWA representatives to leave the city. Upon their departure, the ACWA organizers vowed "to return to direct the opening of the real strike of 25,000 workers for the 44 hour week" but they insisted that there be "no organized" opposition to the ACWA's presence. And when the ACWA leadership learned that the IWW continued to object to their participation, the ACWA withdrew rather than become involved in further interorganizational bickering.[119]

The ACWA's withdrawal came just prior to the announcement of the "short hours" decision. The IWW and the WIIU tried publicly to paper over their differences but the rift was far too deep to allow for any true cooperation. A correspondent for the socialist newspaper *The New York Call* noted: "In Paterson there is a great body—sensitive indeed—but a body without a head." *The Rebel Worker*, the IWW's New York City organ, agreed that "factional quarrels" and workers' "distrust of their own leaders" had prevented effective resistance in Paterson.[120] Weakened and divided by this wrangling, Paterson's workers returned to the mills to await the final NWLB decision.

The Final NWLB Decision

At the NWLB hearings held in mid-March, the UTW once again changed its position and argued that the board should grant a forty-four-hour week as the union's representatives claimed that the forty-seven-hour compromise had only been offered in order to avoid a violent and prolonged strike. Although they presented evidence as to the hardships caused by the fifty-hour week, for the most part the UTW's arguments focused on the need to counteract the IWW, which Golden, Magnet, and the other UTW representatives usually referred to as "the Bolshevik element."

Now that the workers were back in the mills, the manufacturers' representatives scoffed at the UTW's attempt to make use of the Red Scare and argued that the fifty-hour week had to be maintained so as not to further the competitive advantage enjoyed by the Pennsylvania mills. The manufacturers pressed this issue because contrary to Henry Doherty's and the UTW's expectation, few Pennsylvania mills had actually signed the joint submission agreement to the NWLB. But talk of moving out of Paterson threatened the consensus that had brought both sides to Washington because the mill owners had raised issues that the UTW representatives "thought would never come up." The air of cordiality that marked the beginning of the hearings had largely dissipated by their conclusion and even Thomas Morgan, the normally placid head of the Loomfixers and Twisters Local, wondered how the manufacturers managed to afford the "five thousand dollar automobiles that they drove around Paterson."[121] Although at this point both sides had their own reasons for avoiding a break, the disagreements that surfaced at this meeting foreshadowed the employers' 1920–1921 open-shop offensive that ended peaceful relations between the manufacturers and the UTW.

The final NWLB decision came on April 9 when the board set the workweek at forty-eight hours. The ruling specified that the forty-eight-hour week would remain in effect for the "duration of the war" with the provision that either party could reopen the case at intervals of six months.[122] The manufacturers expressed general satisfaction with the edict and the UTW leadership, continuing its public playacting, voiced great disappointment. Meanwhile, the *Paterson Evening News* reported that workers were "stunned" that they had received a mere two-hour cut in hours—a reduction that in the words of one Wobbly gave them an extra "20 minutes a day—just enough for another cup of coffee and a glance at the newspaper headlines."[123] Despite the evident dissatisfaction, little overt opposition to the NWLB ruling surfaced as by mid-April, the Eight Hour Workday Conference had been disbanded and the rank and file showed no inclination to disobey the board's ruling on their own. The left's impotence appeared all the more striking since the IWW and the WIIU had vowed to resist the NWLB and the final decision confirmed the radical unionists' prediction as to the role that the board would play.

The outcome seemed to vindicate the decision of the manufacturers and the UTW to take the case to the NWLB as it is highly unlikely that a locally arranged settlement could have convinced workers to accept the forty-eight-hour week.[124] Weakened by sectarianism and by sectoralism, Paterson's workers would not fully realize their goals until July and August 1919 when they threw off the UTW leadership. By way of contrast workers in the neighboring city of Passaic, who also struck on February 3, proved far more determined and united in their quest to realize the promises held out by the war.

Chapter Four

PASSAIC:
FOREIGN MANUFACTURERS AND
FOREIGN WORKERS

The Passaic Mills

Located a few miles south of Paterson, Passaic stood at the heart of a highly industrialized district that also included Garfield, Wallington, Lodi, and part of the city of Clifton. Although a number of small cotton and woolen mills had been built in Passaic in the 1860s and 1870s, the city's textile industry did not really develop until 1889 when Congress increased the duties on worsteds. In response to this measure, the Botany company, which had its headquarters in Leipzig, Germany, decided to open a branch plant in Passaic. The firm selected the location because of its proximity to New York City and its rapidly expanding garment industry, to which Botany planned to sell most of its cloth, and because, as was true of silk, the waters of the Passaic River were ideal for the washing and dyeing of woolen materials.

Botany started operations in 1890 and enjoyed instant success. After that date, it steadily expanded its plant, which came to sprawl over sixty acres in the Dundee section of Passaic and the neighboring city of Clifton. Practical and experienced managers ran its operations as Ferdinand Kuhn, the firm's president, was an expert wool buyer and Carl Heinrich Schlacter, the general superintendent, was a mechanical engineer. German nationals filled almost all of the other top positions and German soon became known as the "managerial language" of Passaic.[1]

Forstmann & Huffmann, which opened in 1903, was the other large mill in the city. Julius Forstmann, who headed the firm, traced his family's connection to the woolen industry back to sixteenth-century weaving guilds but the first plant to bear the Forstmann name was erected in 1793. From that date, the Forstmanns had been highly successful woolen and worsted manufacturers in Germany. A stickler for detail, Julius Forstmann demanded exactness and he imported most of the new plant's machinery from Germany as he considered American textile equipment to be of inferior quality. To Botany's distress, Forstmann, in keeping with his goal of producing goods equal in quality to those made in Germany, also recruited many of the rival firm's top superintendents.

Forstmann operated two plants. The larger mill was in Garfield, directly across the Passaic River from Passaic, and the other factory was located in the center of Passaic's mill district. As president of the company, Forstmann assumed personal responsibility for the operation of the firm. Unlike Botany's executive officers, Forstmann resided in Passaic and he took a direct hand whenever labor problems loomed at the mills. Paternalistic in his approach, he often spoke to his employees as if they were serfs whose interest would be protected by the lord of the manor.[2]

By 1918, the Botany and the Forstmann & Huffmann mills employed 6,000 and 4,500 operatives respectively. These two mills dominated textile production in Passaic as they were the only plants that took raw wool through each process until finished cloth had been produced. Passaic also had a number of smaller mills. Christian Bahnsen, a Dane who had received his technical training in Germany, directed three of the more specialized plants. Bahnsen owned controlling stock in the Gera and Passaic Worsted Spinning firms, which were located in Dundee, and the New Jersey Worsted Spinning Company, which was based in Garfield. Gera and New Jersey Worsted Spinning mills employed 1,500 workers apiece and Passaic Worsted employed 450 mill hands. All three plants had opened between 1900 and 1911. The Garfield Worsted Company was the sixth woolen mill in the Passaic area. This firm had been incorporated in 1902, the first mill to be based in Garfield. Its 1,100 employees did only weaving and finishing work and most of the yarn came from the Passaic spinning mills.[3]

All of these mills concentrated on the production of worsteds. These goods were both lighter and softer than woolens, and between 1890 and 1920 their popularity with consumers grew tremendously. Since worsted production, unlike woolens, required the use of combing machinery to eliminate the short fibers in the wool, it took considerably more capital to run a worsted than a woolen plant. And since worsteds had only emerged in the 1880s, their manufacturers were able to take full advantage of the latest textile technology. Consequently, worsted mills came to be distinguished by the use of automatic machinery, intense speed of their operations, and large size.

Managed by tough, smart, and shrewd businessmen, the Passaic mills produced top-quality cloth. Even during the First World War, the Passaic mill owners had resisted adding shoddy to their virgin wool. This emphasis on excellence made Passaic a national center for the manufacture of fine worsteds for both men's and women's wear.[4]

The war put the German-owned mills in a vulnerable position and in 1918, the Alien Property Custodian took over the running of Botany, Gera, Passaic Worsted, and New Jersey Worsted because the majority of their stock was held by German citizens. After the war, the federal government sold these shares although Botany remained under government control through the early 1920s. Since Forstmann had become an American citizen, his company remained under his control although the Bureau of Investigation suspected that his retreat in the Catskills was being used as a wireless station by the Germans, and the Alien Property Custodian (and future attorney general), A. Mitchell Palmer, had inaccurately charged that the Forstmann & Huffmann company was "German owned, dominated and controlled."[5] In general, the federal takeovers had little impact on the day-to-day operation of the mills but their German connections did place them in an unusually defensive position on the local level.

The war also marked the end of this period of phenomenal growth as in the 1920s worsteds lost some of their market strength. In 1918, though, in the United States, only the American Woolen Company, the Amoskeag Company (located in Manchester, New Hampshire) and the Arlington and the Pacific mills produced more woolen and worsted goods.[6] Nine thousand and eighty-four of Passaic's 21,396 wage earners worked in the worsted industry and another 3,500 textile mill hands worked in Garfield.[7] The Dundee area of Passaic, the "Botany District" of Clifton, and Garfield actually comprised a single textile district that had grown enormously because of the expansion of the worsted industry.[8]

An Immigrant Community

Passaic, like Paterson, was a city of immigrants, but there the similarity largely ends. Since industrial development had been sporadic before 1890, Passaic's population in that year totaled only 13,028 and was largely composed of residents of English, Scotch, Irish, and Dutch origin. The building of the Botany mill meant that thousands of jobs had opened up almost overnight. Many of the supervisory and skilled positions in Botany had been filled by immigrants from Leipzig and according to the U.S. Immigration Commission, all those who left Germany between 1890 and 1895 "were assured positions in the mill." Many of these German residents and more recent arrivals also filled supervisory and highly skilled positions at Passaic's other plants.[9]

The worsted mills also served as a magnet for thousands of Slavic immigrants who lacked previous industrial experience and who came from contiguous areas of the Austro-Hungarian and Russian empires. Poles comprised the largest percentage of these new arrivals and by 1920 Passaic had become home to over 17,000 people of Polish origin. This ethnic group formed such a large part of the working-class community that outsiders often referred to Passaic's immigrant district as if it were entirely Polish, but Passaic's and Clifton's population also included 5,857 Slovaks, 2,958 Russians, and 2,600 Ruthenians.[10]

The terminology used above was employed by the Census Bureau, but it is a poor indicator of peoples' own national identities. Almost all of Passaic's "Russians" were Ukrainians who hailed from eastern Galicia (present-day western Ukraine), which was then under Austrian rule. They had lived in close proximity to Passaic's Poles, who came almost entirely from western Galicia.[11] And the Ruthenians, who at this time were just as likely to identify themselves as Carpatho-Rusyns, came from Galicia or from the same Hungarian-ruled provinces of Zemplín, Spis, and Săriš in eastern Slovakia as Passaic's Slovaks.[12]

Both Galicia and Slovakia (which were separated by the Tatra Mountains) ranked among the poorest and least industrialized areas of Europe. The economies of both regions had been damaged by the extension of the railroads, which had brought a flood of cheap manufactured goods and farm produce. Since neither Galicia nor Slovakia had sufficient industry to absorb their rapidly increasing populations, many peasants in the 1870s had begun to journey to other areas of Austria-Hungary and to Germany in search of work. In this sense, their decision to come to Passaic only represented an extension of this migratory pattern as their goal remained the same—save enough money to buy land in their native provinces.[13]

On the surface, then, Passaic resembled other Slavic communities such as Steelton and Johnstown, Pennsylvania, that have been described by John Bodnar and Ewa Morawska.[14] There was one significant difference between Passaic and these cities as the Pennsylvania towns produced steel and Passaic manufactured textiles. Since textiles employed large numbers of women, this meant that contrary to the normal migratory pattern, single women had often preceded single men to Passaic. Many of these women had come to America on their own and in some cases they had even left their husbands behind in Europe. Many of the Galician women lived in boarding houses that had been sponsored by a Roman Catholic religious order and worked in the woolen and worsted plants or in the city's handkerchief factories. The presence of large numbers of single women, in turn, had attracted men from the steel-mill towns and from the anthracite coal region of Pennsylvania and they found employment in the textile mills or in the male-employing rubber and wire factories.[15]

Whatever their original intentions, many of the Slavic immigrants decided to remain in the city and, like their compatriots in other industrial communities in America, they built a dense network of institutions that centered on the saloons, the sokols, and the church. The saloon functioned as far more than an eating and drinking place since many of these establishments had halls attached to them that served as sites for social gatherings, dances, and political meetings. When strikes occurred, this last function proved extremely important as police often forbade workers from meeting on the street or in supposedly public halls. Often owned by former mill workers, the saloon provided one of the few places where men could escape the harshness of mill and tenement life, but women often suffered the consequences of this "release" as wife beating could often follow drinking bouts.[16]

The sokols (often called falcons in the Polish community) had originated in Prague in 1862 and had helped kindle the Czech national spirit. By the late nineteenth century they had spread to most other Slavic areas. In the United States, mutual benefit societies often affiliated with them and they also served as centers for gymnastics, cultural performances, and agitation centering on the homeland cause. Passaic's Slovaks, in particular, participated in the sokol movement since the city served as the national headquarters for the Slovak Catholic Sokol, which had split from a secular-oriented sokol in 1905.[17]

The churches, above all, played a central role in the Slavic community and their prominence helps explain why a wide gulf separated the Passaic and Paterson working classes. The massive Gothic cathedrals that towered over Dundee represented a form of ethnic assertion in a city where immigrants were usually treated as second-class citizens. Whether Greek or Latin Rite, Russian Orthodox, or affiliated with the Polish National Catholic Church, the churches structured much of the Slavic immigrants' community life—as they provided for emergency as well as for day-to-day needs. Since the parochial schools instructed children in their parents' language and history, they aided in the preservation of culture and since the churches had often opposed efforts by governmental authorities to impose an alien way of life, they had become identified with national causes and struggles. And unlike the saloons and many of the ethnic clubs, the churches were not strictly male preserves; for women, the innumerable church-related societies provided a social outlet outside of the home and christenings and weddings provided a form of recreation.[18]

Since churches were organized on an ethnic basis, the parishes often became embroiled in nationality disputes. For example, the priest at the Slovak St. Marie's of the Assumption Roman Catholic Church, Father Imrich Haitinger, had been locked in a long-standing battle with many of his parishioners. Though Father Haitinger was a Slovak, many of the church members considered him to be a Magyarone, a Slovak who had adopted Magyar culture and customs. His lack of support for Slovak national aspirations had led to a number of fist fights in the church and police on a number of occasions had to be called to restore order. The dispute was not settled until Father Haitinger's opponents in 1922 seceded and organized the Holy Name Slovak Catholic Church.[19]

A similar battle rocked the Polish Roman Catholic Church, St. Joseph's, when in February 1912, the bishop of the Newark Diocese appointed Father Julius Monteuffel to head this large parish. Thousands of church members objected to this selection, arguing that a Pole rather than a German should have been chosen for this position.[20] As often occurred in church fights, rebellious parishioners supported a dynamic young priest, Father Stanislaus Kruczek, who had only recently arrived in America and who came from the same region of Austrian Galicia as most of Passaic's Polish residents. Father Kruczek's supporters actively campaigned on his behalf. They distributed circulars, conducted petition drives, and organized mass meetings. Rather than boycott the services, the protestors refused to make the customary ten-cents contribution, sang

Polish hymns, and ridiculed Father Monteuffel by singing, talking, and laughing whenever he rose to speak. Most of Father Kruczek's supporters were recent arrivals and they berated older church members for wearing American-style clothes and hats rather than shawls. Female parishioners played a leading role in the entire affair and spread the turmoil to the Acheson-Harden Handkerchief Company when they demanded that the firm fire an employee who they said had acted as a police spy during the church strife. To back up their demand, 300 of the Polish women conducted a "church strike" that lasted until the company fired the suspected employee.

The conflict dragged on for months and was not settled until the Newark Diocese in 1913 incorporated Holy Rosary Church as a second Polish parish. This concession stemmed defections to Passaic's Polish National Catholic Church SS. Peter and Paul, which had been established in 1903 and which had taken advantage of the fray to gain members. Instead, when Holy Rosary finally opened its doors in 1919, it had 7,000 parishioners and the Polish National Catholic Church, which often served as a center for nationalist and even socialist activities, never grew to any considerable size in Passaic.[21]

The intensity of these church battles indicates that to the Slavic immigrants, the church mattered. When necessary, the parishioners defied both bishops and city authorities to gain control of the institution that had been built through their "blisters" and "hard earned contributions."[22] In the process priests emerged as the most visible defenders of the ethnic community as Passaic had only a small Slavic middle class before the 1920s. Standing up for the interests of the immigrant population led the priests to protest the city's neglect of sanitation conditions in Dundee, to criticize city officials' failure to distribute coal to the poor, to condemn blue laws that deprived their working-class parishioners from seeing movies on their only free day, and to band together in 1918 to demand that the mills who were "making plenty of money" provide compensation for crippling accidents.[23] Priests also served as channels of information as they informed church members of on-going strikes, of pay rates in different mills, and of banks that could not be trusted.[24]

The influence of the church helps to account for why socialism had gained few adherents among Slavic mill workers in Passaic. Ukrainians proved an exception because they had forged their national consciousness in opposition to the Polish nobility that owned much of the land in eastern Galicia. In the process many Ukrainians had embraced socialism. Many of Passaic's Ukrainian residents maintained this identity upon their arrival in the United States and leftists exercised a great deal of influence in this community.[25] Poles and Slovaks though remained largely outside the socialist sphere. This did not prevent them from accepting radical leadership at the time of strikes, but it meant left-wing unionists faced a formidable task in recruiting members whose own church denied the sacraments to socialists.[26]

Besides the Slavic groups, large numbers of Magyars and Italians worked in the mills. Passaic's 6,000 Magyar residents lived in the same Dundee neighborhood as the Slavs but many of them had a far different orientation. Close to one-third belonged to the Hungarian Reformed Church but more significantly, whether Protestant or Catholic, they organized much of their community life outside of the church. Groups such as the Hungarian Workingmen's Club and Hungarian Sick and Death Benefit Society and numerous singing and dramatic societies had a definite secular as well as socialist flavor. Passaic also became home to the Hungarian weekly *Szabad Sajtó* (Free press), which gave strong support to workers' causes and which served as the strikers' organ in 1919. Magyars gave support to the left even though about 80 percent of Passaic's Magyar residents came from the rural provinces of Szabolcs, Borsod, Abauj-Torna, and Ung that varied little from the home regions of Slovaks. Here, one can only be speculative, but it appears that since Magyars had not been a subject people, the church had been unable to assume the role of a defender of an oppressed national minority. In this context it is worth noting that both Roman Catholic and Reformed churches had received financial support from the Hungarian government and had not been built totally from the bottom up.[27] Another 20 percent of Passaic's Hungarian residents were German-Hungarians who had been German-speaking residents of Hungary. Known also as Swabians, their ancestors had moved down the Danube and settled in regions near Budapest. These immigrants met in their own halls, supported their own fraternals, and were the most socialistically inclined of any ethnic group in Passaic.[28]

The more radical orientation of Passaic's Magyar community became evident when Count Michael Károlyi visited the city in April 1914. At this time, Count Károlyi headed the liberal Independent party in Hungary, but his American tour had been cosponsored by the Hungarian Social Democratic Party as Károlyi knew this was the only way he could win broad support from Hungarian workers in America. When he came to Passaic, representatives of the Hungarian socialist newspaper, *Elöre*, accompanied Károlyi and his address received a "resounding reception" from the 2,500 Magyars who packed the hall.[29] As will be seen in chapter 8, Magyar workers also responded with great enthusiasm to the Hungarian Revolution of 1919, although such zeal could estrange Poles and Slavs who did not embrace radical causes.

The Italian population lived apart from the Magyars and the Slavs. Within Passaic itself, most Italians lived on the edge of the east side rather than in Dundee. Many Italians also lived in Clifton and Garfield, and Italians composed the largest number of foreign-born in each of these cities. For the most part Italian workers proved extremely supportive of strikes but the residential and cultural barriers that separated them from the Magyar and Slavic immigrants prevented them from playing a central role in labor activity.[30]

Almost all of Passaic's Jewish residents came from the same areas of east central Europe as the Magyars and the Slavs. But unlike in Paterson, very few of these Jewish immigrants worked in the textile mills. Instead, many of them found employment in garment factories or in the building trades. Others chose to work as peddlers, much as they had done in Hungary or Galicia. By the time of the war, these "multi-lingual salesmen" owned much of the real estate in Dundee and owned almost all of the small shops that lined Second Street, the district's principal shopping artery. This perpetuation of an Old World relationship in the New World made Jews vulnerable to accusations of cheating mill hands as many of Dundee's residents believed they paid "scandalously high" prices for provisions.[31]

Regardless of national origins, most of Passaic's immigrants faced the same harsh living conditions because the community had one of the poorest and most congested living quarters of any industrial city in the United States: five-sixths of the population lived on the east side, which comprised only one-sixth of the city's area. A housing survey sponsored by the Passaic Board of Trade found that this district's wood-frame tenements lacked adequate lighting or sanitation and often housed as many as twelve families. The study concluded that "at best these tenement houses were miserable abodes," at their worst, they were "mere dens into which human beings crawl to eat and sleep after long hours of monotonous toil."[32]

Dundee, which was really a city unto itself, comprised the poorest and most congested part of the immigrant quarter. Located on a narrow strip of land between a canal and the Passaic River, this district was home to many of the city's mills and to most of the Magyar and Slavic residents. Besides crowded housing conditions, residents also had to endure the stink of chemicals dumped into the river. Nevertheless, life in such a district had its compensations as within its borders, immigrants drank, shopped, prayed, and socialized together. Especially on Saturday nights and Sunday mornings, its streets came alive as residents sought relief from the daily grind of mill work.[33]

Few of Dundee's residents ventured very far from the neighborhood since trolley lines had been built only on the west side. By 1900, middle-class residents had fled the district, creating a city firmly divided by class and ethnicity. Up until 1911, immigrants had some voice on the city council as each of the city's five wards had been allotted one seat. Under the district system, the first Slavic councilman, Edward Levendusky, had been elected in 1909. In order to deny immigrants all representation, Charles F. H. Johnson, who was then secretary of the Passaic Board of Trade, and other business leaders successfully campaigned to have the city adopt a commission form of government. The new charter provided for a five-person council to be elected at large and the mayor was now to be selected by council members rather than elected by the populace. Once the new system took effect in 1913, the east side lost all representation on the council. All efforts to return to the old system failed and the west siders' domination of city government reinforced east siders' belief that middle-class residents considered them to be second-class citizens.[34]

Many of the Slavic, Magyar, and Italian workers also settled in Garfield, whose 1920 population of 19,371 included 8,521 foreign-born residents. Originally developed to provide housing for Passaic's workers, Garfield had become an industrial community with the erection of the Forstmann & Huffmann mill. Garfield lacked tenements, and thus the community gave immigrants an opportunity to satisfy some of their longing for the rural society they had left behind. Many workers grew vegetables and kept ducks, geese, and chickens in back of their small cottages. Garfield's working class also exerted political power as the city had only a very small middle class, and the city's voters in 1910 rejected a commission form of government and retained a ward system of representation. Due to the working-class political influence, Garfield's mill hands could count on the sympathy of both the city council and local police at the time of strikes—an aspect that proved of considerable importance during every walkout between 1912 and 1926.[35]

Working Conditions in the Worsted Mills

The production of worsted goods required far more steps than silk before the finished product could be turned out.[36] A typical worsted mill separated workers into thirteen distinct job categories.[37] (Table 4.1). Between scouring and finishing, all of the operations were machine processes and most workers—called "operatives" and "machine tenders" for good reason—did the same repetitive task hour after hour and day after day.

Carding was the dirtiest, dustiest, and most disagreeable job because carding machines had a set of teeth that opened the fibers of the wool and arranged them in a mixture of uniform density. Combing and drawing came next. A combing department contained combing, backwashing, and gill box machines that separated the short fibers, known as tops, from the curly fibers. Only the tops were used in worsted production. During the drawing process, the material passed through a series of machines that made the strands longer and thinner. Spinning varied greatly depending on whether or not mules were used. Forstmann &

Table 4.1
Division of Labor in a Worsted Mill

Process	Percentage of Workers Assigned
Sorting	2.9
Scouring	0.5
Carding	2.4
Combing	5.8
Drawing	11.1
Cap Spinning	11.2
Mule Spinning	0.4
Twisting	5.1
Reeling, Winding, Spooling	12.5
Dressing	1.2
Weaving	18.6
Finishing (includes mending, burling and dyeing)	20.6
Other	8.4

Source: National Industrial Conference Board, *Hours of Work as Related to the Output and Health of Workers* (Boston, 1918), 69.

Huffmann produced some French-spun cloth that required the employment of highly skilled mule spinners, but the other Passaic and Lawrence firms mainly used the Bradford system, which required the operative to do little more than tend the machine. Twisting, reeling, and winding, during which operations the material was passed from one machine to another and the ends tied together, were the last processes before weaving.

Weave rooms were at the heart of a worsted mill; this process employed the largest number of workers and was the crucial step in determining the final quality of the product. Though requiring less skill than in silk, weavers could never leave their looms untended as wool was a relatively fine material and subject to frequent breakages. For this reason, worsted weavers usually tended four looms as opposed to cotton weavers who, in this era, tended as many as sixteen looms. As in silk, worsted weaving could be filled with petty annoyances as supervisors played "favorites" in assigning work, machines often needed repairs, and weavers had to wait several hours for new warps after the bolts of cloth had been taken off the loom and sent over to the percher for examination. Weavers were paid on a piecework basis so delays could cause a considerable loss of earnings. And unlike in many other operations that employers had defined as male or female jobs, both sexes worked in relatively equal numbers in weave rooms and men and women often joined together in strike actions.

All of the machine processes were carried out in large rooms that could be over 200 yards in length. Those who saw them for the first time thought they resembled a chamber of horrors. The noise was deafening, the rooms thick with dust and lint, and workers' hands could easily become caught in the closely packed and unguarded machinery. On hot days, it became impossible to continue to work because of the lack of ventilation, and the constant supervision created a prison-like atmosphere in which a worker hesitated even to ask permission to go to the lavatory.

Besides loom fixing, which involved the same type of work as in the silk industry, some worsted-mill jobs did not require the operation of machinery. These included woolsorting and the finishing processes of mending and burling. Woolsorting was the very first step in worsted production and was a skilled position; a woolsorter had to know how to separate wool into different grades. Unlike many of the other jobs, the work had to be done in well-lighted rooms or near windows since the wool had to be graded by both texture and color. On the other hand, the raw wool was foul-smelling and greasy and workers often contracted anthrax, which had come to be known as "woolsorter's disease."

Mending and burling were finishing processes performed entirely by women. Burlers removed knots and lumps that weavers had left in the cloth.[38] Mending required a great deal of skill since these "hand weavers" had to replace the threads that the burlers had removed with new threads that matched the color, quality, and design of the cloth. After these workers finished their jobs, the cloth then passed through further machine processes before being sent to the dyers.[39]

As was the rule in the textile industry, Passaic employers had devised an extremely complex system of pay rates.[40] In 1918, most jobs paid between twenty-five and thirty-five cents per hour and between eighteen and twenty-six dollars per week.[41] Mill workers had to depend on a family wage because families could not survive on the earnings of a sole wage earner. Thus in Passaic, as in the entire worsted industry, women comprised approximately one-half of the work force.

Passaic differed from Lawrence and most other textile communities because large numbers of women continued to work after being married and bearing children. The majority of these young mothers worked on a special night shift that ran from 8:00 PM to 6:00 AM as New Jersey, partly due to the textile manufacturers' vigorous lobbying efforts, was one of the few northern states not to ban night work by women. The mills attracted these young mothers by offering a special 10 percent premium to those who worked at night. Mothers also preferred to work at night as they could leave their young children under some parental supervision while they were in the mills. Fathers may have watched over the children but women did all of the housework and kept schedules that astonished visitors to Passaic. After standing on their feet for ten hours (except for the midnight one-half hour "lunch" break), they returned home to prepare their husbands' breakfasts and then spent the rest of the day cooking, washing, and caring for their children. When asked when she slept, one of these mothers laughed and replied, "Oh, there's no time to sleep" but most managed to catnap or sleep for three to four hours per day.[42]

Night work allowed for little of the socializing that Tamara Hareven and Randolph Langenbach found in Manchester's Amoskeag Mill as Botany and Forstmann & Huffmann used this shift for rush orders and for the preparatory processes of carding, combing, and spinning.[43] Female employees often fell asleep at their machines and suffered from backaches, headaches, chest pains, and sore knees and hips.[44] Women worked up until the moment of giving birth and resumed employment soon after their deliveries—partly accounting for Passaic's extremely high infant mortality rate.[45]

We know very little about how these women perceived their own lives and must rely on the observations of outsiders. Some of the visitors to Passaic commented on the night workers' "stoical acceptance of their lot" but others noted in a more positive vein that they took pride in their work and welcomed the opportunity to be employed outside of the home.[46] Significantly, Passaic workers in 1919 did not demand the abolition of night work. This suggests that given the limited employment opportunities for female workers, they may have come to depend on night work and did not necessarily welcome the efforts of reform organizations such as the New Jersey Consumers' League to have it banned.[47] Regardless of this aspect, the women who survived the double day developed tremendous inner strength and contributed mightily to the great Passaic walkouts of 1919 and 1926.

Before the 1919 strike, none of the Passaic mill owners had shown much interest in welfare work. The contrast between manufacturers' concern for the quality of their cloth and their lack of concern for the work environment appeared the sharpest at the Botany company, which a 1918 National Consumers' League investigation found to be "notoriously lacking in provisions for the welfare of its workers." Behind its high walls, workers ate at their machines as there were no lunchrooms, changed in the workrooms as there were no dressing rooms, took their noon naps on the floors as there were no chairs, and used toilets that were no more than "holes" that were "set over a common trough."[48]

Conditions at Forstmann & Huffmann were not quite as bad, but before the war the company had not spent one cent on welfare work. As noted in chapter 2, Julius Forstmann, motivated by a desire to reduce turnover, had in 1917 installed a cafeteria in the Garfield plant. Forstmann considered this to have been a "satisfactory financial investment" as it had shown "workers our interest in their welfare" and made them "more contented."[49]

Forstmann's positive response to this small change presaged the reversal of the company's position that came in the wake of the 1919 strike. But on the eve of the big walkout nothing more had been done, and most importantly, the manufacturers had sternly opposed all efforts made by workers to gain a voice in the day-to-day operation of the mills.

The 1912 Strikes

Before 1912, despite the grim conditions, the Passaic mills experienced little labor unrest. The availability of surplus labor made it risky to walk out and the steady work and fifty-five-to-sixty-hour workweeks met the needs of many of those who did not plan to remain in the United States on a permanent basis. The series of strikes that occurred in 1912 thus mark a turning point in the city's labor relations as after that date, Passaic workers staged a series of walkouts that grew in intensity until the climactic strike of 1926.

Coming on the heels of the great Lawrence victory, the 1912 strikes owed their inspiration to the Bread and Roses triumph. In an immediate sense they also resulted from the diligent efforts of the same Detroit IWW leaders who were then conducting Paterson's broad-silk strikes. The walkouts began on March 14 when 300 weavers struck the Forstmann & Huffmann plant and eventually 4,000 of Passaic's 10,000 woolen and worsted workers became involved. The demands reflected grievances that workers had accumulated over the years and centered on wages and complaints concerning the use of fines, piecework payments, and bonus systems. Strikers also fought for the recognition of shop committees—a sure sign that workers were beginning to think of themselves as permanent employees. The work stoppages lacked the mass activity and revolutionary fervor that characterized the Lawrence struggle and only the Garfield Worsted Company was forced to shut down.[50] Compared to the Lawrence walkout, the Passaic strike appeared almost grim. An SLP member who observed the workers' largest parade noted: "It was a sight to see file after file of the women march past with their careworn faces, quiet without a word and without a smile."[51]

Michael Ebner has documented the confusion and disarray that occurred when the IWW, fresh from the Lawrence triumph, came to Passaic. The Wobblies did not just try to take over the leadership of the strike, they also advocated a different strategy than that favored by the Detroit IWW. Instead of departmental walkouts, the Wobblies pushed for a mass strike; instead of token picketing, they advocated the "endless chain" method of picketing; instead of grouping workers by mill, they favored the nationality form of organization that had been used so successfully in Lawrence. Both unions also traded insults that alienated and confused many workers. According to the *New York Call*, "Hungarian and Italian strikers" who had been "the most militant" gave an enthusiastic response to Big Bill Haywood and other Wobblies who spoke in Garfield, but other workers became "demoralized" by the infighting that reached such lengths that the IWW accused the Detroit IWW of being "stool pigeons of the mill owners." [52]

The factional fighting allowed the manufacturers to lure their employees back to the mills with the promise of small wage increases. None of the mills made any significant changes in working conditions and none recognized shop committees. And once the employees returned, management took steps to insure that the call for union recognition would not be heard again. Botany fired ninety-seven workers whom it pinpointed as ringleaders; Gera dismissed all those who failed to report to work after the company issued an ultimatum; and Julius Forstmann, responding to the first challenge to his authority the way any martinet would, fired an entire shop committee that complained about the retention of strikebreakers. [53]

It would be hard to imagine a more disheartening scenario. As soon as the walkouts ended, both IWWs gave up all efforts to organize in Passaic. The withdrawal of both unions left the Passaic branch of the Socialist party as the only left-wing group in the city that reached beyond a single ethnic group. But the SP was in no position to offer leadership to Passaic's working class and this was not because the Socialist party stressed electoral rather than industrial action. Instead, the Passaic Socialist Party had limited appeal for Passaic's mill workers because its leaders displayed an antipathy for the Slavs and for their religion. For example, when the 1912 outbreaks occurred, the Passaic SP's organ, *The Issue*, referred to workers' "minds darkened for the lack of education, their souls held in the grip of a medieval superstitious religion, the humbleness of centuries ingrained in them" and commented that the walkouts demonstrated that there was "a latent spark of manhood even in a hunkie." *The Issue* also expressed hope that workers would cast off their religion as soon as their "eyes" were "opened." [54] Such attitudes were hardly uncommon in an era when socialists took pride in their identity as freethinkers and viewed the Catholic Church as a remnant of medievalism. But this perspective meant that even though the Passaic Socialist Party had taken the lead in opposing the commission form of government, it could not lead mass struggles of Slavic workers. [55] Along with the anger generated by the sectarian fighting of the two IWWs, the SP's lack of contact with mill workers guaranteed that when a new round of strikes occurred in Passaic, they would be led by the employees themselves.

The 1916 Strikes and the Passaic Council of Wool Manufacturers

Once the mills began to hum in 1916, Passaic workers launched a new series of strikes that were for the most part more successful than the previous work stoppages. As in 1912, weavers at the Forstmann & Huffmann company took the initiative as they struck the Garfield plant on March 12. The weavers sought to replace the various piecework systems with a minimum wage of $14 per week. When informed of this demand, Julius Forstmann responded:

The idea of a general flat rate is nonsense. Labor is a commodity and the company buys it from the workers according to quality and quantity. To pay a flat rate of $14 a week to all weavers would be as senseless as for one of the weavers to pay the same price for any loaf of bread regardless of size, weight and quantity.[56]

Calling the demand "absurd," Forstmann threatened to fire all of the strikers if they continued the walkout.

Undeterred by Forstmann's hard-line stance, workers in the other mills also walked out although all efforts to organize a general textile strike failed when Botany granted its employees a hefty pay hike. On the other hand, the work stoppages spread to over twenty-five different factories as the ties that bound workers together in the entire Passaic industrial region became apparent. As one group of employees gained wage increases, workers in other mills walked out. In some cases, such as at the Manhattan Rubber Company and Brighton Cotton Mill, workers in unrelated but contiguous plants carried out joint actions to prevent strikebreakers from entering the mills. Strikers shared the same ethnic meeting halls and raised many of the same demands. For a while, before the agitation calmed down, new strikes broke out almost on a daily basis.

Most of the departmental strikes at the woolen and worsted plants lasted for two or three weeks. To solidify their ranks, the immigrant strikers used a wide range of tactics. They threw red pepper at scabs and appealed to local grocers for food and other forms of aid. At daily mass meetings, leaders encouraged each worker "to express any idea he or she may have." Women picketed and demonstrated alongside men and actively participated in the street battles. Many Forstmann & Huffmann weavers took other jobs in order to support their fellow strikers. Gera employees picketed the mill day and night in order to know exactly how many strikebreakers entered the plant. Passaic Worsted employees published the names of those who refused to strike in a local Polish newspaper to make the "'scabs' feel so ashamed of themselves" that they would join the walkout. Strikers picked up their back pay in a body to prevent any individual worker from being singled out and to demonstrate their solidarity.

Of most significance, when weavers banded together to form a union they insisted that it be "purely local." Although they welcomed outside Slovak, Italian, Polish, and Hungarian speakers, workers strongly opposed any intervention by outside organizations. This animosity, which stemmed from the 1912 fiasco, extended to all outside unions regardless of ideological orientation when workers told both the UTW and the IWW to stay out.

Most of the strikes led to pay hikes though some retaliatory firings did occur. As in 1912, weavers at the Forstmann & Huffmann company stood at the center of the most bitter dispute. After holding firm for six weeks these workers won a 20 percent wage increase and a guarantee of improved working conditions. But when they returned to work the weavers discovered that contrary to the agreement six of the strikebreakers had not been discharged, and the weavers left the plants again. The company responded to the second walkout by firing all those who left their looms and by placing prominently displayed "help wanted" advertisements in the Passaic newspapers. These threats proved successful as 200 Forstmann & Huffmann weavers returned to the mill and reportedly apologized for their behavior. By the first of May, the strike lost its momentum and Julius Forstmann expressed great satisfaction that the workers "begged to be taken back."

Events at Forstmann & Huffmann followed a prearranged plan as Forstmann deliberately lured workers back into the mill, secure in the knowledge that a second strike would be extremely difficult to organize. A similar ruse had been used in 1912 and would be employed again in 1919. But, regardless of this result, workers had gained much from the series of walkouts and most importantly, from the perspective of the future, the settlements vindicated the decision to rely on internal rather than external leadership.[57]

Faced with the partial success of the strikes, the Passaic mill owners reassessed their labor policies. They needed a new modus operandi because workers had taken advantage of the manufacturers' lack of coordination to gain more favorable settlements in some plants than in others. This in turn had led to dissatisfaction in the mills that paid lower wages. The problem had surfaced even before the walkouts as some mills had begun "enticing employees away from one mill to another by promises of higher pay, better conditions, etc." [58]

Before 1916, a formidable barrier had blocked cooperation among the mill owners—"they hated one another cordially." [59] But Julius Forstmann had become determined that workers would never again be able to play "one mill against the other." For this reason, he convened a series of meetings of Passaic's woolen manufacturers that aimed at healing the old divisions. The key conference came on 21 June 1916 when manufacturers reached a consensus on a number of points. For one, they agreed that no longer would employees be allowed to "shift" from one woolen mill to another as that "destroyed" any "stability of employment." Second, they agreed to standardize wages and to try to avoid giving large pay hikes in the future as "experience" showed that "a very liberal increase of wages did not mean a corresponding benefit to the workers, because many of the workers took it so much easier and did not work as industriously as formerly." Last, the manufacturers decided to hire "a so-called corporation officer, that is a man trained in police and detective work" who "would scrutinize all help engaged, point out undesirable people, etc." [60]

To implement these recommendations, the manufacturers formed a new organization called the Industrial Council of Passaic Wool Manuturers, which came to be known in Passaic simply as the Wool Council. [61] The new organization's first task was to standardize wage rates and in December 1916, all six mills posted notices with identical wording announcing new wage schedules and "uniform Christmas gratuities." [62] From this date until Botany broke from the Wool Council in 1925, the mills acted in concert in all questions dealing with wages and hours. A central bureau of employment accomplished the Wool Council's other objectives. Before the establishment of this bureau, those seeking employment had applied at each mill separately. Under the new procedures all applicants for work had first to report to the bureau and there answer a series of questions. If bureau employees deemed the responses to be satisfactory, the applicant received a card that was good for one week. Without this card no one could even enter a mill to look for work. These procedures sought to reduce turnover, a common employer objective at this time, as employees could not switch jobs without going through the central office. [63] Most importantly, however these procedures aimed at preventing any potential labor organizers from finding employment in the mills. [64]

The employment bureau opened on 1 March 1917 and in just four months 8,395 prospective employees had had their records checked. The mills actually hired 4,404 of these applicants. The council's secretary expressed satisfaction with the bureau as it had "resulted in the mills obtaining a desirable class" of labor.[65] On the other hand, it took barely a year before workers openly protested against the bureau's operation. Seventy-five loom fixers who sent a message to Alien Property Custodian A. Mitchell Palmer voiced the first public objections. In support of their petition, the workers said a loom fixer had been told that if he switched jobs, his pay would be cut from $32 to $13 per week. Very possibly having the mills' German ownership in mind, the workers also denounced the bureau's thorough physical exam for not being the "American way."[66] Criticism of the Wool Council also figured in the June 1918 Forstmann & Huffmann work stoppage (discussed in Chap. 2) as strikers charged that the employment bureau functioned as a "blacklist bureau" and they demanded its abolishment.[67]

Despite these protests, the employment office was firmly ensconced in Passaic by the end of the war and the blacklist, along with the retaliatory firings, enabled the woolen and worsted manufacturers to remain free of unions. The establishment of the entire Wool Council apparatus signaled a new determination by employers to put aside past differences in order to confront the labor movement. After 1916, workers faced an employing class that was both more united and more determined to resist any encroachments upon its power.

1919—Independent Action and Organization

When the UTW passed its eight-hour resolution at the November 1918 convention, the Passaic mills operated on a fifty-five-hour-per-week schedule (ten hours per day and five hours on Saturday). Though the union had pledged to win eight hours "for all textile workers" it naturally focused its attention on cities with UTW locals. This excluded Passaic as the city had almost no British or Irish workers, who usually formed the core of the UTW's membership. Feeble organizing efforts had been made in 1902 and 1914, but they had amounted to nothing and Passaic played no part in the UTW's wartime resurgence.[68] But, UTW organizers did not have to be present for the slogan "8 hours, February 3rd" to capture the imagination of textile workers when in December, Gera Mill officials reported finding eight-hour signs posted in their weave rooms—a good indication that Passaic workers had become aware of the UTW demand.[69]

When February 3 arrived, the Wool Council surprised many Passaic residents by announcing the adoption of the forty-eight-hour week. At the same time, the mill owners informed workers that they planned to continue running fifty-five hours, but would now pay time and a half for all work beyond forty-eight hours. This meant that for a fifty-five-hour week, workers would receive a sizable increase over their present wages.[70] The council's hand had been forced by the decision of the American Woolen Company to grant its workers the forty-eight-hour week. As Ferdinand Kuhn ruefully noted: "Once this was done by the American Woolen Company it was deemed wise by the Council of Passaic mills" to adopt the same measure.[71]

Already fearful that the end of the war would cost many of them their jobs, Passaic's workers strongly objected to the mill owners' intention to continue operating on a fifty-five-hour-per-week basis. Gera Mill weavers took the first action at 4:00 PM on February 3, when they "suddenly threw off the power on their looms and announced they had worked eight hours." Large numbers of other Gera workers followed the weavers and the entire plant was shut down by the next day. During the rest of the week, Garfield Worsted, Botany, New Jersey Worsted, and Forstmann & Huffmann employees quickly joined the first general textile strike ever to occur in Passaic. Strikers held rallies at Maciag's (a Polish saloon), the Slovak Sokol Hall, and other ethnic meeting places, and the exciting week of activity was capped when 10,000 workers met at First Ward Park for "the greatest gathering of strikers in the city's history."[72]

Such a total strike did not often occur in the textile industry. One key to the unified response in Passaic lies in the relative ethnic homogeneity of the Passaic work force. Since the mills had all been built after 1889, they had almost no "old" immigrants and even such highly paid jobs as boiler firemen, reserved for British and Irish workers in Lawrence, had been filled by Polish and Hungarian employees in Passaic. Lacking what historians have termed a cultural division of labor, when big strikes occurred in Passaic, mill hands did not have to contend with blocs of workers who by remaining in the mills acted as strikebreakers.[73] The second key lies in the Wool Council itself: faced with a united body of employers workers in the six mills recognized they had a common foe—a point they often made during the strike when workers mockingly thanked the employers for showing them the importance of unity.

As Passaic mill hands lacked any formal organization, they first had to form or find a union to lead the walkout. As one might expect, IWW and WIIU leaders in Paterson, where the eight-hour fight was also underway, came over to Passaic to plead the merits of their respective organizations. City officials led by the public safety commissioner, John Kehoe, and the captain of detectives, Benjamin Turner, quickly served notice that left-wing activists would not be welcomed in Passaic and seized radical literature and banned foreign-language speakers except for "men whom we know."[74] Though some workers welcomed the Wobblies, many others opposed the participation of non-Passaic organizations. The hostility of outsiders continued to be based on unpleasant memories of 1912 as the internecine warfare of the two IWW's remained implanted in workers' minds. One woman told the mass meeting of 10,000 workers that "We don't want the IWW or the WIIU. They are robbers. They lost the 1912 strike and we don't want to have anything to do with them. If we take them we will lose the strike." Another shop leader addressed the gathering in similar terms:

We don't want any outsiders, neither from Paterson, nor from Chicago nor from any other place. We want an organization of the woolen and worsted mills of Passaic, Clifton and Garfield. We have men among ourselves who can lead the strike. We want the dues we pay to stay right in Passaic and don't want our money to go to New York or any other place.[75]

Feuding that occurred as soon as the rival WIIU and IWW leaders arrived in Passaic further revivified memories of 1912, and Passaic workers became angered when they saw Paterson's divisions once again brought to their city.[76] As in 1916, the distrust of outsiders transcended ideology and workers said they were opposed to the UTW as well as to the more radical unions.

The intense localist orientation led strikers to form their own organization called the Independent Union of General Workers of the Textile Industries of Passaic and Vicinity, which became known as the Independent Union. In keeping with Passaic workers' preference for a workplace rather than a nationality form of organization, all members of the union's central committee worked in the mills and served as representatives of a particular mill. To insure that no outsiders gained control of this "home-made organization," the union's constitution contained a clause that provided that "any official or member found talking, working or acting in favor of any outside union" would "immediately and automatically be expelled from the organization"—a provision that caused considerable problems later when some workers did seek outside help.[77]

To lead this union, workers turned to Matthew Pluhar, who chaired

67

the very first general strike committee and who became the union's president by acclamation. A markedly cosmopolitan man who shared much with those who eventually led the CIO battles of the 1930s, Pluhar's background explains why he was in a position to assume leadership of 12,000 striking textile workers. Born in a small village in Bohemia of migrant farm parents, he received little formal schooling. At the age of fourteen, he went to work in a Czech woolen mill and later was employed as a spinner in a number of factories before coming to America. In Bohemia, he joined the Socialist party and became involved in myriad political and cultural activities before choosing to emigrate in 1909, a decision made in part because he feared that tensions in the Balkans would lead to a European war. He settled in Garfield, where he found work at the New Jersey Worsted plant, but in 1912 he lost his job due to his participation in the strike and moved to Lawrence in search of work. He was in Lawrence during the exciting months that followed the Bread and Roses strike and during the repressive period of October 1912. In 1913, he rejoined his family in Garfield and found work with Botany. Soon thereafter, he switched to the Forstmann & Huffmann company, where he was still employed as a spinner when the 1919 strike broke out.[78]

Pluhar's range of concerns typified those of many Czech radicals who, unlike most Slavs, were often deeply anticlerical. He participated in many singing societies and drama groups that commonly served as the training ground for immigrant, working-class leaders. He was a committed pacifist, and the war had deepened his conviction that such conflicts only benefited "those people who were going to profit from them." "Cynical" about religion, he never attended church and considered himself a freethinker. Above all, he identified himself as a socialist and trade unionist and believed that workers needed to submerge their national identity so as to build class unity.[79]

Given this personal history, it is no surprise that Pluhar assumed a position of leadership in 1919 even though Passaic had only a handful of Czech residents. As a longtime textile worker, he was familiar with the shop-level concerns of mill hands, and workers knew he was not afraid to talk back to the bosses. He also earned workers' respect because he took "great pride" in his work and believed that "his work had to be good, no matter how he was being exploited." He was familiar with the various Slavic languages and could communicate with most Passaic workers who shared a lingua franca.[80] Workers' acceptance of Pluhar's position demonstrates that even those who were tied to the church would follow radical leaders at the time of strikes. But this would not necessarily hold true in the aftermath of the work stoppage when Pluhar's socialistic and secularistic orientation made him vulnerable to attacks by religious and/or chauvinistic elements. And most significantly, Passaic's workers appeared inclined to let Pluhar assume an inordinate amount of the decision making. This is a sure sign that Passaic's Polish and Slovak communities, in particular, did not produce the type of leftist, assertive, and self-confident leaders that emerged in Paterson and Lawrence and this too would lead to problems at the end of the strike when many workers would blame Pluhar for the less-than-satisfactory outcome.

After selecting their leaders, workers next had to settle on their chief goals. The walkout had led to an outpouring of shop-level complaints but by the second week of the strike, the union settled on the following key demands: (1) recognition of the union and union shop committees; (2) 44/55, or a forty-four-hour week with a wage increase to make up for the lost hours; (3) double time for overtime; and (4) reemployment of all those fired because of strike activity. Workers made the last demand because they said they "remembered the last strike in Passaic" when the mill owners "fired every man and woman that was a member of the union."[81] The demands for shorter hours and increased pay flowed from a concern over the postwar layoffs and from a quest for a higher standard of living. Very often, operatives expressed their hopes for a better life in America in exceedingly modest terms. One worker talked about being able to afford a "shave" and another said that workers struck so that "we can have at least one dollar at the end of the week so that we can enjoy ourselves on Sunday."[82] A young Botany employee best summarized these aspirations:

We are being worked too hard by the manufacturers. Fifty-five hours a week are too much. We want a living wage. Look at the high cost of everything. We have to live. We work and we want to get paid for it and keep our health. We want to work only forty-four hours, so as to give those who are idle a chance to work.[83]

Of all the demands, the call for union recognition received the most attention. The emphasis that strikers placed upon this goal serves as a good indication that Passaic workers had "settled in" and had come to think of themselves as permanent members of a working class rather than as temporary employees in a foreign land.[84] As mentioned, the prominence given the call for union recognition also shows that workers knew they needed their own organization in order to counter the bosses' union. Pluhar put it most succinctly: "If we don't have a union in the shops, it is useless to live in Passaic."[85] Furthermore, the heady postwar atmosphere stimulated workers' audaciousness and strikers warned those who refused to pay union dues that they would be "the losers in the end" as in the future only union members would be employed by the mills.[86]

Building a Strike Movement

Far more than in 1916, the rumble of discontent spread throughout the entire Passaic industrial region so that by mid-March practically every large mill in Passaic, Garfield, Lodi, and other nearby communities had been affected. For a while the situation approached that of a general strike although workers did not use that term to describe the series of events.

Passaic's 2,000 handkerchief employees became the first to be affected by the strike contagion as they joined the picket lines during the second week of February. These Polish female workers had displayed great militancy during strikes in 1916 and 1917 and their participation added strength to the picket lines.[87] During the rest of the month, wire, rubber, cigar, cotton, and other workers joined the walkouts as ethnic working-class and family networks helped to spread the strikes from plant to plant. All of the employees demanded 44/55 and union recognition. In some cases, union sentiment ran ahead of practical organizing work as Okonite Wire company workers struck and then told their boss that the union "was not organized yet but they wanted it recognized as soon as it was." As each group left the mills, they formed their own branch of the Independent Union, whose membership swelled to 12,000 by the end of February. Even though this multi-industrial structure proved ephemeral, such a display of solidarity greatly invigorated the walkout of woolen and worsted workers.[88]

The union first had to develop a relief fund so that hunger would not drive the workers back to the mills. Much of the needed funds were supplied by the numerous ethnic societies in the Passaic area. The long list of contributors included Slovenska Jednota, Hungarian Sick and Death Benefit Society, Polish People's Home, Polish White Eagle Society, Ukrainian Society, Italian-American Citizens Club, and the Russian National Home. Local merchants and grocers also provided aid. Some of these groups gave considerable sums. For example, the Eastside Liquor Dealers' Association, composed of sixty-two saloon owners, contributed

$600. Peter Glita helped organize this committee and his hall served as strike headquarters. The Polish Merchants Association and the Jewish-dominated Eastside Businessmen's Association also made contributions. Many grocers donated foodstuffs or extended credit for the duration of the strike. Other merchants furnished bail for arrested workers or paid their fines, and William Schwartzbach earned the title "strike druggist" by supplying workers with free prescriptions.[89]

Enlightened self-interest as much as genuine sympathy for the workers' cause impelled the shopkeepers to lend their help. One grocer admitted that he had no choice but to aid the strikers as the "women" would "refuse to recognize their former accounts" if he turned down the request. Another merchant claimed that strikers threatened to steal his merchandise if he did not make a contribution. A sign carried at a demonstration asked: "We are spending our money with you. Where are the stockholders spending theirs?"[90] The point was not lost on Dundee's merchants who feared the permanent loss of customers if they did not make a contribution to the strike fund.

The priests also gave strong support to the walkout and Fathers Haitinger, Kruczek, Monteuffel, and Stephanko (of the Russian Orthodox Church) all came to the meeting halls to endorse the strike and Father Monteuffel pointedly reminded the manufacturers that "they should remember that all men are equal before God and law." At one point the local press publicized rumors that the manufacturers were attempting to "buy up the priests" in order to get them to urge a cessation of the walkout. In response, the union released a statement that noted: "We, the workers know our priests better. They are not for sale to the manufacturers, they stick to the working people."[91]

The sizable community resources that the strikers marshalled to their cause guaranteed that the workers could remain out for some time. On the other hand, the ethnic middle class and the priests supported the walkout because outside organizations were not involved. Once the ACWA and the ATWA entered the picture much of the aid evaporated and many of these former supporters became opponents of efforts to build a socialist-oriented union in Passaic.

The strength and scope of the strike meant that workers could mount highly effective picket lines and all of the mills had to cease operations by the second week of February. Office help could not get near the plants and even Gustav Schmid, who was president of both the Garfield Worsted Company and the Wool Council, had to twice abandon efforts to enter the factories after strikers surrounded his car and threatened him.[92]

Despite these displays of solidarity, the mill owners decided to resume production on Monday, March 3. Evidently, they hoped to stimulate a back-to-work movement but the Wool Council seriously underestimated workers' resolve. The night before the scheduled reopening, pickets gathered and by 7:00 AM large crowds, with women in front, blocked all the mill entrances. The strategy rendered local police "helpless" and they could barely keep the crowds moving. The immense throng jeered each mill whistle and much to the embarrassment of company officials almost no workers entered the plants.[93]

A week after the union's show of strength, divisions emerged in the strikers' ranks that threatened to undermine much of this positive organizational work. The split occurred when Gus Roth and Louis Kymack, members of the union's relief and negotiating teams, resigned from the union. Both men had been prominent leaders since the beginning of the walkout and both had been instrumental in building the strike movement. Even before his resignation, Kymack had faulted the leadership for their failure to properly emphasize "Americanism," and three days prior to their departures, both Kymack and Roth had accused Pluhar of not being a "true red-blooded American."[94] This allegation came just as Pluhar had begun to talk with the ACWA about the possibility of the clothing workers' union granting financial aid to the strike.[95] To further sow suspicions, anonymous persons circulated leaflets accusing the strike leadership of stealing $1,000 from a recent tag-day collection. Printed in Polish and Hungarian, the leaflets claimed that "somebody" was "getting rich" off the workers and that Roth and Kymack had resigned in order to "protect" the rank and file.[96] The leaflets, which were markedly similar in style and content to those later used against Passaic's ATWA local, also alluded to Pluhar's discussions with the ACWA and criticized a purported plan "to turn the money over to other leaders with the members and the money."[97]

Pluhar and the rest of the union leadership at this time repulsed their enemies' attempts to invoke Americanism and localism. In order to rebuild morale and to demonstrate the union's resolve, the strikers held a mammoth parade on March 17. The participants included handkerchief, cotton, rubber, wire, and cigar employees as well as the woolen and worsted workers. Brass bands and army veterans holding American flags headed each line of march and workers set off to the sound of church bells as they snaked their way through the narrow streets of the east side where dense throngs greeted them. Their signs told the story of the strike as workers carried banners that read: "10 hours dead: 8 hours now born," "Good Night blacklist, good morning union shop," "Manufacturers democracy. Six autocrats thinking, 30,000 hands working." Most boldly, in a move that one associates more with late-nineteenth-century labor conflicts, the demonstrators set off for the west side and as they passed the home of Julius Forstmann, workers stopped to "hoot" and "shout" although the mill baron failed to come to the window.[98]

The parade was a tremendous success but it caused a rift in the strikers' ranks—a rift that also revealed the difficulties that women experienced when trying to exercise leadership roles during walkouts. This dispute occurred after a photograph of Margaret Haray appeared on the front page of the *Passaic Daily Herald*. Haray, who was born in Budapest, served as secretary of the Independent Union and she was one of four women who served on the twenty-member central committee.[99] In the words of the *Passaic Daily News*, she had "ably handled the records and affairs of the union since it was organized." But the publication of her photo led a number of workers to charge her with seeking publicity and she was forced to resign her post, though she remained secretary of the Botany strike committee. It appears highly unlikely that a male leader would have faced opposition on these grounds, and as we will see, it also proved difficult for women to play leadership roles during the Lawrence strike as well.[100]

Haray's forced resignation meant the Independent Union had lost three of its top leaders in the space of one week. But the parade had injected new vigor into the walkout and the union's membership remained firm. The leadership held the rank and file together despite the differences. As Pluhar commented at the inception of the strike: "It is easy enough for six men with one idea—to make money—to organize for one purpose, but it is hard to organize thousands of people with a thousand ideas."[101] By focusing the work stoppage on immediate issues, the strike committee overcame centrifugal forces and the quest for union recognition remained the glue that held 10,000 woolen and worsted workers together.

Federal Intervention and the First Settlement

When the walkout began, the Wool Council termed the workers' demands "preposterous." In rejecting the notion of union recognition, Julius Forstmann commented: "Shop committees backed by a union, mean shop dictation of hiring and discharging and we cannot allow that."[102]

As Passaic's employers believed workers should have no voice in determining working conditions, this tough stance was only to be expected. And since the 1919 strike was the first labor crisis ever faced by the Wool Council, its raison d'être would have been undermined if council members had failed to remain firm.

By March, then, the two sides had become deadlocked. In hopes of settling the strike, the U.S. Department of Labor's Conciliation Division assigned a mediator, Charles J. Fury, to Passaic. Upon coming to the city, Fury spent most of his time trying to get workers to return to the mills. He criticized the union's insistence on what he termed the "closed shop" and berated the leaders for having "told the workers so much about the union" that they believed it was "absolutely necessary for them to have the union recognized." [103] As in the Paterson silk strike, federal intervention had one central goal: to defuse a potentially dangerous strike situation so as to prevent radicals from gaining influence.

Fury played a key role in breaking the stalemate: shortly after the giant union demonstration he met with three representatives of the Wool Council, including Julius Forstmann, and hammered out an agreement with them. Fury then met with the union's negotiating team and pressed them to accept the settlement. He told the workers that the manufacturers had agreed to deal with shop committees although they would not recognize the union. He asked the committee members to "go back and explain" to the workers that "the strong organization and the shop committees" would "serve the same purpose" as union recognition. He assured them that "the manufacturers have agreed not to discriminate against anybody for his or her part in the strike" and the United States government was "in back of the agreement." [104]

Members of the union negotiating team questioned this offer but after a second meeting Fury convinced them to accept the accord. The concessions relating to the union question that both sides supposedly accepted read:

1. The woolen manufacturers recognize the right of their employees to combine together in a union for their mutual benefit.
2. The workers shall have the right to organize a shop committee in each department of the employers' mills, which shall receive all complaints or grievances and submit same to the management for an amicable adjustment. No discrimination shall be exercised by the employers because of union activity on the part of any individual or committee.

Manufacturers also agreed to submit the wage question to an "arbitration committee" that would be made up of two representatives of the manufacturers, two representatives of the strikers, and one other person who was "acceptable to both sides." In addition, manufacturers agreed that if the Lawrence workers, who were still on strike, won a pay hike, they would grant the same percentage increase. They set hours at forty-eight per week with time and a half for overtime, and the manufacturers guaranteed that "all workers who wish to return to their work will be taken back without any discrimination against anyone who has gone on strike or taken any lawful part in organization, work, meetings, etc." [105]

Workers greeted this news with jubilation, but the Wool Council's secretary, J. Frank Andres, put a damper on the celebration when he commented that somehow strikers had received the "erroneous impression" that manufacturers had actually recognized the union. To clarify the agreement he issued the following statement:

The Wool Council will not recognize the union. Make that point clear. However shop committees may confer with the manufacturers in any disputed question at any time, but not union committees. We recognize the fact that they have a right to combine. [106]

Andres's declaration set off an uproar. Many strikers talked about staying out of the mills and one Passaic employee summed up the thoughts of thousands: "We want recognition of the union and no camouflage." Workers directed much of their anger at Pluhar, who continued to defend the accord. Piqued by their criticism, he even tendered his resignation. Although workers insisted that Pluhar remain as head of the union, the controversy over the agreement's terms foreshadowed the increasingly difficult time that the leadership would face in holding workers together. [107]

Andres's statement only clarified what should have been obvious since the document made no mention of union recognition and Fury had made it clear that the manufacturers only intended to deal with shop committees. Fury claimed that this was tantamount to union recognition, but strike leaders had no illusions about this aspect of the accord. Why then, despite their reservations, did the negotiating team urge acceptance of the settlement? For one, the worst rioting of the entire strike had occurred on the very day the committee met with Fury when ten persons had been arrested as a crowd of 4,000 workers tried to prevent Botany clerical employees from entering the mill. The rioters vented much of their anger on the army veterans who had been serving as special police and the confrontation signaled that the strike committee, which had always discouraged violence, was losing control over the rank and file. Second, the union leadership had grown concerned about the worsening relief situation as increasing numbers of families were in need of aid and food lines had grown longer outside of the Glita Hall headquarters. The resignations of Kymack and Roth had damaged fund-raising efforts and even without this difficulty, only a limited amount of funds could be raised within Passaic itself. Although contact had been established with the ACWA, no aid had yet been received from the clothing workers' union. The decision not to call on outsiders had put the union in a tactical as well as a financial bind; local leaders could not make up for the absence of "charismatic radicals" who so often raised sagging spirits in strikes of immigrant workers.[108]

Fury's relentless pressure also took its toll. Although Pluhar and other union representatives had already begun to consult on a regular basis with the ACWA leadership, they found it difficult to resist the blandishments of a federal mediator who was prepared to blame them for prolonging the walkout.[109] Finally, even without union recognition, there were good reasons to view the agreement in a positive light; it seemed to insure that mill owners would meet on a regular basis with shop committees; it appeared to guarantee a wage increase by making use of arbitration and by tying the settlement to the Lawrence strike. Above all, the union membership now included 9,000 woolen and worsted workers, which left it in a strong position to press for union recognition in the future.

Pluhar knew that the Armistice had presented Passaic workers with a unique opportunity. Wartime frustrations and expectations had led to the first general textile strike in Passaic's history. It appeared highly unlikely that there would ever again be such an opportunity to close down the mills and win major concessions. Thus, it was not easy to accept a settlement that did not include the union's major goal. Nevertheless, Passaic workers appeared to have won a major victory over the mill owners and to have seriously weakened the Wool Council's ability to control every aspect of their working lives.

The Second Strike

Whatever their doubts about the meaning of the agreement, all of the workers returned to the mills on March 25, but they were only back on their jobs for a few hours before new trouble broke out. The dispute centered on the Garfield Worsted Company, where plant officials told sixteen workers that they had been fired. When the Garfield Worsted shop committee heard of these dismissals, ten representatives went to see Gustav Schmid, who cynically responded: "If I knew you were coming I would have had coffee and cake for you." In the meantime, word spread through the mill that officials "were showing discrimination and breaking their agreement" and all 900 employees walked out in protest.[110]

News of the discharges spread quickly through the mill district and that night, workers held a "wild" round of meetings. At these gatherings, mill hands heard reports that Botany and Forstmann & Huffmann officials had prevented workers from soliciting union members on the job and many speakers expressed support for the Garfield Worsted employees. Other woolen and worsted workers expressed chagrin that rubber, wire, and cigar strikers had all won forty-eight hours with fifty-five hours' pay while they had no iron-clad guarantee of a wage increase. Pluhar, though, urged restraint, opposed any walkout in sympathy with the Garfield Worsted workers and "scolded" strikers for breaking faith with Fury and the manufacturers. A number of leaders offered their resignations as a way of showing their dissatisfaction with the precipitous action. But the militants were in no mood to listen to the voices of moderation and the next day mill hands, demanding "positively no discrimination" and union recognition, poured out of the Botany and the Forstmann & Huffmann mills.[111]

There is every likelihood that the Wool Council deliberately provoked the second strike as in 1912 and again in 1916 when mill owners had lured workers back to the plants by making promises that they had no intention of keeping. Julius Forstmann, in particular, had used this tactic quite effectively. Employers remained confident that this strategy would succeed because they knew that the most militant workers would insist that the union take a stand against any violation of the agreement while more cautious employees would have little taste for a new conflict.[112]

The Wool Council's strategy received the support of both local and federal officials. Fury reacted with anger to news that workers had abandoned negotiations; he charged that strikers were "conspiring with citizens of foreign states" and threatened to bring federal charges against anyone who "molested" an employee who wished to work. More importantly, city authorities did an about-face. Up to this point, the team of Kehoe and Turner had won the trust of workers by giving them a relatively free hand in collecting money, picketing, and parading. In return the Independent Union had allowed Turner and Kehoe to sit on the plantform during meetings, to approve of all speakers, and to care for $12,000 of the union's dues and initiation fees.[113]

When the second strike began, Turner and Kehoe realized that they had lost all control over the workers and blamed "Bolsheviki" for the new outbursts. Kehoe used his official position to take concrete action and issued a strongly worded proclamation stating that "every person" who desired "to return to work" would be "fully protected" and that any person who attempted "to prevent a worker from exercising his right to go to work" would have "to bear the consequences of such unlawful acts."[114] Although mill owners had expressed some displeasure with city authorities' lenient attitudes towards the strikers, they certainly had counted on this support when they decided to provoke the new walkout. Back in 1916, Julius Forstmann had been so impressed by Turner's "exceptional ability" in handling labor disputes that he had then suggested that Turner be hired as the Wool Council's chief detective.[115] And now, the mill owners' confidence in Turner proved well placed as the policeman's handshake was replaced by a nightstick as soon as workers overstepped the boundaries that he and Kehoe had drawn for them.[116]

The mill owners proved to be extremely smart strategists. As soon as workers left the Botany and Forstmann & Huffmann mills, they closed all six plants and announced they would reopen on April 1 under open-shop conditions. But as an enticement to weaker union members and to those whose savings had evaporated, they now offered forty-eight hours' work with fifty-five hours' pay.[117]

The Independent Union had been put in a bind. Pluhar and his top assistant, Fred Frankle, issued a statement that acknowledged that the "bosses" had "treated workers so shamefully" that it was "impossible to stay" in the factories "any longer," but they urged workers to "sleep in" rather than confront police on April 1. Partly as a result of the leadership's uncertainty, when that day arrived, large numbers of employees protected by Passaic and Clifton police entered the mills. When the Independent Union tried to rally those who remained committed to the strike, Kehoe and Turner refused to permit any outdoor meetings or demonstrations. And by the end of the week, the Passaic and Clifton mills had practically resumed normal operations.[118]

For a while a different situation prevailed in Garfield, where workers had often displayed considerably more militancy than those in Passaic. Garfield's Mayor Dahnert had issued a proclamation similar to Kehoe's warning but the Garfield City Council refused to appoint special deputies to enforce the order and one council member commented: "Let the mills pay for their own protection if they want it." Consequently, Dahnert had called on Bergen County deputies to police Garfield's streets. Emboldened by the support of their own city council, far fewer workers returned to Garfield than to Passaic plants as strikers lined the arteries leading to the mills and intimidated those who wished to return to work. Some of those who opposed the strike had their homes stoned and numerous brawls broke out between the two factions. But even in Garfield, after a week, strong opposition developed to continuing the strike. Sensing the new walkout's weakness, Pluhar met with the Wool Council's secretary to see if he would consider taking back all of those who remained out. Andres told him that all returning mill hands would be treated as "new" employees—meaning that once again the bosses could pick off the militants.[119]

As the Garfield outcome demonstrates, even when they had the backing of local authorities workers were losing their will to continue the battle. The key lies in the Wool Council's granting of forty-eight hours' work with fifty-five hours' pay. This was an adroit maneuver, especially since Lawrence workers, who had received a tremendous amount of outside aid and whose strike was front-page news in Passaic, were still walking the picket lines for almost the exact same demand. The higher wages proved particularly tempting since many workers had exhausted their savings. Even union spokespersons who endorsed the second strike noted that it would be "a hard proposition to strike with an empty pocket." One Forstmann & Huffmann spinner who refused to join the second walkout asked its advocates: "Who's going to take care of my family?"[120] This question was probably on the minds of most workers faced with the prospect of another lengthy work stoppage.

The outcome showed that the Wool Council had been able to outwit their employees. A more experienced leadership would have probably insisted upon a firmer agreement before recommending that workers return to the plants. The total reliance on local resources had deletrious consequences in other ways. The priests who had been strong supporters of the first strike, were now using their influence to discourage the second walkout. Effective Polish, Slovak, and Italian speakers were needed but they were generally not available within Passaic. Immigrant businessmen, who had done much to aid the first walkout, remained in the background once the second strike began.[121] Many workers took note of the withdrawal of the local support and increasingly began to look beyond the city's borders for assistance.

The Turn to the ACWA and the ATWA

Even before the first strike ended a committee of Passaic workers had contacted the ACWA. Since the Independent Union's constitution prohibited talking with outside unions all of those involved had to be prudent in their actions. Pluhar said he was only seeking financial aid but commented: "We need help and we will take it from anywhere we can get it."[122] Shortly after these initial discussions, Pluhar began to meet with the New York-based ACWA leadership on a regular basis though he still remained hesitant about establishing the ACWA connection. The defections of Roth and Kymack had already made it clear that acceptance of the ACWA's aid would lead to a split in the local union. Moreover, the trust of city authorities had been won by agreeing to bar outsiders and this also would be lost by establishing close ties with the ACWA. Pluhar's ambivalence stood in marked contrast to the outward-looking perspective of Lawrence workers who had embraced the ACWA and won a pledge of major financial aid by the third week of March.

The mill owners' violation of the agreement ended much of the union's wavering. As soon as the second walkout began, the central committee passed a resolution authorizing Pluhar and nine other workers to visit the ACWA headquarters to discuss furthering the ties between the two organizations. Following this meeting, Amalgamated representatives Julius Powers and Frank Cancellieri visited Passaic to address a strike gathering. They were the first outside organizers to come to Passaic since the first week of the strike and their talks, which focused on the need for a strong union and the advantages of a connection with the ACWA, were well-received by the several hundred workers who came to Glita's to hear them.[123]

Despite this favorable reception, Pluhar still hesitated to establish ties with the ACWA. While city police had allowed the Amalgamated's organizers to speak, when Turner heard that the local union might join with the ACWA he said: "If this affiliation is brought about and any attempt is made to exclude the police, we will close the halls tight." Kehoe flatly announced that he would not allow the ACWA to conduct the strike and Fury warned those who crossed state lines that they risked federal prosecution.[124] Whether because of these threats or because Pluhar doubted the very wisdom of the second strike, no more ACWA leaders went to Passaic to aid the new walkout.

Finally, amid the growing disarray of the second strike, Pluhar cast off all hesitancy about establishing ties with the ACWA, and on April 4 he signed the call for the founding convention of the ATWA. City authorities' bitter hostility to the second walkout had removed all remaining doubts. The ties that had been cultivated locally had now been broken and workers had to turn elsewhere for support in their fight with the mill owners. Though many workers still expressed strong reservations about outside organizations, the belief had grown that Passaic workers could no longer fight alone. According to Mollie Pluhar, her father had hoped "to keep it a local union" but saw no alternative once employers "reneged" on the agreement. At this point, he decided that "we needed a stronger, nationally known union." Pluhar used almost the same words at the time in replying to the critics of the ACWA: "We felt that the local union was not quite strong enough, that a bigger organization was necessary." Another worker put it more simply: "We can't win with no backing." In answer to Kymack's continuing objections to outside aid, an ACWA supporter replied that the "workers' affair" was "a movement throughout the country" that Passaic workers needed to join. All three workers expressed lessons learned during the two months' strife.[125]

The ACWA was certainly the logical union to turn to as Passaic workers had little confidence in either the UTW or the IWW. The clothing and textile industries were closely allied and during the second strike, the ACWA announced that its shops would boycott Passaic cloth unless workers there were granted union recognition.[126] Already, the ACWA's support for the Lawrence walkout had demonstrated that it was prepared to back up its words with action. Indeed, numerous fund-raisers had been held in New York City for the Lawrence strikers while Passaic mill hands had made no effort to take advantage of this nearby support. The irony was not missed by the Passaic leadership. The ACWA's independent status also appealed to Passaic workers who viewed with suspicion Fury's efforts to push the AFL upon them.[127] Finally, Pluhar played a decisive role in the turn to the ACWA. When he finally saw the need for a "national organization" he "picked the one that he had great faith in" as its perspective closely resembled his own.[128]

The Passaic representatives played an important role at the ATWA's founding convention since Passaic and Paterson were allotted the second largest number of delegates after Lawrence. As an indication of the respect that the ACWA leadership had for him, Pluhar was named treasurer of the new union and the ATWA expected the Passaic local to be one of its strongest branches.

Despite the disappointing ending of the second strike there were good grounds for optimism as Passaic mill hands had now fought the manufacturers in 1912, 1916, and 1919 and each strike had been stronger than the previous one. Certainly, this struggle had not reached its denouement. As one worker put it at the conclusion of the second work stoppage: "The strike is not over. It will start again for the people want the union. Nor will there be any rest so long as the industrial office is there."[129] Passaic's workers turned to the ATWA because they hoped that it could remove this agency of fear from their lives and the ATWA's fate would be determined by its ability to challenge the Wool Council. And yet many Polish workers, in particular, continued to distrust outside unions, especially one that was Jewish-led and socialistically inclined. A far different situation prevailed in Lawrence where workers lacked the unity of Passaic employees during strikes but where those workers who accepted radical leadership looked almost automatically beyond the city's borders for aid.

Chapter Five

LAWRENCE:
THE BATTLE RENEWED

The Lawrence Mills

The site of three of the four largest textile mills in the United States, Lawrence had been an industrial center ever since 1845 when a group of Boston investors decided to erect factories on a plot of land along the Merrimack River. As had been true of the Boston Associates, who had built the nearby Lowell cotton mills, these early capitalists hoped that their enterprises would provide for the cultural and educational needs of their employees. But by 1860, when over eighty workers lost their lives in the collapse of the Pemberton Mill, little remained of the original vision. Conditions were so dismal by 1868 that the city served as the setting for Winslow Homer's dramatic woodcut that depicted men, women, and children sadly trudging to work in America's version of the "dark satanic mills."[1]

The Pacific Mills, the Arlington Mills, and the American Woolen Company were the three dominant firms in Lawrence. The Pacific had been established as a cotton mill in 1853 and from the beginning had combined all cloth-making operations under one roof. In the 1880's, worsteds had become its primary product and by 1910 it·had also begun to turn out large quantities of printed cloth as well. Well managed from the outset, the firm's unusual product mix had enabled it to pay dividends on a steady basis, and by 1918, it employed 8,000 Lawrence mill hands in its varied operations.[2]

The Arlington, founded in 1865, shared much in common with the Pacific as it had an experienced Boston-based management and integrated operations from its inception, and in 1900, it ranked as one of the twenty-five largest industrial employers in the United States. Unlike the Pacific, the Arlington had come to concentrate almost entirely on producing worsteds for the men's ready-to-wear trade and in 1917 it had separated its cotton from its worsted department. By the time of World War I, it employed 6,500 operatives who lived and worked in a distinct section of the city—known as the Arlington District—which adjoined the town of Methuen, two miles away from Lawrence's center where the other mills were based.[3]

The American Woolen Company was the city's largest employer. When this firm was established in 1899, it merged eight separate plants; by 1919, it operated over fifty factories. Frederick Ayer served as the company's first president but ever since its founding, William M. Wood had been its guiding hand. Born of poor, immigrant parents, Wood first captured Ayer's attention when he helped rescue the Washington Mill from bankruptcy and he further gained Ayer's attention when he married his daughter. Determined to become the Andrew Carnegie of the textile industry, Wood believed in running his plants at peak capacity, using bonus systems to maximize production, reducing prices in order to undersell the competition, and making use of multiplant operations. As noted, before the war this strategy had not proven particularly successful but the European conflict offered Wood the opportunity to realize his dream of making the American Woolen Company the first textile trust. By 1918, net profits soared over the $12-million mark, dividends had increased appreciably, and "intoxicated by war profits," the American Woolen Company had purchased eleven additional mills.

Lawrence served as the hub of the American Woolen Company's operations.The large Washington Mill remained under the firm's control but the corporation's productive capacity had expanded enormously when the Wood Mill—named after the recently appointed president—was completed in 1906. This was the world's largest worsted mill and its twin six-floor red-brick buildings stretched for one-quarter of a mile along the

Merrimack River. Equipped with the most modern textile machinery and with escalators to rush its 7,000 employees to their workrooms, the Wood Mill manufactured vast quantities of blue serge, the firm's staple, and supplied yarn to other American Woolen plants. By 1910, when the Ayer Mill was built, the American Woolen Company employed over 12,000 operatives in the city of Lawrence.[4]

The Arlington and the Pacific firms looked askance at the American Woolen Company's moves. Fearing to fall behind, both firms between 1900 and 1910 increased their worsted operations and the Pacific built its vast plant to manufacture printed cloth. Both corporations also distrusted Wood's labor policies since he generally paid his employees wages that were slightly above the industry norm. Of greater consequence, Pacific and Arlington both preferred to let their agents deal with labor, but Wood, in the style of Julius Forstmann, became involved in every work stoppage. Wood might have wanted to be a Forstmann but he lacked the savvy and in 1912 had even been implicated in a clumsy effort to pin a dynamite explosion on the strikers. An attempt had been made in 1916 to create an organization similar to the Industrial Council of Passaic Wool Manufacturers but it had gotten nowhere, and much to the distress of Arlington and Pacific, Wood continued to act on his own when dealing with labor.[5]

Besides the three big firms, there were a number of other textile mills in Lawrence. The Everett, which employed 2,000 workers, was the next largest plant and was one of the few Lawrence factories devoted exclusively to cotton manufacture. It opened in 1860 but expanded greatly in 1909 when a huge mill building was completed. Other firms, such as The George E. Kunhardt Corporation, Katama Mills, Plymouth Mills, Lawrence Duck Company, and the U.S. Worsted Company, employed between 500 and 1,500 operatives each in the manufacture of cotton and woolen products. Kunhardt was unusual in that it was owned by a local resident and though it had only a small work force its president, George Kunhardt, played a prominent role in all of the manufacturers' deliberations.[6]

These mills made Lawrence one of the leading textile cities in the United States and probably no other textile community had so many plants clustered close together. Approximately 30,000 of the city's 94,000 residents labored in these immense factories and the city's skyline was fittingly dominated by the Ayer Mill clock tower which could be seen miles away. In the words of one observer: "The mills are Lawrence and you cannot escape them."[7]

Immigration and a Fragmented Working Class

As in the cases of Passaic and Paterson, Lawrence's work force had always been largely composed of immigrants. The Irish excavated the city itself and by 1910, there were 14,000 people of Irish descent in Lawrence. Between 1860 and 1890, Lawrence had also received successive waves of English, Scotch, French-Canadian, and German immigrants. Though historians have often followed the pattern set forth by the U.S. Immigration Commission and have lumped all of these groups together as "old" immigrants, they actually differed greatly in their backgrounds. Most of the English newcomers hailed from the textile center of Bradford and, much like those who came to Paterson from Macclesfield, they were no strangers to trade union battles and some of them remained active in the radical labor movement right through 1919. For the most part, the German immigrants came from the industrial regions of Saxony, Bavaria, and Silesia and also had years of experience in the textile industry. Upon coming to Lawrence, they settled in a distinct section of the city known as Prospect Hill, where much of their community life centered on the turnverein and a highly successful German Cooperative Association. The Germans, in particular, played a leading role in strikes that broke out in Lawrence in 1882, 1894, and 1902 and they dominated the local branches of the SLP and later of the SP.[8]

Although many of the Irish immigrants had worked in English factories, they had less prior textile experience than either the English or the Germans. As in Lowell, upon their arrival, those of the famine era filled the less-skilled positions in the mills. According to Alice O'Connor, who wrote an insightful study of immigrant life in Lawrence, Irish immigrants who came after 1865 were less likely to work in the mills as in positions in the building trades and city government that had opened up for them.[9] For this reason, though the Irish dominated the lower level supervisory positions in the Lawrence textile plants, it is unlikely that they composed more than 15 percent of the work force in 1919, when they were well into their fourth generation of residency in the city.[10]

The Irish had not exactly been welcomed with open arms. Although Lawrence lacked any true older inhabitants, those New Englanders (or Yankees as they liked to be called) who migrated to the city joined in anti-Irish rioting and backed the nativist Know Nothing movement in the mid-1850s. A new wave of anti-Irish sentiment developed in the 1870s and in the early 1890s when the rabidly anti-Catholic American Protective Association attracted great support.[11] And in a pattern that characterized

New England mill towns, the Irish met hostility with hostility and in the course of time lashed out at Yankee reformers, French-Canadians, leftist labor leaders, and all others who stood outside the clan.

Irish resentments had political ramifications because their large numbers and cohesiveness gave them great voting power. In 1882, Lawrence became the first Massachusetts city to elect an Irish Catholic mayor and after that date local politics became divided between "Mick" and "anti-Mick" factions. The Irish solidified their political hold on the city in 1911 when Lawrence adopted the commission form of government, which meant that the Irish, who had themselves once been the victims of gerrymandering, could easily elect all five city councilmen (now chosen at large) and the mayor. The losers in all of this were the French-Canadians and especially the Germans who under the old ward system had elected a number of representatives to the council. After 1912, this "miniature Tammany Hall" turned Lawrence into an Irish political preserve as the Irish dominated the police, fire, and sanitation departments as well as the school system. Other ethnic groups withdrew from city politics rather than engage in a fight they could not win and much of the middle class withdrew to the surrounding suburbs.[12]

The Irish also exercised considerable power within the local Roman Catholic Church. Although those who came in the 1840s and 1850s had been relatively unchurched, by 1900 the Irish in Lawrence and elsewhere had created an extensive parish network, which, as with other ardently Catholic groups, touched all aspects of daily life. Most importantly, the more liberal and open Roman Catholic Church of the 1870s had by 1900 given way to the church militant that stressed obedience to papal authority and boldly crusaded against secularism, socialism, and all other forms of modernism.[13] Within Lawrence, Father James T. O'Reilly, who had been pastor of St. Mary's for over thirty years, ruled the church with an iron hand, and Boston's William Cardinal O'Connell made no decision concerning local church matters without first consulting him. Within the Irish community, Father O'Reilly had earned great respect especially since as an ardent Irish nationalist he had warmly welcomed opponents of British rule over Ireland who often journeyed to Lawrence for speaking appearances.[14]

Although the Irish had tasted power on the local level, the community's concerns remained firmly rooted in the working class. Irish trade unionists led the local Central Labor Union (CLU) and Lawrence's representatives to the Massachusetts legislature had strongly supported labor legislation. Three of five members of the 1919 city council had been union members and in the spirit of Pope Leo XIII's encyclical *Rerum Novarum* (on the condition of labor), Father O'Reilly had supported unions so long as they were not led by socialists.[15]

In 1919, Lawrence was also home to over 13,000 residents of French-Canadian origin. Most of the city's French Canadians had arrived between 1860 and 1890 when tens of thousands of destitute inhabitants of rural Quebec rode the rails down to New England. These migrants filled cities such as Woonsockett, Rhode Island, New Bedford, Fall River, and Lowell, Massachusetts, and Manchester, New Hampshire, as the textile mills provided employment for entire families, which often included eight or nine children. Lawrence did not rank as a major center of French-American life; nevertheless the French who created their own "Petit Canadas" in South Lawrence and in the Arlington District placed the distinct stamp of the *Quebequois* upon the city.[16]

Soon after their arrival, the French Canadians developed a reputation in labor circles for being hostile to strikes and to unions, and in 1881 the Massachusetts Bureau of Statistics of Labor referred to them as "the Chinese of New England." Though French-Canadian involvement in the Pulp and Paper Workers Union and in the Massachusetts Carpenters Union shows the falsity of this accusation (not that one should accept the Chinese stereotype either), it is true that in the textile industry, the French Canadians had been less likely than other groups to support efforts at organization even when they were led by conservative unions.[17] Fred Beal, who grew up in Lawrence, called them "born slaves," but such comments hardly explain the reasons for the French Canadians' seeming accommodation to the harsh life in the mills.[18] Tamara Hareven offered a plausible explanation for this phenomenon when she suggested that the mills' irregular schedules actually met the needs of the French Canadians since they often desired to make return trips to Quebec, and that the manufacturers' informal hiring practices benefited them since entire families could often find employment in a single room of a mill. According to Hareven, after 1920, when the labor market tightened and working conditions deteriorated, French Canadians joined other workers in the New England-wide walkout of 1922.[19]

French Canadians' hostility to radical movements is easier to trace as it is largely attributable to their intense Catholicity, which surpassed even that of the Irish, Poles, and Slovaks. The key to understanding this aspect of French-Canadian life lies in the idea of *la survivance*, which inextricably linked French language, culture, and religion. Following the British conquest of Quebec in 1763, religion and language, in particular, had become identified with resistance to alien rule. In order to preserve this cultural inheritance, French Canadians considered it an absolute necessity that their children attend parochial schools. In Lawrence, the French Canadian parishes, St. Anne's and Sacred Heart, had an extensive parochial school network staffed by Quebec-trained teaching orders and by Marists who had fled the anticlerical legislation of the Third French Republic and who lacked the pro-labor perspective of the Irish priests.

The missionary spirit that influenced the approach to the schools affected all other aspects of French-American life as attendance at mass reached the highest proportions of any Catholic group in the United States and parish and neighborhood became synonymous.[20] Especially, the large numbers of French Canadians who lived in the Arlington District, within the boundaries of St. Anne's, had far more contact with their compatriots who lived just over the line in Methuen than with other residents of Lawrence. This parochialism and insular perspective was of a different sort than that of the Irish as the French Canadians did not even enjoy the semblance of power. The French Canadians had few foremen in the mills, few representatives on the CLU, little influence within the Roman Catholic hierarchy, and no representation on the city council. Scorned by the Irish, the French Canadians returned the enmity by voting Republican and by fighting for control over their own parish life against the centralizing tendencies of Father O'Reilly.[21]

The spectacular decade of mill building that stretched from 1900 to 1910 brought entirely new immigrant groups to Lawrence. With the exception of the Franco-Belgians, almost all of whom had prior textile experience, these recent arrivals came mainly from the periphery of capitalist development and from nonindustrial backgrounds. Unlike in Passaic, these "new" immigrants came from extremely diverse areas. (See Table 5.1) In particular, the new mill hands came from four distinct regions: France and Belgium (Franco-Belgians); Eastern Europe (Poles, Jews, Lithuanians, Russians, and Ukrainians); Southern Europe (Italians, Greeks, and Portuguese); and the Middle East (Syrians, Turks, and Armenians).[22]

Since the American Woolen plants had been erected after the Arlington and the Pacific, recent immigrants composed an especially large percentage of the work force at the Washington, Wood, and Ayer mills. In all the plants, though, a cultural division of labor prevailed as "new" immigrants had been assigned to the "simpler, cruder processes" while the English-speakers (a term that in Lawrence's parlance included the French Canadians) dominated nonmachine-tending jobs such as mending and burling.[23] For example, at the Arlington and the Pacific mills

Table 5.1
Country of Origin of Lawrence's "New" Immigrants

Country	Total Foreign Stock Residing in Lawrence in 1920
Belgium	516
France	842
Russia	
(including Poles, Letts, Jews, Lithuanians)	9,252
Italy	14,687
Greece	467
Portugal	707
Turkey in Asia	
(Syrians, Armenians, Turks)	3,833

Source: *1920 Census, Census Population*, 2:952–953.

the dirtiest and most dangerous jobs had been assigned to Poles, Lithuanians, and Italians.[24] These workers chafed at this discriminatory policy, and according to Lawrence's Italian Roman Catholic priest, Father Mariano Milanese, by 1917 "workers with the hard job" wanted the easier job even if it paid less as it was "worth the difference in health."[25]

Older immigrants had their own complaints. Many of them believed the oft-repeated story that William Wood had recruited workers by flooding Italy with posters showing contented employees leaving a mill and entering a bank. In 1917, the CLU loudly protested upon hearing that Wood intended to import Puerto Ricans to work in the mills. No firm evidence existed to support either of the allegations but workers believed them because they were convinced that the American Woolen Company had artificially stimulated immigration in order to reduce wages and to speed up the pace of work. As conditions deteriorated, many "Americans" had come to stigmatize mill employment as "beneath the native born."[26]

Likewise, many of the older residents had become upset at the living conditions of the recent immigrants, who had settled in a tenement house district near the center of the city. This area resembled the Dundee section of Passaic and suffered from poor sanitation and health conditions. Those who had the means moved out but still bemoaned the fact that the residential area near the picturesque Lawrence Common had become one of the most densely populated and dilapidated mill sections to be found anywhere in New England.[27]

The conflict between immigrant groups resulted from an interplay of social, cultural, and psychological factors as well as from the existence of an ethnically split labor market. Consequently, Lawrence workers had become far more divided by ethnicity than those in Passaic and a process of both working-class formation and fragmentation had occurred—a development that was hardly unique to Lawrence but one which meant that a sharply divided working class existed within the confines of the city.[28]

The 1912 Strike and Its Aftermath

The 1912 walkout that earned Lawrence a national and even international reputation as a radical labor center stood as "the era's supreme symbol of militant struggle against industrial oppression."[29] Begun as an effort to win back wages lost as a result of a Massachusetts law that cut maximum hours for women and children from fifty-six to fifty-four, the strike, which involved all of the mills but which centered on the American Woolen Company, had been fought with a revolutionary élan though the actual demands had been relatively modest. The national IWW leaders garnered much of the publicity but the strike succeeded in part because the Wobblies' Local 20 had already cultivated a base among Franco-Belgian and Italian mill employees. The participation of women workers, the IWW's perfection of the endless chain method of picketing, and the city authorities' ineptness in dealing with mass activity also help account for the walkout's success.[30] Workers managed to hold together for two months largely because the Wobblies made use of the nationality form of organization by which each ethnic group met separately and elected its own representatives to the general strike committee. The IWW employed this structure even though Joe Ettor, who had been assigned to Lawrence, had told workers "forget that you are Hebrews, forget that you are Poles, Germans or Russians" and even though upon his arrival in the city Big Bill Haywood told the crowd that welcomed him that he came "with no thought of nationality."[31] Despite the paradoxical state of affairs by which the IWW told workers to forget nationality and then organized them according to nationality, the IWW made no effort to alter the ethnic base of representation used by the general strike committee. On the other hand, as the Wobblies might have predicted, the difficulty of relying on an ethnic structure became more apparent at the end of the work stoppage when the various nationalities became more suspicious of one another. Partly for this reason, in November 1912 the IWW made an effort to break up the language federations, but this met resistance from groups that wished to continue to meet separately.[32]

Melvyn Dubofsky has used material collected by Selig Perlman, who conducted an investigation in Lawrence in 1913, to show that the Wobblies faced other problems besides ethnic jealousies as employers spied on workers, blacklisted leaders, and made use of multiplant operations to shift work to other cities.[33] Other factors also accounted for the Wobblies' rapid demise. Perlman's own investigation showed that the IWW had not been able to establish an effective presence on the shop floor. Cyrille de Tollenaere, a Franco-Belgian leader, told him that foremen harassed weavers by giving them complicated work or by "temporarily" assigning them to an additional loom—a workload that soon became permanent. According to de Tollenaere, Italian workers had staged a number of quickie strikes that had ended when management promised to make adjustments. These actions had been largely symbolic as both sides knew that superintendents would not make any permanent changes and, in some cases, the American Woolen Company may have deliberately provoked the departmental walkouts so as to pick off the militants. Unlike in Paterson, the IWW had no effective means to retaliate against discrimination and workers soon discovered that the organization could not defend them at the workplace.[34] Ideological divisions also beset the Lawrence IWW and many German Wobblies began to reconsider their participation in the union as a result of the dispute between the IWW and the Socialist party.[35]

Any account of the Wobblies' decline needs to consider as well the impact of the "For God and Country Parade" held on Columbus Day 1912 that Elizabeth Gurley Flynn called "a terrible climax to a great victory." This demonstration came a few weeks after Italian workers at the American Woolen Company led a highly successful protest strike in support of the IWW leaders Joe Ettor and Arturo Giovannitti and a local worker Joseph Caruso, who were about to be tried on trumped-up conspiracy-to-commit-murder charges. Father O'Reilly came up with the idea for the For God and Country slogan, which had become a staple of Catholic fraternal groups such as the Knights of Columbus, after some Wobbly demonstrators from Boston appeared in town carrying a banner inscribed with the message "No God, No Master." Father O'Reilly knew what he was doing. The twin religious and nationalistic theme had far more appeal than a call for the support of "For God and Employer" and 30,000 Lawrence residents turned out to cheer the marchers. In the rally's wake, the already daunting task of reaching Irish and French-Canadian workers, who at most had given lukewarm support to the Bread and Roses strike, had become well nigh impossible.[36]

The repressive activity greatly damaged the IWW, but the 1913–1915 depression provided the knockout blow as all hopes that the Wobblies had of rekindling a militant labor movement were lost once massive unemployment came to Lawrence. Whereas there had once been fifteen separate nationality branches in the city, by 1915 none remained.

As Dubofsky has noted, upon the Wobblies' demise, workers more than ever found sustenance within their own ethnic communities, but this did not mean that former Wobbly supporters had rejected the left.[37] In fact, many of Lawrence's immigrant groups supported a wide variety of ethnic societies that sustained the radical vision and served as a focal point for labor agitation once prosperity returned. For the most part, these ethnic organizations had been founded by groups that had developed an anticlerical perspective and their large membership helps explain why Lawrence had emerged as such a radical labor center.

Three groups in particular, the Franco-Belgians, the Lithuanians, and the Italians provided the core support for the left in Lawrence. Franco-Belgians, who hailed from French-speaking areas of Belgium and adjoining areas of France, added a special element to Lawrence's radical labor movement since many of them were highly skilled textile workers whose average earnings exceeded that of some of the "old" immigrant groups. Strong believers in direct action and ardent union advocates, the Franco-Belgians had founded Wobbly Local 20 and their hall served as strike headquarters during the 1912 walkout. At times during the Bread and Roses battle, Franco-Belgian representatives to the general strike committee had actually criticized the Wobblies for lacking militancy.

Completely churchless, Franco-Belgian community life centered around the meeting hall, theatre groups, and the immensely successful *Cooperative Franco-Belge*. Three hundred families belonged to this "social democracy in miniature," which contained a bakery and a grocery store. Modeled on the Belgian *Maisons du Peuple*, the cooperative operated along socialist lines as the managers, bakers, and clerks all earned the same wages and worked the same hours. Ten percent of its "profits" had been earmarked for "Socialist or Cooperative" propaganda and the organization had sent money overseas to aid Belgian strikers and had provided substantial help to Lawrence workers in 1912.[38]

Lithuanian radicalism had different roots. Much like the Jews and Finns, many Lithuanians had come to the United States after the failed Russian Revolution of 1905. Almost entirely of peasant backgrounds and often exploited by Polish landowners, the Lithuanians had fiercely resisted czarist efforts at Russification and had been part of a "protest generation" that had established secret schools to study the Lithuanian language, Lithuanian history, and socialist theory.[39]

Lawrence's Lithuanians developed their own unique blend of community institutions. Many of those who were Roman Catholic had turned against Father Jusaitis, the priest at the Lithuanian Roman Catholic Church, St. Francis. As always in church battles, the dissidents argued that since they had "built the churches," they rather than the bishops were the rightful owners of church property. The schismatics had also become disturbed when Father Jusaitis without their permission used the church basement for antisocialist meetings. Significantly, Paul Chabis, whose hall had served as an important meeting place during the 1912 strike, was the leader of this rebellion. When Father Jusaitis refused to meet the demands of the parishioners, the dissidents in 1916 formed an Independent Lithuanian Church that quickly won over the majority of St. Francis's members and affiliated with the Polish National Catholic Church.[40]

The most radical Lithuanians shunned religion all together; Father Virmauskis, Father Jusaitis's successor, estimated at least one-third of Lawrence's Lithuanians did not attend church at all.[41] These Lithuanians had helped organize a Lithuanian cooperative provision store, a singing group known as the *Liaudes Chorus* and the Lithuanian Social Camp Association. The last-named group had been founded in 1915 when a number of Lawrence's Lithuanians had purchased land in Methuen. Each weekend the members cut down trees and cleared land and kept a careful record of all work performed so that shares were awarded to participants according to the number of hours worked.[42] When the toil had been completed the area was named Maple Park, and it became the site for picnics and political gatherings as well as providing a refuge for Lithuanians who had traded the "healthy and aromatic air" of their homeland for Lawrence's "steam heat and foul air." Father Virmauskis grew so concerned with Maple Park's success that he tried to raise money from the manufacturers so that Roman Catholic Lithuanians could have their own park. According to Father Virmauskis, it had become necessary to counteract the radicals' efforts because Lithuanians of all persuasions had been attracted to Maple Park where "they feel they are at home, nobody is bothering them."[43]

Italians played a crucial role in all labor activity in Lawrence as they formed a high percentage of the work force at the American Woolen plants. Italian IWW leaders such as Carlo Tresca, Ettor, and Giovannitti had played a prominent role in the Bread and Roses strike, which had inspired Italian-American labor activity throughout the nation. Though one should not overgeneralize about the perspective of Lawrence's Italians, who came almost entirely from provinces south of Rome and from Sicily, their great support for the IWW in Lawrence as in Paterson at least partly stemmed from the preference of these early migrants to settle scores through mass rebellions rather than through the slow maneuvering of trade union leaders.[44]

Lawrence's Italians had strong village-based loyalties and their mutual aid societies had been organized along regional lines. As in Paterson, the Sons of Italy had tried to combat Italians' attachment to *campanilismo*. Leftists along with some of the *prominenti* believed that Italians needed to develop a more cosmopolitan perspective, and both Luigi Misserville and Joseph Salerno, who played important roles in the 1912 and 1919 strikes, held high office in the Lawrence Sons of Italy.[45]

The influence of the mutual aid societies and the Sons of Italy stood in stark contrast to the institutional weakness of the Roman Catholic Church since Lawrence had only one very small Italian church, Holy Rosary. Father Milanese had not been able to raise sufficient funds for the church from Lawrence's 14,000 Italian residents and he was constantly casting about for ways to generate revenue. On some occasions he asked Jewish businessmen for contributions, and in 1919 he tried to sell information to agents of the Bureau of Investigation (they turned him down).[46] Father Milanese's one consistent patron had proven to be the mill owners for whom he had done "a good many favors," and in 1918 they gave him $50,000 for a new church building. Although this particular transaction had been kept secret, Father Milanese had not tried to hide his ties to the manufacturers and William Wood had spoken at the dedication of a church addition in 1917. But the more Father Milanese depended on others, the less respect he received within the community and Lawrence's Italian residents had often subjected him to savage ridicule.[47]

Anticlericalism also had an impact on Lawrence's Poles, who came mainly from Russian Poland and who had a different orientation than the Galician Poles. Many Poles had gathered around a branch of the Polish

National Catholic Church that had been founded when the Roman Catholic priest refused his parishioners' request to distribute funds more equitably. In 1919, one police detective considered this to be the "Bolshevik headquarters" in Lawrence because Sunday speakers came from out of town to address meetings on "Bolshevism, Socialism etc."[48] Even those who remained in Lawrence's Polish Roman Catholic Church, Holy Trinity, could hardly be considered enemies of the left. According to a special report prepared for church authorities in 1920, the new parish priest of Holy Trinity had "practically taken sides with the socialists" and when attempts had been made to remove him, church members had threatened to kill anyone who replaced him. Large numbers of these parishioners called themselves "socialists" and this observer concluded that the parish was "undoubtedly the most difficult in this part of the country."[49]

Germans, Jews, and Syrians also supported institutions that harbored leftists. German radical activity centered around the *Arbeiter Verbund Textile* (Textile workers' association) and the Socialistic Workingmen's Society. Karl Vogt, a former Wobbly, was a leader of both of these groups. Jewish workers belonged to a chapter of the Workmen's Circle, and a Workmen's Co-op League and James Brox and Farris Marad, who had been two of the principal Syrian IWW activists, were instrumental in forming the Syrian National Club.[50]

All of these organizations helped insure that radicalism would survive in a city where the newly arrived immigrants shunned electoral politics. The community-based institutions also provided leftists with a haven from repression, a valuable function as the IWW proved an easy mark for federal authorities who in October 1917 raided the last remaining Wobbly clubhouse in Lawrence and arrested Ettore Giannini, one of the few open IWW members left in Lawrence. These same officials closed the Wobbly headquarters and again arrested Giannini on the eve of the 1919 strike. In contrast, federal agents found it difficult to infiltrate Polish and Lithuanian societies because their membership rules either excluded outsiders or required "satisfactory credentials" before admission.[51]

These ethnic clubs provided many of the 1919 strike leaders with valuable experience in public speaking and organizing. But as in Paterson's fraternals, women did not play leadership roles within them and did not have the same opportunity as men to develop these skills. Nevertheless, an alternative culture survived the dismal 1913–1915 period and when a new opportunity for labor organizing emerged, the manufacturers learned that the memory of 1912 remained though the organizational expression had changed.

Wartime Unrest and the Continuing Divisions

As in Paterson and Passaic, once wartime prosperity arrived, workers immediately took advantage of the favorable context and staged fourteen separate strikes between 8 March and 8 June 1916. These walkouts followed a definite pattern as the majority of the participants were older immigrants and most work stoppages occurred at the Pacific and Arlington mills. All of the strikes were confined to certain departments and practically all resulted in pay increases or improved conditions for the participants. Those involved could count on broad community support and Mayor Hurley allowed workers to meet at city hall. Menders and burlers staged the only American Woolen walkout when these female employees struck in order to achieve a readjustment in the way their pay was calculated. Fewer walkouts occurred at the American Woolen plants because the company's management had moved its wage rates ahead of its competitors and, in fact, Pacific and Arlington employees demanded that their pay be equalized to that of the American Woolen workers.[52]

The only strike led by leftists took place at the Pacific Mill where Franco-Belgian loom fixers invited Joe Ettor to direct their walkout. Ettor again responded to the call but Lawrence police seized him and forced him to leave town. The authorities' ability to expel Ettor indicated that the left at this time lacked muscle, and the loom fixers, who were led by the de Tollenaere brothers, had to carry out the strike on their own.[53]

A May 1917 strike at the American Woolen Company showed that despite the renewed militancy, Lawrence's workers remained sharply divided. This walkout began when the company fired two "English-speaking workers" because they complained about a wage hike that gave the unskilled a higher percentage increase than received by the skilled employees. Upon hearing of these dismissals, mechanics, boiler firemen, and employees in the American Woolen's preparatory and finishing departments struck in protest over the discriminatory pay hikes and in order to demonstrate their support for the fired workers. These employees met at a Franco-American hall and distributed leaflets that maintained that skilled workers deserved the same increase as everyone else. A number of letters that appeared in the *Lawrence Sunday Leader*, a weekly directed mainly at Irish residents, supported these workers and the correspondents expressed annoyance that the "white help" which had "stood by" the mills in 1912 had now received a smaller increase than those who had participated in the Bread and Roses strike. One worker wondered if the mills were "afraid of the unskilled foreigner" and if the "white help" would ever again stick by the corporation "as they did in 1912."

The skilled employees' strike set off a walkout by the American Woolen Company's "foreign" employees. These workers, who had not struck for five years, invited Edmondo Rossoni, an IWW hero in 1912, to lead them. When Rossoni failed to appear, the mill hands asked a Mrs. Sproule, a Socialist party leader in Lowell, to direct the walkout. The unskilled workers also invited striking skilled workers at the American Woolen Company to join with them in fighting for the eight-hour day. But the "English speaking" employees said they wanted nothing to do with the radical leadership and they turned down the offer. The strike of the "foreign" workers soon dissipated and the skilled workers returned to the mills after receiving some adjustment in wages.[54]

If anything, the gap separating the Irish and the French Canadian workers from the more recent immigrants had grown wider since 1912. Benjamin Legere, another IWW veteran, blamed the American Woolen Company for having erected this "Chinese wall of prejudice" that separated the "so-called 'white people' and the 'black people' in the mills." According to Legere, the company used "every means possible" to further the hatreds that poisoned the air in Lawrence.[55] Though Legere oversimplified the process by which these divisions had been created, the mill owners had certainly benefited from the fragmentation and workers would remain divided for the duration of the 1919 strike.

48/54—The UTW Loses Control

As in Paterson, many Lawrence workers considered the UTW to be a strikebreaker because of its efforts to undermine the Wobbly-led walkout. But unlike in Paterson, the AFL union had made no attempt to recruit new members when labor activity picked up in 1916 because the UTW remained fearful of Lawrence's foreign-born workers who John Golden said "never" did "anything constructive themselves and spoil the field for an organization which can."[56] Lawrence's woolsorters had formed their own union and the loom fixers had affiliated with the Fall River-based American Federation of Textile Operatives (AFTO). Only the Arlington

Mill dyers and finishers gave strong support to the UTW as most of these employees enrolled in the union during a November 1918 strike.[57]

Despite its weak base, the UTW brought its eight-hour campaign to Lawrence. Rather than taking direct control of the movement, it had given the Central Labor Union responsibility for forming a general organizing committee to which most ethnic groups had elected representatives. The CLU-led group had asked the manufacturers to meet with its representatives but the mill owners said they would not meet with "outsiders" though they promised to discuss the hours issue with their own employees. The American Woolen Company took the next step on January 20 when it placed provocatively worded circulars in each worker's pay envelope. The letters took note of the UTW demand and asked: "We wonder whether all of you understand that the request of the United Textile Workers means a reduction in earnings of all our employees? Do you want this done? Do you want to work shorter hours and earn less."[58]

Even before the American Woolen Company distributed these circulars, small knots of workers meeting in pool halls, barber shops, coffee shops, and saloons had expressed dissatisfaction with the UTW's limited demands and had talked about conducting a battle for shorter hours and a wage increase.[59] Once the American Woolen Company suggested that a pay cut would accompany a reduction in hours, this movement gained momentum and delegates at the next CLU meeting voted to change the demand to 48/54—fifty-four hours' pay for forty-eight hours' work. Nevertheless, the UTW tried to maintain control over the movement and UTW vice president Tom McMahon came to Lawrence to urge workers "to forget the wage question and fight for the principle of eight hours." McMahon's words fell on deaf ears as the 1,500 workers at the meeting voted unanimously to seek 48/54. This slogan quickly captured the imaginations of many Lawrence workers and during the last week in January, Syrian, Italian, Russian, Franco-Belgian, German, Polish, and Lithuanian workers voted in separate meetings to endorse this demand. All efforts began to be directed towards building a February 3 walkout and strike sentiment became so powerful that when a reporter asked UTW organizer Horace Riviere if he would still urge acceptance of 48/48, he replied: "I am afraid my life would be in danger if I did so."[60]

As workers carried out their strike preparations, the American Woolen Company surprised everyone by announcing its intention to begin operating on a forty-eight-hour schedule on February 3. Although the company said it would not grant a wage increase, it pledged to pay time and a half for all overtime employment. The unilateral decision conformed with the company's policy of acting on its own in labor matters and undercut the various textile associations' hopes of acting in concert on this issue. As late as January 23, the Pacific company had been running full-page advertisements against the forty-eight-hour week and other manufacturers had stated privately that a cut of six hours was too great to be absorbed at once.[61] But once the American Woolen Company, which had no southern competition to worry about and which believed that it could more easily absorb higher costs of production than other manufacturers, had made this decision the Arlington, Pacific, and most other northern cotton and woolen mills had no choice but to go along as they knew their workers would now certainly strike to achieve the forty-eight-hour week.[62]

The American Woolen Company's concession for the most part brought the UTW's phase of the northern campaign to a successful close. In Lowell, 25,000 cotton-mill employees reported to work on the new basis on February 3. The forty-eight-hour schedule also went into effect in Manchester, the Fall River/New Bedford area, and throughout Rhode Island's Blackstone Valley. Though some Woonsocket, Rhode Island, workers briefly walked out for 48/54, Lawrence became the only city where a major strike movement emerged, even though workers everywhere faced the same cut in their weekly wages.[63]

Although their own radical labor traditions in themselves accounted for the new outbreak, cutbacks in employment that came almost immediately upon the heels of the Armistice further fueled labor protest. Most of the Lawrence mills had gone on three- and four-day-per-week schedules and the American Woolen Company, which often dismissed workers as soon as orders dropped, had laid off thousands of employees altogether.[64] These actions followed the American Woolen Company's declaration of a special dividend for stockholders and publication of a U.S. Treasury Department report that listed the firm as one of the country's leading war profiteers.[65] To workers who faced a continuing rise in the cost of living and who now feared a return to the hard times of 1913–1915, the company's callousness served as a further spur to take to the streets to conduct "a protest against unemployment."[66]

Normally, it would have been difficult to win a strike begun at a time when many workers were laid off, but February was actually a propitious time for a walkout. Due to the steady wartime work, many employees had accumulated savings that could tide them over for a period of months.[67] Moreover, Lawrence workers had always initiated their strikes between January and April. This was true in 1882, 1894, 1902, and 1912 as well as in 1919.[68] The goal had been to insure that workers would be on the streets when orders for the spring season arrived from the ready-to-wear manufacturers. In 1919, workers anticipated that if their movement mustered sufficient support, this strategy would once again prove successful.

The Strike Leadership

On February 3, workers responded enthusiastically to the 48/54 call when close to 10,000 pickets surrounded the mills. The Pemberton, Lawrence Duck, and Everett mills were forced to close, the American Woolen Company was badly crippled, and the Pacific and Arlington mills struggled to maintain a semblance of normal production. Because of experience gained during the 1912 struggle, workers knew instantly how to put a strike organization into place and they formed a police committee (to monitor police conduct), a finance committee, and a relief committee. Picket lines organized on a nationality basis created an immediate sense of mass involvement and activity. There was one major departure from 1912 as all sessions of the general and executive strike committees were private—a futile effort as it turned out—to prevent police from gaining information.[69]

The selection of Samuel Bramhall as chairperson of the strike committee signaled the movement's new direction. Somewhat of a maverick, the Lancashire-born Bramhall headed a local of the carpenters union. A first-rate soapbox orator, a committed socialist, an opponent of the war, and a fierce anticlerical, Bramhall had often defied city authorities and in June 1916 chaired a rally that protested Ettor's deportation from Lawrence. His selection as the head of the strike committee aroused enthusiasm among many Italians who had previously remained somewhat aloof from the 48/54 movement.[70]

Ime Kaplan, who was named secretary of the general strike committee, was the sole holdover from the original CLU group. Kaplan, who was born in Russia, arrived in the United States in 1906 and had been a member of the Jewish branch of the IWW and the Socialist party. In 1918, he had joined a small mule spinners local and the UTW had employed him to spread eight-hour sentiment in the Merrimack Valley. He had "been well thought of" by John Golden and the CLU had considered him one who "could reach the people" but federal agents also reported that in

January, Kaplan had been distributing "radical propaganda" and talking up the need for a general strike.[71]

Workers turned to Bramhall and Kaplan because they were known as supporters of both socialism and of trade unions. On the other hand, the task of mobilizing the strikers had to be assumed by representatives of the various nationality groups. From the very beginning of the walkout, Joseph Salerno emerged as the leading spokesperson for the Italians and his prominence suggests that many Italian workers had begun to look toward an ACWA-style unionism rather than towards the IWW. Born in the sulfur-mining region of central Sicily, Salerno had held the title of *Oratore* in the Sons of Italy and had been a close associate of Reverend Ariel Bellondi, a Baptist minister from nearby Haverhill. Considered "anti-priest" by the federal operatives, Salerno had often feuded with Father Milanese. Salerno was a socialist but a fairly moderate one and he demanded that the strike be conducted in an entirely peaceful and orderly way.[72] Lena Cacici led a minority faction of Italians that considered Salerno's approach to be too mild. Well educated and an excellent speaker, she issued her own circulars during the strike and engaged in scathing denunciations of priests. Unlike Salerno, she still openly supported the IWW and had close ties with the anarchist community in Lynn.[73] Other prominent Italian activists included Edward Franchesi, a weaver at the Pacific plant who had been secretary of the Italian branch of the IWW and who had helped lead the 1918 work stoppage at the American Woolen Company; Frank Coco, a fiery speaker who headed Lawrence's Italian barbers union; and Luigi Misserville, who also held office in the Sons of Italy.[74]

Mike Bolis and William Blazonis emerged as the leading spokespersons for the Lithuanian workers. Bolis had been an officer in the Lithuanian branch of the IWW and had run a small art supply store since the 1912 strike.[75] Blazonis had been active in radical agitation for a number of years. He came to the United States in 1907 and had been dishonorably discharged from the Marine Corps in 1918 for refusing to obey orders. He had worked briefly at Lowell's Appleton Mill until being fired for spreading left-wing propaganda and had led a brief strike at the Lawrence plant of the U.S. Worsted Company in September 1918. Greatly influenced by the Bolshevik Revolution, he openly espoused revolutionary views.[76]

Most other nationality groups had two or three persons who emerged as the most prominent public spokespersons though each group elected five representatives to the general strike committee. Many of the best-known leaders had some command of English as those who knew only their native tongue could not exercise influence beyond their own community. No Lawrence woman held as high a position as Margaret Haray did in Passaic but at least eight women overcame gender barriers and served on the strike committee.[77] One of these female workers, Annie Trina, spoke to Anthony Capraro, who interviewed a number of workers during the strike. Trina had come to the United States from Latvia in 1906 but retained a keen interest in her homeland. A believer in both trade unionism and socialism, she supported the Bolshevik Revolution and was proud that Lettish women had won the right to vote. She was elected as one of the Lettish representatives to the central strike body, and her interview reveals her as a vibrant, self-confident woman whose range of concerns typified those most active in the walkout.[78]

An impressive number of the 1919 leaders had been members of the IWW. Besides Kaplan, Franchesi, and Bolis, this included Emile Lemaire (a Franco-Belgian), the de Tolleneares, Carl Vogt, and Thomas Holliday and Archie Adamson, who were British-born socialists and had worked as weavers in the mills.[79] Many of them had been "hero worshipers" of the Wobblies but because they were either too young or had only recently arrived in the United States, they had played only a secondary role in 1912. By 1919, they were ready to replace the members of the 1912 general strike committee who had been forced by the blacklist to leave the city.[80]

That former Wobblies assumed leadership positions indicates that despite all of the poststrike repression, the Bread and Roses walkout had left a lasting imprint on the Lawrence working class. But the IWW could do no more than wistfully send its greetings as the organization was busy combating massive federal repression.[81] Yet, Lawrence workers continued to hope that aid would arrive as they knew that outside support had been a crucial factor in the winning of the 1912 strike.

In 1919, this assistance came from a most unlikely source when three Protestant ministers, A. J. Muste, Cedric Long, and Harold Rotzel, came to Lawrence as soon as the strike began and quickly assumed leadership positions. Dubbed the "intellectual gang" by the press, none of them had ever been involved in a walkout. But all three had recently paid a price for their dissenting views: Muste and Rotzel had been forced to give up their pulpits because of their antiwar stand and Long had angered his Epping, New Hampshire, congregation because of his outspoken support for local shoe workers who were out on strike. All three had also been active in the League for Democratic Control that strove to develop a postwar reconstruction program that could unite liberals and radicals. In 1918, with the financial help of wealthy supporters, Muste and Rotzel had moved to a house in the Back Bay section of Boston that became the base for a small group known as "the Comrades of the New World." They hoped this collective would serve as the foundation for a new "preaching order" that through concrete action would demonstrate that social change could be accomplished through nonviolent means.[82]

Since they desired to participate in some form of "deliberate propaganda," the ministers had gone up to Lawrence as soon as workers left the mills. When they arrived, they discovered that the strikers eagerly welcomed their assistance and they busied themselves addressing envelopes, distributing circulars, sending out appeals for relief, and explaining the workers' cause to reporters. They immediately earned the trust of the mill hands and by the second week of the walkout, Muste had been asked to become executive secretary of the general strike committee.[83]

Both Cedric Long and Harold Rotzel also assumed leadership positions. Rotzel became chairperson of the general relief committee, which distributed over $90,000 during the strike. This was an important post because police agents often used charges of theft to discredit strike leaders. Its membership consisted of the heads of the nationality relief committees and the chairpersons of the soup kitchens, coffee stations, and medical relief committees. The structure helped avoid allegations that any one nationality was being favored in the distribution of funds. Rotzel saw one of its functions as "training" workers for "future responsibilities" and despite the plans of infiltrators, the leadership avoided all taint of scandal.[84] Cedric Long also became a member of the general strike committee and took charge of youth activities, entertainment, and the strikers' guard that had responsibility for keeping order on the picket lines and watching for cases of police misconduct. Ironically, part of Long's expertise in this area came from having patrolled Lawrence's streets as a member of the state militia in 1912.[85]

Given their lack of experience, it is remarkable that these three "innocent appearing" ministers could assume leadership positions. According to Muste, workers accepted them because they had earned respect for having opposed the war, because they returned to Lawrence after their initial visits, and because they provided a convenient "cover" for strikers.[86] Muste's personal magnetism also should not be discounted as he was an inspiring and forceful speaker who quickly learned how to express the strikers' own aspirations. Indeed, at his very first speaking appearance in Lawrence he told the assembled workers: "You should learn all you can about the textile industry because very soon you are going to take it over for your own."[87]

Groups connected to the ministers also provided valuable aid. The Comrades of the New World raised $15,000 and organized a special delegation of supporters who travelled to Lawrence. The Boston-based magazine *The Forward,* whose political perspective resembled that of the League for Democratic Control, printed three special editions that gave the strike valuable publicity. These organizations also formed a "Boston Committee for the Lawrence Strike" that gave workers access to left/liberal financial support.[88]

Elizabeth Glendower Evans also contributed much to the strike movement. Known as the "angel of the strikers," Evans, a Boston resident, stayed in Lawrence during much of the conflict. No ordinary upper-class sympathizer with a fleeting interest in workers' causes, Evans, who later became a major figure on the Sacco-Vanzetti Defense Committee, frequently visited workers' homes to distribute milk or other forms of aid. She walked the picket lines to watch for incidents of police brutality and testified in court on behalf of those who were arrested. One morning she and Bramhall even managed to defy city authorities and led an impromptu parade through Lawrence's main business street that proved to be the largest demonstration of the entire strike. Herself an Arlington Mill stockholder, she and her comrade Anna Davis gave thousands of dollars to the strike committee.[89] All of this assistance confounded the expectations of observers such as U.S. commissioner of immigration, H. J. Skeffington, who had confidently reported back to Washington: "I do not believe that they will be able to get anything near the funds adequate to carry on this strike . . . by February 25th at the latest, the bottom will drop out of the whole thing."[90]

A number of other radicals came on their own to the city but only those associated with the *Revolutionary Age* in Boston made a concerted effort to lead the strike. This newspaper, which was edited by Louis Fraina, began publication in November 1918 and became the leading organ of the left wing within the Socialist party. Its first issues focused exclusively on revolutionary developments in Europe and ignored events in the United States. But the Lawrence strike captured its attention and a number of left-wing socialists came to the city as soon as the walkout began. Eamon McAlpine, an associate editor of the *Revolutionary Age,* P. P. Cosgrove of the Marine Firemen's Union, and Jim Larkin, former head of the Irish Transport and General Workers' Union, all gave speeches at mass meetings during the first week of the work stoppage. Since all three were Irish, they also made special appeals to that sector of the population to support the strike. The Lawrence press speculated that Larkin would assume primary leadership of the struggle and, given his organizing experience, the Lawrence work stoppage appeared to present the perfect opportunity for Larkin to gain support for his party grouping.[91] Larkin, though, was reluctant to assume this position since he thought Americans should "take charge of their business" and feared that police interference would be stepped up if the strike was led by a foreigner.[92] Both Larkin and McAlpine failed to return to Lawrence after their initial visit although Cosgrove, as well as Richard Hansen, another left-wing socialist, remained and became members of the general strike committee.[93]

On the surface, the *Revolutionary Age* supporters served harmoniously with the ministers on the committee as both sides tried to avoid disputes. This does not mean they shared the same approach. Muste's speeches sounded relatively moderate compared to those of Hansen who upon his arrival in the city told workers: "The American workingman is learning something every day from the Russian Bolsheviki, where the red flag is the symbol of the working man."[94] But nothing illustrated the differences more than Louis Fraina's dramatic appearance in Lawrence. When Fraina addressed a large crowd, he told the assembled throng that they should be fighting for "94-36" rather than a mere 48/54. He further urged workers "to smash the fat belly of the capitalists until they are down and out." In part of his speech, contrary to the strike committee's policy of not defying police regulations, he told workers "to parade and if they refuse it to you, take it. The streets are yours." When he concluded his talk, a disturbance broke out and eight workers were arrested. Fraina was immediately indicted for inciting a riot. Muste testified on his behalf but he was probably uncomfortable with Fraina's rhetoric.[95] Fraina did not return to Lawrence after his preliminary hearing although Hansen and Cosgrove continued to serve on the general strike committee.

Throughout the strike, Hansen and Cosgrove did much of the nuts and bolts work necessary to insure a victory. On the other hand, Fraina's brief foray into Lawrence indicates that some of the left-wing socialists, who were soon to move into the communist movement, had been too smitten by the Bolshevik Revolution to provide effective leadership. Ultimately, the left wingers' inability to raise funds may have prevented them from playing a more influential role. Lawrence strikers needed leadership that could furnish financial aid and the ministers and eventually the ACWA were in a better position to provide this than the *Revolutionary Age* group.

The willingness of supporters to come to Lawrence played a decisive role in the walkout. In a small industrial city, the mere presence of outsiders could significantly raise strikers' morale. Moreover, the inability of local police to keep these people out demonstrated that state authority could be challenged. In itself, the name established by Lawrence as a result of the 1912 strike attracted many persons who were anxious to lend a hand or merely to look around—all of which added to workers' sense of importance.

The relationship of outsiders to a strike is often far more complex than appears on the surface. Some observers on the left lamented the substitution of Christian ethics for the revolutionary élan of the IWW.[96] Some liberals credited the ministers with weaning workers "away from the doctrines of revolutionary socialism."[97] But both perspectives exaggerate the ministers' impact. In 1919, Lawrence workers were again eager to accept outside leadership and they embraced the first group that offered them tangible aid. This does not mean that strikers had adopted the Christian nonviolent philosophy of the ministers any more than they had all embraced the IWW in 1912. As was to become clear during the course of the strike, Lawrence workers had many disagreements among themselves and any organization or union that emerged in a dominant position would inevitably face a challenge from those who held a differing viewpoint.

The Differing Responses to the Strike

Although the general strike committee, as in 1912, attempted to reach out to all groups of workers and accepted representatives elected by the smaller mills and by particular crafts, the strike movement failed to win the support of large chunks of the mill population. After the first week, only the Everett Mill remained totally shutdown as this plant, which had a large number of Polish and Lithuanian workers, was located next to the major immigrant residential district and was an easy target for pickets and missiles. All of the other mills remained open although with widely varying abilities to approach normal production. The best estimate is that 15,000 or about 60 percent of Lawrence's textile mill employees were out on strike.[98] Other than Everett, the American Woolen Company was hurt the most by the walkout while Arlington and Pacific employees were the least prone to strike. Both of these mills employed large numbers of French-Canadian and Irish workers. According to Edward

Franchesi, the Irish employees of these plants were "nearly all scabbing" and the French who were "in favor of the priest" also stayed at work.[99] The incompleteness of the walkout was, of course, normal for Lawrence but presented a sharp contrast to Passaic where workers had closed all of the plants.

None of the mills could even approach normal operations as tie-ups in one room affected the entire flow of production. Ironically, the manufacturers paid a price for their discriminatory hiring policies as the Arlington Mill's combing department, which was principally composed of Polish and Lithuanian workers, and the Kunhardt Mill's carding department, which was almost entirely Italian, had been completely shut down. Some firms even had to pay "loyal" employees who reported to work even if there was little for them to do.[100]

As often occurred in the textile industry, many skilled employees preferred to carry out their own departmental battles. For example, boiler firemen at the Pacific Mill twice conducted their own walkouts in the midst of the 48/54 strike and Arlington Mill dyehouse employees staged an unsuccessful five-week work stoppage for new wage rates. Although the AFTO voted to accept the 48/48 offer, a number of members objected to this position and in the seventh week of the strike, American Woolen loom fixers staged their own walkout for a wage increase. Despite being organized separately, this work stoppage strengthened the 48/54 movement and the loom fixers even voted to send a delegate to the ATWA's founding convention.[101]

The general strike committee never abandoned its efforts to get everyone to leave the mills. One "Victory Bulletin" addressed "to you Irish, French Canadians, English, American, Lovers of Freedom" called upon these groups to cease scabbing on themselves: "They call the strikers now out 'foreigners.' That is throwing dust in your eyes. Do you think your wages will stay up if the wages of the 'foreigners' are reduced." Another bulletin issued on the eve of May Day claimed that if all of the workers "come out of the mills in a body . . . in 24 hours the workers will have substantial increases in pay."[102] These efforts had little impact and those English-speakers who joined the walkout continued to be gibed for siding with "wops" and "hunkies."[103] This does not mean that the holdouts wanted the strike to lose. When Franchesi spoke before the Massachusetts Consumers' League, he told its members that the "Irish girls" would not go out but they hoped that the strikers would win so they could gain a wage increase.[104]

Some nationality groups played a role far disproportionate to their numbers. This was especially true of the Lithuanian community as strikers met at Maple Park, a Lithuanian food store was converted into a strikers' cooperative, and a Lithuanian hall became the general strike committee's headquarters.[105] Although the most active supporters belonged to the Lithuanian Social Camp Association and the Independent Catholic Church, Roman Catholic Lithuanians also backed the cause. Father Virmauskis was a former mill worker and in 1918 he established the St. Joseph's Roman Catholic Labor Association to combat leftists in the Lithuanian community. During the work stoppage, this lay organization set up a fund to support those on strike and issued an appeal for aid that was circulated throughout New England. When the city banned public meetings, the Lithuanian Roman Catholic Church offered its privately owned lot to strikers. When queried about this aid, Father Virmauskis told Bureau of Investigation agents that he had to act in this way as he feared that "the agitators were picturing the clergy" as the enemies of the workers.[106]

While the Lithuanian participation flowed from the community's connection to the left, special factors could affect the involvement of other groups. For example, many German workers resented the hostility they faced during the war. One of the most annoying incidents occurred on Armistice Day when a number of German mending-room employees had been humiliated by their "American" coworkers who forced them to stand on their heads and sing the national anthem. The case, which became known as Lawrence's "German she war," had come before Judge Mahoney who found three of the seven defendants guilty of assault. But, he imposed no penalties and the perpetrators had been treated as heroines by the Lawrence press and by a big crowd that greeted the accused women following the trial.[107] Partly because of their anger over incidents such as this, large numbers of German workers supported the strike even though the manufacturers told them that "they must atone for atrocities committed by the German government in the European war" by scabbing on their fellow workers.[108]

Lawrence, then, remained a city where workers struck by nationality. According to Harold Rotzel, besides the Lithuanians and the Germans, the Italians, Poles, Russians, Syrians, Franco-Belgians, and Jews remained solid through the "16 long weeks of the strike."[109] Holding the various nationalties together was not an easy task but the general strike committee showed some imagination in this area. A joint Polish-Russian meeting tried to heal ethnic divisions and a German-Belgian picnic salved wartime tensions.[110] Poles remained firm in their support of the work stoppage even though the Massachusetts Adjutant General's Office assigned a special operative representing the fictitious "Central Polish Citizens Committee" to Lawrence and instructed him to speak against the strike and warn workers against "Jewish Bolshevik agitators."[111]

Above all, the pattern that had been evident in 1912 repeated itself in 1919. In both years, workers at the American Woolen Company comprised the backbone of the strike movement. Significantly, when the 1922 strike occurred, Lawrence became the only New England city where two ideologically opposed unions (the UTW and the One Big Union) competed with one another for influence. Furthermore, when the CIO came to Lawrence in the 1930's, it gained only a foothold at the Wood and Ayer mills as the Arlington and Pacific workers refused to join the "wop union."[112] These divisions existed because two separate working class cultures had evolved in Lawrence. One was mainly composed of French-Canadian and Irish workers who were closely tied to the church, sympathetic to craft unions, and determinedly antiradical. The other was composed of workers who were often anticlerical, open to leftist ideas, and advocates of industrial unionism.[113] These two groups conducted their battles separately and had little contact with one another. As a result, workers who had left the mills in 1919 had to develop tactics that could enable them to win an incomplete walkout.

Strike Tactics

Lawrence was not a city where striking mill hands would turn over their dues to city officials and workers knew they would face the unrelenting opposition of the police. The local authorities were far better positioned than in 1912 to combat the walkout as the Bread and Roses work stoppage came immediately after the adoption of the commission form of government and the municipal authorities had not been prepared to deal with the outbreak. No such confusion existed in 1919. Having learned in 1912 the vital role parades played in building morale, the director of public safety, Peter Carr, banned all such demonstrations. After the first week of the strike, he prohibited all meetings on public grounds and workers had to gather on vacant lots, ash dumps, and mudholes. Instead of calling upon the state militia, city officials placed far more reliance on police from neighboring Massachusetts and New Hampshire cities who had only been used on a token basis in 1912. These officers, who were indistinguishable from local police, proved more efficient in crowd control and aroused less public indignation than the bayonet-equipped state troopers.[114] Authorities exercised their power in other ways. On the first day of the strike, local officials took Frank Coco in for "questioning" and in mid-February, federal agents removed Ime Kaplan to Boston and charged him with draft evasion. Although federal officials, to their embarrassment, had to release Kaplan when he produced proof of registration, they continued to threaten "undesirable aliens" with deportation. And it soon became clear that a "war psychology" prevailed in Lawrence.[115]

As in 1912, mass picketing provided the best means to combat the harassment and to build morale. The biggest crowds usually gathered on Mondays as strikers believed that if employees did not report on that day, they would not work for the rest of the week. In order to discourage people from working, strikers threw bottles, ashes, or pepper at strike-breakers, snatched their lunch baskets, subjected them to verbal abuse, and broke windows in their homes. Most of these incidents occurred in the central immigrant district as strikers rarely ventured into Irish or French-Canadian neighborhoods. In retaliation, the police arrested over 300 strikers during the course of the conflict but the frightful beatings they administered to workers proved to be the most effective deterrent to strike activity.[116]

The ministers tried to look the other way whenever strikers committed aggressive acts. Muste, in particular, used specious reasoning to justify workers' actions. For example, at Fraina's trial, he told the court: "I am opposed to violent violence."[117] Though Muste helped convince the strike committee not to openly defy the ban on parades the strikers themselves actually had little desire to lock horns with police. This stance did not result from the ministers' influence but was a product of the workers' own sense of tactics. The Lawrence working class used very little violence in either the 1912 or the 1919 strike. Faced by hostile city authorities, confrontations with police could only invite mass retaliation and repression. In the sort of unequal struggle imposed by industrial capitalism, a policy of restraint crossed many an ideological boundary.[118]

As in all long strikes, the conflict had an ebb and flow and when spirits sagged, the leadership had to rebuild morale. The "Victory Bulletins" promised a "surprise at every meeting" and proclaimed that "we wear the smile that won't come off." The strike committee publicized unusual acts of solidarity such as when Polish workers donated $1,000 in Liberty Bonds to the strike fund and Italians collectively refused relief for a week. Ex-soldiers formed a "Soldiers, Sailors and Marines Protective

Association" and children boycotted classes in protest of teachers' efforts to discourage the walkout. On May Day, workers held a "peoples festival" and festooned themselves in red.[119] In one of the walkout's more dramatic moments, Muste and Long headed a picket line at a time when spirits appeared to be low. Police knocked Long unconscious and arrested both men, but the incident earned the ministers new respect.[120]

As in 1912, strikers decided to send some of their children to sympathizers in other cities. This idea had been considered since the beginning of the strike but was put off until the tenth week of the work stoppage when many children began to feel the ill effects of the walkout. Not only did they need food and clothing but the entreaties of young children could force people back to work. The operation had to be carried out with the utmost care as no incident from the 1912 strike had aroused more fear and animosity than when the police stopped children from leaving town and arrested their parents for child neglect.

A special committee who chose those in need, handled all of the arrangements. The first fifteen children left by auto vans in total secrecy for Boston. The security system worked so well that police "were surprised to learn that any children had left." Shortly afterwards, two other vans took approximately eighty children from the city. For the fourth truck load, the strikers decided to "shake off the police fear" and organized a public demonstration. They placed signs on the trucks reading "we will make Lawrence fit to live in" and "we don't earn enough to feed our children." But as in 1912, a terrible scene developed. Police began to hassle one of the drivers and removed the signs from his car. Upon hearing of the interference, Polish workers left a meeting hall, marched to the scene, and almost clashed with authorities. Although police allowed the autos to leave, strikers fearing for the safety of their children ceased making use of this tactic.[121] Despite the suspension of the motorcades, workers had been able to demonstrate both tangibly and symbolically that they would not allow hunger to drive them back to the mills. The conscious imitation of 1912 also served a purpose as it showed the manufacturers and city authorities that the Wobbly spirit lived on.

The strike committee also tried to spread the 48/54 movement to other cities as the failure of other New England textile workers to walk out had weakened their cause. The first efforts came in Lowell, but mill employees there evinced little inclination to support their coworkers in Lawrence. Quite naturally, the UTW's Lowell Textile Council strenuously objected to the strike call and circulars urged Lowell workers "to stand by your city" rather than listen to "outsiders Kaplan and Long." The 10,000 Greek mill employees also proved to be unresponsive and a strike could not be organized without their support.[122]

During the second week of April, fearing that the Americn Woolen Company was using its multi-plant operations to break the walkout, Lawrence workers issued a new call for a sympathy strike. The leaflets resonated with the language of the 48/54 movement and called upon workers to "communicate" their plans at once to the general strike committee:

Arise then ye men and women of the mills of the loom and spinning frames. Be ready to stop work, strike in great numbers, all and everyone of you. Organize one big walkout and line up in battle array with the strikers of Lawrence and for a shorter work day and more pay, in order to live and enjoy the good things of life.

Drudge no longer. Band Together.

Lend a hand to the Lawrence strikers, send in funds for the needy and for the inevitable one big strike in the textile industry. Get ready for the time is ripe. One big Strike! One big union! One big victory![123]

The strike committee put the most effort into the Providence and Olneyville, Rhode Island, area, and P. P. Cosgrove, who was convinced that workers needed to extend the "industrial battlefield," took charge of the agitation. Again, the results proved disappointing and despite speaking appearances by a number of Lawrence leaders, few workers left any of the Rhode Island mills. As in Lowell, appeals to localism proved damaging and the brief sympathy strikes ended amid reports that workers had been "fooled by the general strike call."[124]

The failure to generate support came after Lawrence workers had predicted "that within a very short time the employees of every plant owned by the American Woolen Company in New England would be on strike."[125] It is hardly surprising that the movement flopped as Lowell and Providence workers had little ongoing contact with those in Lawrence and it is often difficult to spread locally rooted labor militancy from one city to another. From the perspective of Lawrence workers, the inability to widen the strike movement meant they had to muster other forms of support for their cause.

The Ethnic Elite: Opponents or Supporters?

As in Passaic, immigrant shopkeepers granted aid to the strikers. Workers held meetings in a Syrian barber shop and a Russian drug store and a Syrian rooming house offered free board to those who faced eviction. A number of ethnic grocers extended credit to the strikers and a committee of Franco-Belgian merchants donated $500 to the strike fund. A number of these supporters formed a Business and Professional Men's Committee that endorsed the strikers' demands as being to the "ultimate welfare of the city" and that offered "moral and financial support" to those who were out on strike. At their founding meeting, Muste and Long spoke about the reciprocal relationship between workers and small-business people and thanked them for their aid.[126]

As their financial losses mounted, the Business and Professional Men's Committee tried to negotiate an agreement. Against the advice of the general strike committee, "the Non-English Speaking Business Men" as they also called themselves proposed that the walkout be settled through shop committees composed exclusively of workers employed in the mills. To implement this plan, they met with representatives of the mill owners. At one point, both parties appeared to have approved of an agreement by which the workers would return to the plants and wages would be readjusted through shop committees, but the discussions ceased when the businessmen's group insisted on a no-discrimination clause. The manufacturers rejected this proposal and publicly suggested that the committee could "best demonstrate its influence with the people it represents . . . if it will endeavor to bring as many people as possible back to the mills." The patronizing and insulting language stung a group that had risked its status by proposing a compromise that undercut the strike committee. In reply, the immigrant business organization criticized the manufacturers for trying to "trick" them into playing a strikebreaking role and renewed their support for the walkout.[127]

The conflicting pressures that tore at the ethnic bourgeoisie can best be viewed within the Italian community, which due to its considerable size supported a number of banks, steamship agencies, pharmacies, bakers, grocers, and a few doctors and lawyers. The *prominenti's* standing had been enhanced by the war as they directed Liberty Loan drives, organized "Italian Days," and greeted Italian war missions.[128] Fearing a loss of this influence and dependent on workers' patronage for their livelihood, they extended aid to the strikers though sometimes it took threats of boycotts or pressure from the Italian consul in Boston before they did so.[129] Other factors caused the middle class to extend a sympathetic hand. Dr. Constant Calitri nursed a personal grudge because he had been removed from his city position; many Italian residents resented their lack of representation in city government; practically everyone became indignant when mounted police rode through the immigrant community and wantonly attacked strikers and bystanders alike.[130]

Some of the *prominenti* played both sides. Dr. Constant Calitri, Antonio Colombo, who owned a print shop, and Salerno's close friend Reverend Bellondi all publicly supported the strike and also supplied information to federal agents.[131] Angelo Rocco provides the best example of how conflicting forces could push an individual in two directions. Rocco had been a textile worker in 1912 and had been instrumental in getting the IWW leaders to come to Lawrence. By 1919, he had completed night law school, become an attorney and established his own practice. In an autobiographical account written for the *Lawrence Evening Tribune*, he now described America as having "the best practical form of government in the world today."[132] Not surprisingly then, he hoped the strike would not last long and had been one of the prime movers in efforts to settle the walkout through shop committees. Strike leaders considered him to be an enemy of the work stoppage. And yet Rocco defended strikers in court, spoke out against police brutality, and helped sneak Carlo Tresca, a hero to the most radical Italian workers, into the city.[133]

Some clan leaders doggedly opposed the work stoppage. This was especially true of Fabrizio Pitochelli and Father Milanese. Pitochelli was one of the city's wealthiest Italian residents; he had been a banker, real estate broker, and employment agent. For a number of years he had been a "reliable informant" for the Bureau of Investigation and strikers —who may have known this—had fired shots into a funeral parlor operated by the Pitochelli Brothers.[134] Father Milanese had backed the 1912 walkout but by 1919 he had moved completely within the orbit of the manufacturers. William Wood publicly thanked him for speaking out against the strike and Father Milanese urged the mill owners to hold out against the "radical element."[135] Ironically, the manufacturers' efforts to use Father Milanese may have backfired as Wood in particular seemed unaware of the fact that many Italian residents had nothing but scorn for him. During the work stoppage, workers broke windows in Holy Rosary, boycotted religious functions, and accused Father Milanese of "immorality and extortion."[136]

Most of the *prominenti* were caught in the same bind as many of Lawrence's other middle-class residents since they considered the demand for a wage increase to be just and yet did "not want socialism to triumph."[137] Because their help was given grudgingly, Lawrence workers knew they could not count on the support of the ethnic bourgeoisie indefinitely. This made it all the more imperative that further outside assistance be secured so workers could win the prolonged battle.

The ACWA's Entry

The ACWA provided the aid that proved critical to the winning of the strike. As soon as the walkout began, the Amalgamated printed an appeal by the Lawrence workers in its newspaper. By early March, the ACWA expressed definite interest in the Lawrence situation and soon thereafter assigned staff members August and Frank Bellanca, Joseph Kleinman, Leo Robbins, Gioacchino Artoni, H. J. Rubenstein, and Anthony Capraro to the city.[138] Rubenstein, who had only recently resigned from the Paterson branch of the WIIU, took over much of the day-to-day running of the strike. Capraro, who was one of a number of Italian anarcho-syndicalists who had joined the ACWA, played an even more important role. A dedicated socialist who had spent time in Sing-Sing, the Sicilian-born Capraro became head of the finance committee and convinced many Italian workers to support the ACWA.[139] The ministers deferred to the Amalgamated's representatives, and Bramhall and Kaplan, who may have harbored doubts about the ACWA's role, were no match for the experienced cadre. Soon after coming to Lawrence, Capraro reported that "the whole situation is in our hands" and the strike became a crucial test of the Amalgamated's ability to extend its influence to the textile field.[140]

The ACWA moved immediately to provide the strikers with financial aid. The New York office of the Amalgamated assessed its members "one hour's" wage for every week for the duration of the strike and Amalgamated locals in other cities set their own assessments. The union's general executive board also promised to send money. These pledges came at a time when Italian shopkeepers were pressing for payment for food supplies and landlords were insisting that workers give at least partial rent payments. Although the ACWA's contributions did not live up to expectations, this aid and monies supplied through benefits arranged by the Socialist party newspaper *The New York Call* helped tide workers over and gave the movement a badly needed lift.[141]

Upon leaving the mills, workers had formed their own union, but once the ACWA representatives came to the city, and upon Capraro's urging, the general strike committee voted that it would be preferable to affiliate with the Amalgamated. To consider this request, the union's general executive board chose a three-person committee consisting of the ACWA treasurer David Wolf and board members Henry Cohen and August Bellanca. Capraro expressed great optimism that the ACWA would approve of the merger of the Lawrence textile workers with the clothing workers.[142] But after deliberating for two weeks, the special committee decided against affiliation because the board members thought "that the time of a strike was not the proper time" for such an important decision that should only be made after "calm and careful deliberation" rather than during a period of "excitement."[143]

The decision proved disappointing to Lawrence workers but it did not dampen their desire to establish a connection with the ACWA. This sentiment, of course, continued to be generated by the ACWA cadre who had come to Lawrence precisely for this purpose. Following the advice of the ACWA representatives, Lawrence workers joined with those in Passaic and Paterson in the call for a new textile workers' union, which held its founding convention in New York City on 12 and 13 April 1919. After the gathering, the winning of the Lawrence walkout became the ATWA's top priority. The union's newspaper established temporary headquarters in Lawrence under the editorship of Capraro, Hansen, and Rubenstein and 10,000 workers enrolled in the Lawrence ATWA local, making it the union's largest branch.[144]

Conflicting Views on the Left

Lawrence mill employees did not respond positively to the ACWA simply because it happened to be the first union to arrive on the scene. As David Montgomery has noted, since the IWW's decline many foreign-born workers had begun to seek out unions that provided more than "oratory and strike leadership."[145] These ex-Wobblies had adopted a more practical orientation but they were hardly bread-and-butter union-ists. According to an investigator for the Federal Council of Churches, the leaders of the Lawrence strike "adhere[d] to a syndicalist philosophy— they believe[d] that an industry should be socially owned and managed by the workers and for the workers."[146] Calls for worker control of industry never ceased during the sixteen weeks of the walkout. This was not the control sought by skilled workers who often fought for autonomy on the job while accepting the overall capitalist framework. Instead this was a call for nothing less than "the abolition of capitalism and the system of wage slavery."[147]

Workers expressed their revolutionary beliefs in a number of ways. They sang the *Internationale* before every strike meeting and pictures of Marx, Lenin and Karl Liebknecht adorned various meeting halls. Victory bulletins celebrated other struggles such as the Havana general strike and the fight of British workers for the six-hour day. Strikers referred to the mill owners as "Our Masters and Capitalists" and one call for 48/54 ended with the prediction that "the earth shall rise on new foundations." The first issue of the ATWA newspaper printed the "Declaration of the Soviet Republic of Bavaria" and workers addressed Capraro as "Comrade Fellow Worker Anarchist Communist Revolutionary Anthony Capraro."[148]

These revolutionary sentiments had been evident during the Bread and Roses walkout. In 1919, the Bolshevik Revolution added new inspiration for many workers. As the Council of Churches' report pointed out: "The Russian situation constituted a backdrop for the industrial battle."[149] This presented a problem for Salerno and others who did not necessarily see a direct parallel between the Bolshevik Revolution and the Lawrence strike. But the Lithuanians, in particular, did make this connection as many of them believed that an independent and socialist Lithuania would result from Lenin's promise of self-determination for the subject nationalities of the old Russian empire.[150] During the walkout, the impact of these events became evident as Mike Bolis told workers "You are fighting for a great cause. . . . You should learn to work together. You should learn the business because very soon you will take it over for your own, like the Russians are doing in Russia," and William Blazonis told them not to worry that the press called them Bolsheviks because "Bolsheviki is all right. Bolshevik government is all right."[151]

A number of strike observers noted that workers had their eyes on Europe (and the Middle East) as well as on Lawrence. This was a recurrent theme in interviews that Anthony Capraro conducted. A Syrian woman, Mrs. Bastyani, wished to return home partly because of her curiosity about political changes in her homeland; John Holopich wanted to go back to Russia because he thought America was only "free for capitalists"; Mary Glinka was "crying all the time to go back home" and she thought the Lithuanians were "almost of one mind to go back to Europe."[152] Jerome Davis, who was employed by the Federal Council of Churches, also found that many Russians wished to return to their native country which "they now dream of as the land of opportunity and freedom." Many were embittered by the presence of Allied troops on Russian soil and wanted to know "why do they fight our poor country of Russia?" Others expressed a new pride in being Russian and one worker noted that "if you are Russian, you must believe in a government where the workers rule." Another Russian told Davis: "I only came back from France last week. In the entire war I was not wounded but when I come back and picket I am clubbed back into unconsciousness."[153] Ruth Pickering, a writer for the radical journal *The Liberator*, found the same sentiments during her stay in Lawrence, although she thought the looking towards Europe had a damaging impact on workers' consciousness as it led workers to ask "why change America?"[154]

Pickering had a point. Capraro talked to one worker, Fred Telucik, who was "well informed about Russian events" but had "no idea of this great country beyond Lawrence." Other strikers held American workers in contempt. Annie Trina wondered why people said "America first" as she said "America last" and thought that "working people in this country have no brains."[155] Polish workers passed resolutions that mockingly asked the government "to open up the iron bars of immigration by which we are confined and we will gladly leave your boasted freedom and country."[156] A more bitter mood prevailed than in 1912 when immigrant workers applauded Big Bill Haywood's comment that the only foreigners in Lawrence were the capitalists; in 1919, many may have agreed with Richard Hansen that "even an American-born worker is not a citizen, that they were all foreigners, foreigners in their own country."[157]

Regardless of the rhetoric, most of Lawrence's left-leaning workers intended to remain in the United States. But as the ATWA was to discover many distrusted the more "practical" ACWA approach. During the strike itself, the leadership managed to fend off all challenges to its power. The most serious threat to Salerno's position came from Lena Cacici, who in defiance of the strike committee distributed her own inflammatory leaflets. At one meeting he "forced her to sit down and keep quiet" and Salerno exacted an oath from the Italians that they would remain nonviolent for the duration of the strike.[158] At another point, various nationality meetings voted to change the 48/54 demand to 44/54, a switch partly inspired by the presence of the ACWA representatives, as the Amalgamated had recently won a major forty-four-hour strike in New York City. However, the strike committee opposed changing the demand and the goal remained 48/54.[159] Other conflicts occurred behind the scenes as even Capraro, who worked closely with Muste, was

"troubled" by his "Christian rhetoric."[160] One worker responded cynically to Elizabeth Glendower Evans's financial aid by noting: " Why
shouldn't she? It is our money she was using. She got her money
through dividends in the mills and it was only right that she should give
it back to us."[161] Certainly, many Lawrence workers must have cringed
when Evans told them: "When they say Bolshevik, you say 'No American, Abraham Lincoln's country'" though strike leaders also understood
that one did not appeal for public support by advertising sympathy for
the Russian Revolution.[162]

As John Fitch commented, the Lawrence struggle was "a strike for
wages carried on in a revolutionary atmosphere."[163] But not everyone
defined revolution in the same way. The ministers favored a variant
of guild socialism and others looked toward communism or anarcho-
syndicalism. After the strike, these ideological divisions racked the Lawrence ATWA chapter until its demise in 1921. But between February and
May 1919, practically everyone managed to paper over these differences
in order to defeat a common set of enemies.

Victory

In January, the mill owners had agreed among themselves that "under
no circumstances would 54 hours' pay be given for 48 hours' work" and
they reaffirmed this stand when they met again on April 1.[164] Henry
Endicott, the Massachusetts Board of Arbitration, and the Business and
Professional Men's Committee made efforts to arrange a settlement but
they failed because the manufacturers remained confident that eventually
workers would have to return to the mills without receiving concessions.[165]

Ever since the walkout began, the leadership had been "holding out
promises to the strikers, always prophesying that something would
happen the following week," but by May 1 it had become difficult to
come up with new morale-building tactics.[166] From the first day of the
walkout, the most radical Italian workers had pressed the strike committee to invite Carlo Tresca to come to the city. No one could fire up a
crowd like Tresca, but before May, the leadership refused to invite him.
Lawrence police had vowed to arrest Tresca on sight since they had
never forgotten how he had led a parade of workers through a police
cordon during the 1912 "No God No Master" demonstration. The strike

committee feared for Tresca's personal safety and also feared that a visit by him would bolster the status of Cacici and other extreme leftists. Finally, as enthusiasm waned, the strike committee relented and agreed to invite Tresca so long as Capraro had complete control of the arrangements. Under Capraro's guidance, Rocco and Calitri smuggled Tresca into the city and he made a surprise appearance at a rally when he popped up from under a stage and delivered an electrifying address. In order to give Tresca a head start out of town, no one was allowed to leave the hall for twenty minutes after the meeting. The police had discovered that Tresca was due to arrive in the city and they were searching all cars coming into Lawrence as Tresca and his four bodyguards were departing.[167]

Tresca's appearance set off a new round of repressive activity. A few days after his speech, police mounted a machine gun in the heart of a Syrian neighborhood. Only quick action by the strike committee and by Syrian leaders prevented strikers from responding violently to this act of provocation. Soon thereafter, thugs (who were most likely city police officers) kidnapped Capraro and Kleinman from their hotel rooms. The resort to terroristic methods indicated that antistrike forces had been frustrated by their inability to keep Tresca and other outsiders from coming to the city. The vigilantes released Kleinman after placing a rope around his neck but they administered a terrible beating to Capraro who might have been killed if a passing auto had not scared off the perpetrators.[168]

Such attacks actually generated support. *The Forward* circulated a special edition on the incident entitled "The Ku Klux in Lawrence" and the publicity led to additional contributions to the strike fund. The strike committee also convinced many Lawrence retail establishments to place photos of the badly beaten Capraro in their store windows. Capraro, himself, after spending a week in a Boston hospital, staged a triumphant return to Lawrence where large crowds greeted him.[169]

For all of this help, strikers remained short of funds. By the fourteenth week of the walkout, the money shortage meant that only bread, soup, and coffee could be distributed to those receiving relief. Still, many of the leaders remained confident that the work stoppage could be won. As exactly as they had anticipated ready-to-wear manufacturers in April began to press for delivery of their goods. Even the Pacific Mill reported that it was "overwhelmed by orders" that it could not fill as the company was "not making any substantial gains in the number of their employees."[170] The American Woolen Company faced an even greater crisis because it had embarked on an aggressive foreign and domestic selling approach—yet its key mills were practically shut down.[171]

In a last-ditch effort to break the strike, the Everett Mill announced that it would reopen on May 19. Few workers returned on that date and the display of solidarity finally convinced the manufacturers that they needed a face-saving way to settle the strike. The opportunity was provided to them when the Massachusetts cotton textile manufacturers, in response to a UTW request, granted their employees a 15 percent increase effective on June 2. By granting the same pay hike, the Lawrence manufacturers could actually give their employees more than they had been asking (48/54 equalled a 12.5 percent increase) and they could appear to be doing so in response to the settlement between the cotton manufacturers and the UTW.[172]

At the precise time the leadership had decided that it could no longer ask workers to remain on strike, Walter Lamont of the American Woolen Company summoned Muste to inform him of the manufacturers' decision to grant the increase. Workers decided to accept the terms though only the American Woolen Company had promised to grant any form of recognition to shop committees. Sensing the mill owners' weakness, the strike committee did demand that all workers be taken back without discrimination. Faced with this last burst of militancy, the manufacturers met with their employees at each mill site and agreed to this final condition. Having won this point, the general strike committee called off the walkout as workers celebrated in the streets.[173]

After 107 days, Lawrence workers had done what many neutral observers had considered impossible—they had won a strike for higher wages that began at a time of high unemployment. Despite the success, the real test was still to come as the wage concessions did not affect the underlying balance of power. A formal agreement had not been signed and the promises not to use the blacklist and to recognize shop committees would depend on the ATWA's ability to enforce compliance with these conditions in the future. In 1912, the IWW won the battle but lost the war. The ATWA's hopes for avoiding the IWW's fate depended on the ACWA's success in bringing together the ministers and their allies, former WIIU members, and local labor militants in an organization strong enough and flexible enough to take on the textile giants.

Chapter Six

ESTABLISHING AN ORGANIZATION

The ACWA and The Textile Industry

During the 1919 strikes, workers in all three cities demonstrated an interest in building permanent unions as well as winning shorter hours and higher pay. By 1919, most immigrant textile workers had resided in the United States for at least five years and almost no new arrivals had come between 1914 and 1918. Consequently, the textile work force was far more settled than it had been at the time of the IWW strikes. That workers now considered themselves permanent residents of the United States helps explain why even many former Wobblies now sought out a "radical, yet practical alternative" to the IWW.

The ACWA for a number of reasons had readily responded to the textile workers' request for help. For one, the union had anticipated that employers would try to take back labor's wartime gains and the Amalgamated's leadership believed that labor needed to formulate its own offensive strategy in order to counteract the expected employer onslaught. The ACWA contrasted the AFL's failure to prepare for the postwar period with the far more advanced position of British trade unionists and the Amalgamated even printed the Labour Party's manifesto "Labour and the New Social Order" as part of its 1918 convention proceedings.[1] To the ACWA, the shorter workweek represented a "reconstruction measure" as it would reduce unemployment. Emboldened by the success of New York City clothing workers in winning the forty-four-hour week— an achievement it called "the first great victory" of American labor in the postwar period—the ACWA wanted to help other workers win similar gains.[2]

Furthermore, since its founding the Amalgamated had viewed itself as the emissary of immigrant workers. Led by recent Jewish immigrants, its membership was mainly composed of Jews, Italians, Lithuanians, Poles, and Czechs—and the ACWA's survival proved that diverse nationalities could overcome ethnic differences to build a strong union. To those in the AFL who believed that immigrants had been responsible for lowering the American standard of living, the ACWA cited its success as evidence that immigrants were actually in the forefront of the fight for improved working conditions.[3] The parallel between the hidebound UGW, which had refused to utilize the organizing abilities of former Bundists, and the UTW, which distanced itself from all who carried the taint of radicalism, appeared quite exact. As an editorial in the ACWA's organ *Advance* pointed out: "The experiences of the textile workers are the experiences of the clothing workers before they had their own union."[4]

In addition, the ACWA along with the International Ladies Garment Workers Union (ILGWU) had proven that women workers could be organized since beginning with the "Uprising of Twenty Thousand" New York City shirtwaist workers in 1909, tens of thousands of female clothing workers had joined both the ILGWU and the ACWA. Patriarchal attitudes had only been dented as men dominated leadership positions in both organizations and women had to fight to gain the appointment of female organizers, but by 1918, no one could reasonably claim that women's temporary position in the work force or responsibilities in the home meant that they were not interested in unions.[5]

Finally, the ACWA's interest in expanding beyond the clothing field resulted from its own extraordinary organizing success. Since its founding in 1914, the ACWA had enrolled over 100,000 workers, many of whom worked in large factories as well as small shops. The greatest membership gains came after the United States entered the war when the ACWA had benefited from its close working relationship with the secretary of war, Newton D. Baker, who required that the U. S. Army's uniforms be purchased from shops that maintained union conditions. Using this edict to its maximal advantage, the ACWA had launched a wartime organizing drive that brought in large numbers of new members in 1917 and 1918.[6] In return for the governmental aid, the ACWA refrained from conducting walkouts during the war and punished dissidents who disobeyed this policy. Recognizing that the union had to keep its end of the bargain, the Amalgamated's president, Sidney Hillman ordered that the *Advance* not print editorials critical of the war and insisted that the ACWA withdraw from the antiwar People's Council for Peace and Democracy. Particularly after President Wilson's Fourteen Points address, the ACWA became an enthusiastic supporter of the war and pledged to raise large sums for the third Liberty Loan drive.[7] To a certain extent, these policies derived from Hillman's belief that the Kaiser's defeat would unleash democratic forces within Germany, but they also stemmed from his preference for taking pragmatic stands that aided the union rather than principled positions that might run counter to the organization's needs.

The ACWA's success stood in marked contrast to the IWW's decline. Although both organizations advocated industrial unionism and stood outside of the AFL, the ACWA and the IWW had some sharp disagreements, such as the fact that the Amalgamated signed contracts and believed in the need for unions to cooperate with employers in establishing standards of production. In keeping with this stance, the ACWA had little sympathy for workers who engaged in slowdowns or who interfered with production as it viewed such actions as harmful to employers who signed agreements and as a hindrance to the union's long-term goal of psychologically preparing workers to run industry on their own. Also in contrast to the IWW, the ACWA employed a large staff that was well paid by the standards of many unions and praised features of American democracy that it viewed in a positive light.[8]

The IWW and the ACWA had never worked together and the Bellanca brothers had often engaged in "vitriolic attacks" on the Wobblies. But the IWW had few members in the clothing industry and the two unions had rarely engaged in open rivalry. The major exception to this had occurred in Baltimore in 1916 when the ACWA and the IWW became involved in a bitter struggle for the unionization of the men's clothing industry. After the ACWA emerged victorious in this battle, the IWW stepped up its polemical attacks and criticized the ACWA for believing merely in "a fair day's pay for a fair day's work," for taking away workers' right to strike, and for being "another boss" because the Amalgamated disciplined those who tried to limit output.[9]

By January 1919, the federal government's repression of the IWW and the ACWA's organizing success meant that the Amalgamated was now the strongest union with an explicitly socialist philosophy in the United States. As a sign of its leading role on the left, Italian activists such as Carlo Tresca, Arturo Giovannitti, and Joe Ettor—all of whom had been prominent members of the IWW—now gave their support to the ACWA. The union's reputation attracted many other activists such as Anthony Bimba, who edited the ACWA's Lithuanian organ.[10] The IWW's failure to establish a permanent foothold in the textile industry led many of these radicals to look more sympathetically upon the ACWA, and the Amalgamated's strong emphasis on workers' self-education and self-emancipation appealed to many leftists who otherwise looked askance at the union's advocacy of political action. The working relationship that had developed between Hillman and the general secretary, Joseph Schlossberg, symbolized the ACWA's own delicate balance between reformist and a more revolutionary version of unionism. While Hillman remained in firm control of the organization, the more radical and idealistic Schlossberg was given relatively free reign (except during the war) to use the pages of *Advance* to articulate the socialist future for which the ACWA strove.

As Steve Fraser has pointed out, the ACWA did not hesitate to punish its own militants. But on a wider scale, the ACWA was a strong advocate of the need for labor to practice solidarity. After its January 1919 success, the Amalgamated pledged that it would "assist other members of our class in attaining what we have already attained for ourselves," and the ACWA's contribution of $100,000 later in 1919 to the AFL-led steel workers' strike showed this was not mere talk.[11] Since the textile industry was closely connected to the clothing industry, the ACWA had a particular interest in aiding workers in Paterson, Passaic, and Lawrence since a twin alliance of clothing and textile workers held out great hopes for the unionization of every step in the production of men's clothing.

Despite these expectations, the ACWA's special committee that was convened during the Lawrence strike decided against incorporating the textile workers and this decision was reaffirmed at the union's 1920 convention. This policy was fully in keeping with the ACWA's pragmatic approach. A decision in favor of affiliation would have opened up the possibility of organizing America's one million textile workers into a single clothing and textile union. On the other hand, there were grave risks in such a strategy as it had yet to be proven that permanent industrial unions of textile workers could be built. If the textile effort failed, the ACWA's resources would have been spread so thin that the union itself would have been severely damaged. To a union as cautious as the ACWA, a half-way solution proved preferable to one that might have been appealing in theory yet posed grave dangers.[12]

For these reasons, the ACWA believed that textile workers should form a separate union modeled on the ACWA, which if successful could then merge with the clothing workers. The ACWA fully intended to guide this effort; Schlossberg and August Bellanca delivered the principal addresses at the ATWA's founding convention and the ACWA representatives directed much of the behind-the-scenes maneuvering at this gathering.[13] The ATWA chose New York City for its headquarters so its leadership could remain in close touch with the ACWA, and both unions anticipated that the ATWA would quickly demonstrate that the ACWA model was fully applicable to the textile field.

The ATWA Leadership

Founded at a time when the American left was being reshaped, the new union attracted an unusual blend of local labor radicals, former WIIU members, and intellectuals.[14] Although coming from remarkably diverse backgrounds, all of the ATWA's core supporters had come together as a result of their participation in the 1919 textile strikes and as part of their search for new organizational forms that would allow workers to challenge the power of capital.

At the ATWA convention, August and Frank Bellanca stage-managed A. J. Muste's selection as the new union's general secretary, the top leadership position in the organization. One would hardly have expected a former minister to have been elevated to this post but the Bellanca brothers had evidently been impressed by Muste's leadership abilities and these two "ethical intellectuals" shared Sidney Hillman's belief that college-educated persons had much to contribute to the union movement.

Muste's assumption of this office capped a period of extraordinarily rapid personal change. Although he had expressed interest in labor issues since 1912, as late as June 1918, Muste had criticized groups that overemphasized the "economic" side of life and had suggested that purely materialistic movements could lead to "new forms of oppression." At this point in his life, Muste still believed that "a spiritual revolution in the Christianity of Jesus" represented the "one hope of the world," and he extolled Jesus Christ because he worked for spiritual change and did "not tell" workers "to organize, strike, fight." [15] His participation in the Lawrence walkout taught Muste the potential of working-class self-organization, and he quickly shed much of his religious language and instead talked about the day when "workers will rule the world." [16] Still, he hesitated to leave the church and in the midst of the strike in response to a query about his plans, he replied that "my present problem is how best I may serve the labor movement and the revolution—in some independent religious movement or directly in the radical labor and political organizations and movement without any religious labels." [17] His selection as the ATWA's general secretary solved this personal dilemma and Muste proceeded to spend the next fifteen years as a prominent member of the American labor movement.

Cedric Long and Harold Rotzel also became converts to the cause of industrial unionism. Like the other left-leaning ministers, Long had been searching for a way to apply his social principles. After his graduation from Harvard in 1913, he had worked in a printing plant and as a day laborer for a Massachusetts construction company. According to his own account, the latter experience had given him a "most decided sympathy for the laboring classes as a whole." In 1915, he had entered Union Theological Seminary in the hope that he could apply religious teachings to industrial and social problems. Much of his time at the seminary had been spent arguing with faculty members and he had been ordained only after he promised "to work inside and not outside the church." As his forced resignation from the Epping, New Hampshire, pastorate demonstrated, this pledge had not ended Long's conflicts with those who held a more traditional notion of a minister's role. [18]

The Lawrence strike provided Long with what he came to consider his proper place in life. At the conclusion of the walkout, the ATWA appointed him manager of the Lawrence local, and in November 1919, he reported to his Harvard classmates that he considered his work to be "more fundamentally Christian" than "anything else" he had ever done and this "conviction" was stronger "than at any time" since he had come to Lawrence. He expressed little hope for the church or for the more "educated" classes: "I see them drawing more and more to the side of capitalism in preparation for the social conflict which is soon to descend upon us. . . . I have given up all hope of seeing culture and higher education on the side of the struggling masses of labor in such a crisis as this. My own future is to be given to work for the laboring classes in society."[19]

Harold Rotzel underwent a similar transformation. A 1910 graduate of the University of Michigan, he had later been ordained as a Methodist minister. In 1918, he had joined the staff of the League of Democratic Control and had spent much of his time aiding conscientious objectors who faced harassment in military prisons. Like Muste and Long, he had precious little experience with labor, but the 48/54 fight also inspired him to cast his lot with the working class and the ATWA appointed him an organizer with special responsibilities for Lawrence. Rotzel based his change of course upon a belief that "middle class agitation" had failed to accomplish much and upon a desire to quit talking and jump in where new forces were actually at work as he considered that the "new world" belonged to and would be made by workers and that college-educated persons should be a part of this movement.[20]

The three ministers used their associational networks to attract other persons with similar interests to the labor movement. One such individual was Evan Thomas, the brother of Norman Thomas. A graduate of Princeton University, Thomas had been in Edinburgh, Scotland, doing postgraduate work when the war broke out. As was true of the other intellectuals, the European conflict had led Thomas to reexamine his beliefs and he was uncertain what direction his life should take. At one point, he even considered enlisting to have his "fling at the Germans" but his work with wounded German prisoners convinced him of the senselessness of the war. Thomas finally resolved his own personal conflicts by returning home, declaring himself a conscientious objector, and refusing induction—a stand that led to his incarceration.[21]

Upon his imprisonment, Thomas continued to apply his nonresistance principles. Along with other conscientious objectors, he argued that he should either be freed or sent to a civilian prison and opposed all efforts to treat him as if he were a soldier. While held at the U. S. Disciplinary Barracks at Fort Leavenworth, Kansas, he participated in a number of hunger strikes, and at times, he had to be force-fed and placed in solitary confinement, where he was manacled to bars in his cell.[22] For his refusal to cooperate with authorities, he had been court-martialed and sentenced to a twenty-five-year term but the army "suddenly and unexpectedly" discharged him in January 1919. Upon his release, Thomas devoted most of his time to speaking out about the plight of conscientious objectors and he did not participate in the textile strikes.[23] Despite this lack of experience, the ATWA chose Thomas to head the Paterson local. A neophyte could not have been assigned to a more difficult place as the city's ideological disputes and the silk industry's complexity posed a difficult challenge to even experienced labor organizers.

Two other young intellectuals, Robert W. Dunn and Paul Blanshard, followed somewhat different paths before being appointed ATWA organizers. Dunn, who came from a small town in Pennsylvania, had been a student at Yale University when the United States entered the war. A brilliant scholar, he had held office in both the Inter-Collegiate Socialist Society and the Collegiate Anti-Militarist League. Compared to the other intellectuals, Dunn had spent considerable time thinking and writing about labor problems. An advocate of class-conscious, industrial unionism, his thinking in 1918–1919 merged radical Christian and socialist values.[24] He had been in Lawrence during the 48/54 strike and in an article that he wrote about the walkout called "At Lawrence—Preparing the Workers for a New World," he expressed the hope that its success would make possible "a virile, victorious Christianity."[25] Given this perspective, it comes as no surprise that the ATWA appointed Dunn as a general organizer.

Blanshard had been employed at a variety of tasks before joining the ATWA. After graduating from the University of Michigan in 1914, he attended Harvard Divinity School and following the footsteps of his father became a Congregational minister. While at Harvard, he joined the Socialist party, assisted the minister of a labor-oriented church and aided striking cordage workers in Plymouth, Massachusetts. In 1916 and 1917, Blanshard served as a minister for a Tampa, Florida, church until he resigned, in part, because parishioners objected to his antiwar views. Blanshard then settled in Philadelphia, where he worked in a settlement house and as a machinist's helper. He was uncertain about what to do next at the time Muste "providentially" called and invited him to become an ATWA staff member.[26]

No American labor union had ever employed so many intellectuals in key positions as did the ATWA. In March 1920, Muste remained in charge of the central office, Rotzel had been chosen as head of the Lawrence local, Long had been assigned to Passaic, Thomas still headed the Paterson branch, and Blanshard had been asked to organize Utica, New York, textile workers. Only Dunn was no longer on the ATWA payroll since he was working for the American Civil Liberities Union (ACLU), but he remained in close touch with the ATWA leadership.[27]

These six activists shared much in common. All had been influenced by the social gospel and based their thinking on a radical interpretation of Christianity; all had been shocked by the harsh punishment meted out to conscientious objectors and to other opponents of the war; all had come to believe that the labor movement would be in the forefront of social change in postwar America; all still considered themselves Christians but had come to question whether there was any point to remaining within the institutional church. Most of the intellectuals belonged to the Fellowship of Reconciliation, which had been founded by British pacifists in 1914 and which established its first American chapters in 1916. Along with many other members of the fellowship, they had paid a price for their beliefs. Thomas had been placed in prison, all four of the ministers had lost their pulpits, and Dunn had been hounded because of his refusal to serve in the Reserve Officer Training Corps.[28] If they had come of age ten years earlier, they most likely would have found an outlet for their social concerns in the settlement house movement. But in 1919, the "industrial field" appeared to provide the best opportunity to apply "the teachings of Jesus"—an opportunity that had been "denied them within the church."[29]

The intellectuals had much to overcome. As products of the social gospel, they shared Walter Rauscenbusch's naive belief that ministers could "soften the increasing class hatred of the working class."[30] Well educated, they at times considered themselves superior to workers who had "never had time to get education nor inclination to attend schools for the training up of moral integrity."[31] As ascetics devoted to the spartan life, they could have trouble understanding workers' materialistic concerns.[32] Prone to introspection and lacking industrial experience, they could be paralyzed by doubts about the correctness of their own decisions. Above all, as Protestant, native-born, college-educated, middle-class Americans, they had backgrounds that differed sharply from those of textile workers. In embracing industrial unionism, they had exchanged the world of peaceful reform for the world of class conflict. Their task was even more difficult than it might have been since the intellectuals had made no effort to disguise their class backgrounds or to obtain mill jobs. Workers knew that if the ATWA failed, the educated cadre had an escape mechanism that was not available to mill hands.

Fortunately for these religiously inspired radicals, they could count on the support of their mentors. Although the ministers derived their inspiration from the Sermon on the Mount and the ACWA leadership derived theirs from Marxism, both groups viewed trade unionism as an "educative enterprise" and both groups admired the British labor movement,

131

whose emphasis on shop control and "common ownership of the means of production" offered an alternative to Wilsonian liberalism and revolutionary socialism.[33] Largely because they shared these points in common, the ACWA viewed the intellectuals—for all of their inexperience and for all of their self-consciousness—as the logical group to place in charge of the new union.

The ATWA also recruited its leadership from persons who had been associated with the WIIU and the SLP in Paterson. Many of these activists had begun to reconsider their membership in both organizations after the SLP expelled Joseph Schlossberg in 1917. Schlossberg, a member of the SLP from 1900, had edited its Jewish organ *Der Arbeiter* and had belonged to the Brooklyn branch of the Jewish Socialist Labor Federation. He had kept up his membership in the SLP even though practically the entire ACWA leadership belonged to the rival Socialist party. Schlossberg's conflict with the SLP began when the party leadership scolded him for endorsing the SP candidate in a 1916 New York City congressional election. Shortly thereafter, Schlossberg incurred the wrath of the SLP again—this time for writing an article in the *New York Call* congratulating the Socialist party for its showing in the November 1917 New York City mayoralty election. For this transgression, the SLP demanded that the Jewish Socialist Labor Federation reprimand Schlossberg. When the federation refused to carry out the instructions, the SLP's national executive committee suspended all five of its branches (including the one in Paterson) and reorganized the entire body. All those who joined the new federation had to sign a "loyalty pledge" in which they promised "to counter-act the pernicious influence of the disrupters." These actions effectively expelled Schlossberg from the SLP. But as was often the case, the dogmatic stand alienated the ever-dwindling ranks of SLP supporters and only a handful of Jewish members in Paterson signed the loyalty pledge.[34]

Jewish and non-Jewish members of the SLP had also been upset ever since they had been ordered to withdraw from the Paterson chapter of the Peoples Council for Peace and Democracy on the grounds that the council was a "mere adjunct" to the Socialist party. To many SLP members, this edict typified the party's habit of making decisions without consulting the membership and of forcing the SLP from important "field[s] of agitation" for purely sectarian reasons.[35] Irritated by these continual "insults" to their "intelligence" and alienated by the SLP's lack of "decent and democratic treatment of one another," some WIIU members in January 1919 had unsuccessfully sought to form "an independent textile workers' union" and in February, Rubenstein had proclaimed that the time had arrived for Paterson to have "one and only one union."[36] The last straw for many long-time supporters came when the WIIU failed to mount an effective opposition to the NWLB intervention. At this point, large numbers of WIIU militants sought out the ACWA's aid, and at the ATWA founding convention at least seven of the sixteen Paterson delegates had been in the WIIU.[37]

A union sponsored by the ACWA had considerable appeal to the former WIIU members. Along with the intellectuals, they too believed unions should expand workers' horizons and develop their minds. The ACWA's emphasis on centralized control and direction also attracted them because they had long opposed what they viewed as undisciplined or anarchic forms of direct action. They hoped that the ATWA could be a WIIU that "worked" since they knew that regardless of the soundness of its principles the WIIU could never move beyond its narrow base.[38]

Two former WIIU members, Russell Palmer and H. J. Rubenstein, joined the ATWA's national staff. A veteran silk weaver, Palmer became associate editor and later editor of the union's organ *The New Textile Worker*. He brought the WIIU perspective to this position and in the early 1920s wrote a number of thoughtful columns on the need for labor to develop a political as well as a workplace strategy to counteract the employers' antiunion offensive.[39] Rubenstein had joined the WIIU in 1912 and federal agents considered him "indefatigable" in his efforts to bring the unionist message to workers. An antiwar militant, he had been indicted (and subsequently found not guilty) for violating the Espionage Act. He had also served as secretary of Local 25, edited the WIIU newspaper *The Silkworker*, and had played a leading role in the coalition of radical, labor, and ethnic groups that led the eight-hour fight in Paterson. Upon his abandonment of the WIIU, the ACWA had assigned Rubenstein to Lawrence for the duration of the 48/54 fight and soon thereafter the ATWA appointed him to its staff. In this capacity, he directed a long Allentown, Pennsylvania, silk workers strike in 1920 and participated in a number of other organizing drivers.[40]

In the long run, the ATWA's success in the three communities depended on its ability to develop effective local cadre. In Passaic and Lawrence, all of the ATWA's leaders had played important roles in the 1919 strikes. Besides Pluhar, the Passaic group included George Protze, Joseph Gianconia, Walter Fischer, and Fred Frankle.[41] In Lawrence, staff members included Joseph Salerno, Frank Coco, Frank Szajna (a Polish leader), Vincent Blazonis, and Mike Bolis, and the Paterson local could count on the support of those who had left the WIIU as well as other workers who deserted either the UTW or IWW.

These leaders constituted the "militant minority" who were in the forefront of all efforts to build industrial unions in the early twentieth century.[42] For the most part, they were socialists as industrial unionism was a socialist cause in this time period. Most of them had to confront the central paradox of this era since their radicalism was rooted in the subcultures of particular immigrant groups and yet they sought to build a multiethnic working-class organization. To do this, they had to battle particularistic elements in their own communities that often used the church, the mutual aid societies, and their business enterprises to encourage ethnic rather than class loyalties. These ethnic socialists walked a tightrope as they wished to combat those they viewed as chauvinists and yet they could not appear to be unsympathetic to their own national causes. Ironically, members of other nationality groups often viewed these immigrant labor activists as representatives of only their own ethnic groups and this along with language barriers limited their influence.[43] To compound matters, nationality tensions often surfaced in the aftermath of a strike when much of the multiethnic solidarity that had been developed in the course of a walkout dissipated.

Rubenstein, Pluhar, and Salerno typified the type of local leaders most attracted to the ACWA. Others who had once belonged to the Wobblies now looked to a union that had more "business sense and stability" than the IWW and yet was "more than a business union." The relative ease with which employers had defeated the IWW also convinced many immigrant radicals that they needed a union that represented a "happy medium" between anarcho-syndicalism and business unionism.[44]

There was no room in the ATWA for those who did not wish to build a union based on the ACWA model. This meant that the *Revolutionary Age* group quickly departed from the union. Cosgrove, Hansen, and John Galley (another left-wing socialist who had been active in the Lawrence strike) had attended the founding convention as Lawrence delegates and Hansen had been made an associate editor of *The New Textile Worker*. But Hansen, who believed that the "present situation" in America was "as revolutionary as in Europe," used this position to attack many of the convention's actions and questioned the need for a paid staff and strong central office.[45] Shortly thereafter, Hansen, Cosgrove, and Galley removed themselves (or were removed) from the union.

Most noticeably, women were totally absent from the union's leadership. At the ATWA's founding convention, there were only two women among the thirty-six Passaic, Paterson, and Lawrence delegates and the union's nine-member executive board was entirely male.[46] The lack of female representation is not too surprising given that only a small number of women had assumed public-leadership roles during the 1919 strikes and that two of these women, Margaret Haray and Lena Cacici, had met opposition that appeared to be based in part on their sex.[47] Even during the strike of Passaic's handkerchief work force, which was 90 percent female, men had assumed the key leadership positions.[48]

The union also failed to appoint any women to its national staff or as organizers. In this respect, the UTW was far ahead of the ATWA as the older union normally appointed one female for every three male organizers.[49] What explains the ATWA's backwardness in this area? To a certain extent, it can be attributed to the intellectuals' inexperience as they were seemingly unaware that potential female members might be more receptive to a female than to a male organizer. Local labor militants also do not appear to have viewed the assignment of women to its staff as a priority. Finally, the ACWA, despite having a female representative on its general executive board and having hired a number of women staff members, evidently did not press the ATWA on this issue. In its negligence, the ATWA was little different from the Wobblies as the IWW in Lawrence had not made any special efforts to guarantee that women would have a place in the union's administration.[50] As we will see, some union social activities in Paterson, Passaic, and Lawrence were designed to make women feel comfortable in the union, but the failure to make special efforts to reach the 50 percent of textile workers who were women greatly diminished the ATWA's chances for success.[51]

Formulating a Program

Meeting at a time of worldwide revolutionary upsurge, the delegates at the ATWA's founding convention sent their greetings to "Soviet Russia, Hungary, Bavaria" and passed a resolution that described "the Soviet form of government" as "the only existing form of government that guarantees and gives to the working class its full rights of representation, control and ownership of the means of production." Caught up in the excitement of the occasion even August Bellanca in his opening remarks hailed Russia as "the symbol of the new civilization and the source of inspiration and guidance to all oppressed peoples." But the next day, Bellanca in criticizing the pro-Soviet resolutions told the delegates: "We

135

don't care what is going on in Russia. We are in the United States and we should organize ourselves and bring about better working conditions and not talk about Bolshevism"—a comment that reflected his own uneasiness with those who were overly enthusiastic about the Russian Revolution.[52]

The convention actually spent little time debating basic principles, as the delegates were content to rely on the ACWA model. With only minor changes, the convention adopted the ACWA's preamble as its own and soon thereafter, the ATWA adopted a constitution that closely resembled the ACWA's. The *New Textile Worker* copied *Advance* in style and content. So imitative was the new union that Muste appeared proud to tell the 1920 ACWA convention that "we make no claim to originality."[53]

As was true of the ACWA, the ATWA's basic outlook portended that of the CIO, and the pro-Soviet resolutions did not reflect the true ideological orientation of the union though local authorities always cited them when attacking the ATWA locals. Once it began organizing in earnest, the ATWA tried to develop its own progressive interpretation of Americanism and talked about bringing "the American principle of democracy into the textile mills." It described itself as "class conscious" and in favor of "social reconstruction" but the ATWA avoided calling itself socialist. Instead, it preferred to talk of the need for workers to organize for "freedom, independence, self-respect, a new status, industrial democracy." Always denying that it sought to make workers "better paid wage slaves," in actuality it based much of its appeal on the promise of winning shorter hours, higher wages, and improved working conditions.[54]

The ATWA criticized the UTW's national office for exercising excessive control over the locals, but the new union also faced these same accusations. Complaints emanated from locals that, out of opposition to Golden's arbitrary exercise of power, had switched their affiliation from the UTW to the ATWA, and from Passaic, Paterson, and Lawrence where mill hands had become used to taking action without consulting a national office.[55] When the ATWA held its first formal convention in October 1919, the question of centralization versus decentralization became a topic of hot debate. At this time, delegates revised the union's constitution so that from then on locals merely had to consult with the national office before going out on strike as the "final decision" rested with "the locals and the locals alone." An editorial in the *New Textile Worker* praised the convention's "determination . . . to keep the organization democratic, to have the seat of government in the rank and file and not in any 'leaders,' any officialdom," but one suspects that the diminishment of the central office's power made Muste extremely uneasy.[56] But at this time, the union's leadership held back from an all-out fight on this issue as it recognized the powerful appeal that local control had for the ATWA members.[57]

Rank and filers raised other nettlesome issues. At its founding convention, the ATWA had voted "that the fact that an organizer is not a textile worker should not bar him from such employment." But at the October 1919 gathering, Lawrence delegates convinced those present to change the constitution so that only actual textile workers could serve on the general executive board. Convention delegates even rejected a proposal to make non-textile workers eligible if they received three-fourths of the votes though Muste did manage to avoid a cut in organizers' salaries (another controversial issue) by persuading those present that a union that sought to end the exploitation of textile workers should not exploit its own members.[58]

Founded at a time when many workers did not accept what became the norm for industrial unions after World War II—a regular dues-payment schedule, a well-paid staff, and central administration—the ATWA was never free of these conflicts. Appeals to localism would be made by direct actionists, by Pluhar's opponents, and by shop-centered ribbon weavers and in each case, many workers would respond positively to the call for rank-and-file control. Lacking a self-confident leadership and a string of victories, the ATWA could never quiet its own dissidents despite Hillman's plea that the union spend less time on "program and resolution" and more on "building power."[59]

The Local Context—Passaic and Lawrence

Ultimately, the ATWA's strategy had to be worked out on the local level. Although the ATWA announced its intention to organize all branches of the textile industry, the union's greatest opportunity appeared to lie in the woolen and worsted sector because the surge of mill building and of profits between 1890 and 1918 had made workers in Passaic and Lawrence confident that employers could easily afford to make concessions. By contrast, cotton-textile workers had not benefited as much from the war and had to take into account the threat posed by southern competition when making demands.[60]

Passaic and Lawrence had many points in common. Large mills employing thousands dominated both cities. Both communities had received a large influx of immigrants from the periphery of capitalist development. Workers in both cities responded to the same market and political forces as they had struck in 1912, 1916, and 1919. In neither city did mill workers have much expectation that participation in electoral politics would bring about significant change. Finally, the UTW had almost no members in either city and thus industrial unions had an opportunity to gain the support of the majority of workers.

For all of these similarities, Lawrence and Passaic differed greatly and the differences highlight how much the local context could vary from city to city and mill town to mill town. In Lawrence, a cultural division of labor prevailed since older residents had the more desirable jobs. In Passaic, Germans dominated the supervisory positions but no ethnic group was excluded from the nonmachine-tending processes. As a result, Passaic lacked Lawrence's bitter ethnic rivalries—a difference that proved crucial in February 1919 when only 60 percent of Lawrence's textile workers joined the strike while the shutdown of Passaic's mills had been complete.

On the other hand, those workers who did strike in Lawrence had been far more influenced by left-wing ideologies than those in Passaic. This difference is largely attributable to the contrasting ethnic composition of the two cities' working classes since Lawrence's Franco-Belgians, Lithuanians, and Italians had all given support to anarcho-syndicalist or socialist movements and been influenced by anticlericalism while Passaic's Polish and Slovak workers gave little backing to radical movements and remained loyal to the church. This difference in ideological orientation explains why Passaic workers in 1919 spoke the language of self-determination and legitimatized their cause by invoking President Wilson and those in Lawrence spoke the language of worker control and often of Bolshevism.[61]

The IWW's contrasting legacy also highlights the difference between Passaic and Lawrence workers. The Wobblies may have been defeated in Lawrence but many workers there still respected them. Passaic workers blamed the feuding between the two IWW's for the 1912 defeat and exhibited little regret over the IWW's disappearance from the city. Partly as a result of the 1912 sectarian battles and partly as a result of the inward-looking perspective of Slavic workers, when Passaic employees began their walkout they looked to the church and to city authorities for support. By way of comparison, Lawrence workers looked instantly beyond the city's borders for the help that would carry them to victory.

A dispute that erupted at the ATWA's founding convention illustrated how much bolder Lawrence workers were than those in Passaic. At this gathering, Lawrence representatives who were still out on strike sponsored a resolution that called on all textile workers to stage a walkout on May 1. Passaic delegates led the opposition to this proposal arguing that it would be "impossible" to get Passaic workers to go out again since they had just returned to work. In reply, one Lawrence delegate called the Passaic representatives "cowards" for refusing to endorse the general-strike call and claimed that a walkout might "start a revolution" which was "just what they want."[62]

The contrast in orientation explains the different patterns of organization in the two centers. Passaic workers placed much greater emphasis on building shop ties and winning union recognition than employees in Lawrence. Lacking ethnic divisions, whenever Passaic's workers had confronted the manufacturers they had organized by mill. In Lawrence, ethnic diversity had led to a nationality form of organization and the ideological concerns of Lawrence workers had often led them to raise issues that went beyond shop-level concerns. Consequently, Lawrence workers openly welcomed the leadership of non-mill hands such as Bramhall, Bolis, and Coco whereas all leadership positions were filled by mill workers in Passaic.

In both cities, the union faced the same dilemma because the ATWA had been founded in the backwash of long strikes. Given the nature of strike cycles, it was not likely that workers in either city would conduct another work stoppage for a while, and yet strikes remained by far the most effective recruiting mechanisms for unions. The union had a better opportunity in Paterson as workers there were seething over the NWLB's sleight of hand and silk workers struck constantly. In all three cities, the ATWA had to develop a program that could hold its own supporters and attract additional members. Given the need to collect monthly dues without some evidence that it provided concrete benefits to workers, the ATWA faced the prospect that only its most committed members would continue to support the union. Conscious of the IWW's fate and anxious to demonstrate that the ACWA model could be applied to the textile industry, the ATWA knew that its ability to win the support of the rank and file would ultimately determine its fate.

Chapter Seven

THE ATWA IN LAWRENCE

Shop Level and Community Organization

As soon as the 48/54 walkout ended, the ATWA set out to do "the sober, constructive work" that it hoped would allow the union to establish a permanent presence in Lawrence. Cedric Long served as head of the local and a paid staff composed of six of the most active representatives of the various nationality groups assisted him. Since the ATWA allowed its locals to determine their own structure, the Lawrence branch was free to choose the organizational form that best met its needs and, following the example set by the Wobblies, the ATWA decided to retain the nationality format. Like the IWW, the ATWA leadership did not wish to tamper with a winning formula, but the decision to stick with the nationality structure contravened the opinion of most trade union officials who by 1919 had come to believe that ethnic locals led to "friction, jealousy, misunderstanding and a tendency to work at cross purposes."[1] On more than one occasion, the Lawrence leaders acknowledged their own dissatisfaction with the format and by January 1920, the ATWA, borrowing from the UTW, had established separate chapters of spinners, weavers, and dyers to complement the ethnic units.[2]

Regardless of its structure, the ATWA had little hope of establishing a shop-floor presence. None of the mills had granted the union any form of recognition and only the most naive of the intellectuals could have taken Walter Lamont's promise to deal with shop committees seriously. Only in the Everett mill did the ATWA exercise enough muscle to call shop meetings, collect dues, and limit the power of foremen.[3] Everett presented exactly the right circumstances for the winning of concessions as it was a relatively small plant that employed a large number of Polish and Lithuanian workers who had a history of labor militancy. In October 1919, the ATWA even forced the mill to grant a 15 percent increase to all of its employees but Everett stood in sharp contrast to the Arlington and Pacific mills and the American Woolen Company, where shop committees had "gone to pieces" a mere six months after the conclusion of the walkout.[4]

Widespread blacklisting of activists served as the clearest signal that power relations in the Lawrence mills remained unchanged. In some cases, superintendents told former employees there was no work available and then turned around and hired new arrivals in the city. Employers could easily pinpoint militants since the financial secretary of the general strike committee, John Mach, had been an employee of the Sherman Detective Agency and had worked closely with Bureau of Investigation agents and other corporate detectives in monitoring strike activity.[5]

To do nothing about discrimination against its members exposed the union's weakness but the ATWA failed to develop a plan to challenge the blacklisting. At one point, the union voted to conduct a one-day work stoppage to protest the refusal of the mills to rehire some strike participants but it never carried out this threat. Thomas Holliday suggested that ATWA members in other cities should come to Lawrence to fill the vacant positions, but the union rejected this innovative though somewhat impractical idea. A union delegation tried to see Lamont in order to protest the American Woolen Company's failure to live up to the agreement but they were turned away from his office. Female employees of the American Woolen Company took the most effective action when they stopped the firing of shop committee members by threatening a walkout.[6] Other incidents of this sort may have taken place but the union for the most part proved powerless to stop this process.

Although the ATWA proved no more successful than the IWW in

establishing a presence on the shop floor, it did establish a presence in the city. It accomplished this by involving itself with a range of educational, social, and cultural institutions that aimed at creating—to apply a phrase from the 1960s—a counterculture. This effort originated from three divergent sources; that of the subcultures of Lawrence's ethnic groups, especially Italians, Lithuanians, and Franco-Belgians; that of the strike itself, which opened new vistas to many workers; and that of the ACWA leadership, especially Anthony Capraro, who acted as an advisor for the ATWA local.

The Workers Cooperative Union (WCU) and Young Peoples International League (YPIL) were the cornerstones of the program. The WCU's founding resulted directly from the 48/54 walkout as Taddeo Cuomo, who had coordinated the strikers' soup kitchens, was the person most responsible for getting it off the ground. A member of the Workingmen's Cooperative Federation of Boston, Cuomo believed that work stoppages because they encouraged self-help activity could serve as incubators for the cooperative concept. To further stimulate enthusiasm for this idea, in the months following the strike the ATWA sponsored addresses by J. P. Warbasse, president of the Cooperative League of America, and by Margaret Bondfield, a prominent English trade unionist and cooperationist.[7] Capraro and the other ACWA leaders gave their wholehearted support as the Amalgamated, along with many other unions, showed great interest in cooperatives at this time period.[8]

Conceived as a "practical school of emancipation from bourgeois psychology," the WCU was based on the syndicalist notion that workers needed to prepare themselves in the present for the running of the future society. Its preamble stated:

The day is at hand when the working class is accomplishing its historical mission of doing away with capitalism. The army of production must start the advance by taking possession of its economic life as the first step toward capturing production while capitalism is being overthrown. The cooperative organization as complementary to the industrial organization is a new civilization within the shell of the old.[9]

The WCU's immediate purpose was to provide low-cost food and other provisions to workers and thereby lessen their dependence on the ethnic bourgeoisie. Rather than begin from scratch, the WCU absorbed an Italian bakery and grocery store and Lithuanian grocery and meat shop. In one three-month period, these four stores did $40,000 worth of business and, in keeping with the WCU's philosophy, the 1,000 members voted to allocate the "profits" for "community benefits." As a portent of future disagreements, the Franco-Belgians refused to give up control of their own cooperatives. Nevertheless, the ATWA talked of building "One Big Cooperative Union" and though the union did not directly control the WCU, Salerno served as the WCU's treasurer and the ATWA's own committee on cooperation worked closely with it.[10]

The YPIL's goal was to demonstrate that a "true union organization" could be "concerned with the social, intellectual and economic welfare of the workers as well as their industrial life within the mills."[11] Capraro was primarily responsible for its establishment as he fervently believed in the importance of education and culture as a mechanism for liberation. To be a member of the YPIL, one had to be under thirty years of age since Capraro, along with the intellectual cadre, believed that youth had a special responsibility to reshape the world. To aid him in this effort, Capraro enlisted the services of Bert Emsley, a recent Brown University graduate who had come to Lawrence to conduct English classes for the ATWA. Emsley assumed most of the day-to-day responsibility for recruiting members and for establishing YPIL programs, which included a workers' forum, a chorus, dances, sporting events, and singing classes. Most of these activities took place at the ATWA's headquarters though the YPIL hoped eventually to build a "Peoples House"—an idea that stemmed from the humiliation of having to meet on dumps and vacant lots when police denied strikers the use of various halls.[12]

In a manner similar to the WCU, the YPIL worked closely with the ATWA while remaining organizationally distinct from it. The union itself sponsored other cultural and educational activities. These included a Sunday School for Workers' Children, which intended to teach topics, such as economics, not covered in the public schools and to give children "every opportunity" to learn about "nature, music, art and the brotherhood of man"; English classes that aimed at teaching workers "Union, Workingman's English" and at enabling different nationalities to become "more efficient units in the American labor struggle"; and a series of skits and plays the union often cohosted with the YPIL.[13] To further stimulate interest in the union, the ATWA held outings at the Lithuanian Social Camp Association and sponsored speaking appearances by nationally prominent leftists such as Arturo Giovannitti, Scott Nearing, and Anna Louise Strong.[14]

The ATWA hoped that its endeavors would counteract the Americanization efforts of the schools, the North American Civic League, and the

YMCA and YWCA since the union recognized that it did little good to criticize these institutions unless workers had a substitute available. These activities also offered women an opportunity to participate in the union since both men and women performed in the choruses and theatricals and attended the educationals.[15] Of course, even the most successful programs could not make up for the union's weakness on the shop floor, but the ATWA hoped that by meeting workers' cultural, educational, and recreational needs the union could sustain strike-inspired enthusiasm and demonstrate that it could contribute to workers' betterment even if it had not won recognition.

Declining Membership

The ATWA encountered a twofold problem in attempting to sustain its Lawrence local; it proved unable to win the support of those mill hands who had not joined the 48/54 walkout, and even many workers who had participated in the strike discontinued their membership in the union.

For the most part, the ATWA proved unable to crack the barrier that separated Lawrence's radical workers from the city's Irish and French-Canadian workers. By the union's own admission, only a "handful" of "English, Irish" workers had joined the Lawrence local and, remarkably, the ATWA reported it had no French-Canadian members.[16] The failure to gain recruits from these nationality groups did not result from a lack of effort because immediately upon the conclusion of the strike, the ATWA held special meetings to try to interest English-speaking workers in the union.[17] In July 1919, when skilled slasher tenders, dressers, and perchers struck, the ATWA supported their efforts and tried to enlist them in the local. The union followed the same strategy when the stationary engineers walked out the following year. At the time of the Boston police strike, the ATWA held rallies to demonstrate their support for the largely Irish police force and in the spring of 1920, the ATWA hired a French-Canadian organizer to reach workers who lived in the Arlington District.[18]

These efforts proved unproductive for a number of reasons. For one, it was difficult to overcome bitterness engendered by the strike and even when the ATWA sought to win the support of the Irish and French Canadians, the union referred to them as the "least enlightened" or "the scabs of strike time"—phraseology that was hardly likely to generate a sympathetic response.[19] As another sign of lingering resentments, the

Lawrence CLU, still smarting from being undercut in February 1919, intervened to prevent the head of the Boston Police Union from addressing the ATWA on the grounds "that it would be an IWW meeting."[20] Second, the ATWA's sponsorship of radical cultural programs did not appeal to the highly churched French-Canadian and Irish population, and the Sunday School for the Workers' Children carried sacrilegious overtones. Last, the UTW in the summer of 1919 began actively to contest the ATWA in Lawrence. The organizing campaign that eventually allowed the union to play an important role in the 1922 strike gained recruits especially since many skilled workers proved responsive; this was best demonstrated in January 1921 when 500 members of an independent woolsorters union voted to join the UTW rather than the ATWA.[21]

The inability to hold its own membership was far more damaging to the union's cause. Just a few weeks after the end of the strike, the American Woolen Company's corporate detective reported there had been a "noticeable decrease" in the union's membership and this slide continued through the summer. In October 1919, the Lawrence local claimed to have 10,000 members but its own roll books showed the actual figure to be 5,200 and the union's staff had been forced to take on the time-consuming task of going door to door to collect dues.[22] Some contemporary observers believed that recent immigrants refused to make these payments because they lacked trade union principles and this may help account why, for example, Syrian workers did not appear to have been involved in the union at all.[23] Other factors need to be considered. According to Father Milanese, many "foreigners" still intended to return to their homelands and, according to Capraro, many workers resented those who held paid staff positions.[24] Other mill hands, having witnessed the ATWA's inability to stop the blacklisting, may have decided the union could never challenge the power of the manufacturers. One point can be discounted—failure to pay dues did not stem from an inability to take the fifty cents per month from family budgets since the swindler Charles Ponzi managed to convince large numbers of Lawrence workers to invest thousands of dollars in his get-rich scheme before his "empire" collapsed in the summer of 1920.[25]

Italian workers proved to be the union's strongest supporters and in September 1919, they composed one-half of the membership of the Lawrence local.[26] But large numbers of Italians who had supported the walkout stopped paying dues to the ATWA as they continued to give their primary loyalties to village-based mutual aid societies.[27] The ATWA also faced competition from the *prominenti* who once the strike was over shed their cautious neutrality and launched an all-out attack on the union. The community's doctors, lawyers, and businessmen had followed a similar strategy after the 1912 strike, but by 1919–1920 Lawrence had a more prosperous and self-confident Italian middle class than before the war, a middle class that had learned how to use both Italian nationalism *and* Americanism against the left.

Dr. Constant Calitri, Angelo Rocco's close associate, led the assault as Calitri began a weekly newspaper, *La Difesa*, which directed much of its fire at the pro-ATWA sheet *La Luce*, edited by Joseph Salerno's brother. Calitri also served as president of the Society of Victor Emanuel Third, which raised money to send to the Italian poet Gabrielle d'Annunzio, whose private army in the fall of 1919 seized the Adriatic port city of Fiume. As a sign of their continuing desire to tap patriotic sentiments, be it American or Italian, the sponsors of the big Fiume Day celebration in September 1920 were precisely the same persons who had led the wartime Liberty Loan drives.[28] Rightists also made efforts to reduce leftist participation in the Sons of Italy and by September 1920, they had gained enough influence in the Lawrence lodge that it now declared its intention to "destroy un-American or unpatriotic tendencies introduced among Italians," and at one meeting when radicals tried to gain the floor, conservatives drowned them out by playing the "Star Spangled Banner."[29]

The campaign against the left really intensified in the Italian community when the ATWA led protests against a severe American Woolen Company pay cut that came in the midst of the 1920–1921 depression. On the inside, "loyal workers" led by Charles Pitochelli defended the need for the cutback and thanked William Wood for all he had done for the "Italian people." On the outside, conservatives sponsored meetings that criticized labor organizers who "do not belong to our people" and who ask us to "de-Americanize ourselves."[30] The ATWA's members succeeded in physically disrupting some of these gatherings but, as was to be true in Passaic, the union was not always able to defend itself against the seemingly contradictory charge that it sought to undermine workers' loyalties to both their new country and to their country of origin.

To halt its decline, the Lawrence branch needed some tangible demonstration of its ability to improve workers' lives. Since it was powerless to stop retaliatory firings, arbitrary foremen, or speedups, the union's best hope appeared to be to gain a further cut in hours and a hike in pay. At the union's founding convention, the ATWA established the forty-four-hour week as its first goal and shortly afterwards, the Lawrence local decided to also seek a 25 percent increase in pay.[31] These demands had great appeal for textile workers as the cost of living continued to sky-rocket throughout 1919. The ATWA though faced a dilemma. The only way to win shorter hours or more pay would be by conducting another long strike and yet it was highly unlikely that Lawrence workers would walk out so soon after the conclusion of the exhausting 48/54 battle. The ACWA organizer Leo Robbins noted this contradictory state of affairs when he went to Lawrence to build forty-four-hour sentiment and yet commented that "talk of another strike was foolish."[32]

Nevertheless, the ATWA set February 1920 as its strike date. But the manufacturers preempted the union when in December 1919 they granted a 12.5 percent increase—a hike that William Wood favored in order "to avoid the danger of having an agitation in favor of a 25 percent increase and 44-hour week."[33] The ATWA then resumed this campaign in spring 1920 when along with locals in other cities, it demanded a forty-four-hour week, 50 percent wage increase, and union recognition. But as was to be true in Paterson and Passaic as well, the intellectual leadership grew skittish when the time to take action approached. When the UTW-affiliated stationary engineers struck in early May, the ATWA called for a general strike but hesitated to initiate it. Instead the ATWA asked each of the city's small craft unions to choose delegates to a conference to consider action. Naturally, the UTW, AFTO, and other independent unions had no interest in cooperating with their rival and once the 1920–1921 depression began, the ATWA abandoned all talk of a strike.[34]

The cessation of the forty-four-hour agitation marked the end of an era in Lawrence since the 1920–1921 depression put a halt to all offensive struggles. After the summer of 1920, unions had to revise their strategies when employers used the economic downturn to take back the gains made by workers between 1916 and 1920, and offensive battles did not resume until the CIO's Textile Workers Organizing Committee, under Sidney Hillman's direction, went to the city in 1937. However, even before the 1920–1921 depression hit, the manufacturers and the federal government had devised new tactics in order to combat the ATWA.

Welfarism

By the time of World War I, many large employers such as International Harvester, Proctor and Gamble, and U.S. Steel had established welfare programs to wean their workers away from unions. With the exception of the Amoskeag Company, northern textile manufacturers had shown little interest in such endeavors.[35] In the wake of the 1919 strikes, some firms reevaluated their employee policies and both the Forstmann & Huffmann Company and the American Woolen Company established welfare programs that rivaled the Amoskeag's in size and scope.

Almost immediately upon the strike's conclusion, the American Woolen Company reconsidered its prior policies. It did this primarily because for the second time in seven years it had lost a major strike but other factors also influenced the company's new direction. In 1918, William Wood had named his son, William M. Wood, Jr., a first vice president and director of the American Woolen Company. Wood's son had studied sociology and industrial relations at Harvard and his academic studies had convinced him that strikes could be prevented if employers showed more interest in their employees. In addition, the company in 1919 embarked on the construction of Shawsheen Village, located in the Lawrence suburb of Andover, that Wood hoped would become the corporation's headquarters and house the firm's white-collar staff.[36] There is no precise evidence on this point, but the Woods also evidently desired to show that their commitment to the Lawrence community now extended to the mill hands as well as to the executives— though this "concern" did not prevent the company from closing all of the Lawrence mills for two months in 1920.

Whatever the motivations, the American Woolen Company in June 1919 began to invest considerable capital in welfare programs. A newly created department of labor, headed by former socialist and trade unionist Ignatius McNulty, coordinated all of the activities, which included a company-funded life insurance plan, a stock subscription program, sickness and accident benefits, a Homestead Association to permit employees to purchase company-built homes at cost, and company-sponsored athletic teams.[37] In order to participate in these programs, a worker had to maintain "continuous" employment—a requirement that companies usually inserted to reduce turnover and to deter strikes. William Wood also made efforts to counter the ATWA's appeal to specific ethnic groups. With no Yugoslavs in Lawrence to alienate, the American Woolen Company launched its own "Help Fiume" drive, and feature articles such as "Proud Poland" and "Reconstruction of Lithuania" appeared in the company's glossy, attractive and photo-filled monthly magazine.[38] Almost in direct imitation of the YPIL, in the spring of 1920 the company founded a Cosmopolitan Club that took charge of many of the preexisting welfare activities and sponsored "nights" for various nationalities, outings, dances, and classes for which it awarded diplomas.[39]

The American Woolen Company designed a number of new initiatives specifically for women workers. These included maternity insurance, mill nurseries, a summer camp for workers' children, homemaking classes, and women's clubs. The company sponsored activities of this sort partly because it needed to attract female employees during the prosperous May 1919–May 1920 period. It also knew that the ATWA had not established any programs specifically for women workers and that unions often neglected to arrange meetings or activities to accommodate women who had household responsibilities. Not coincidentally, at the height of the forty-four-hour agitation, the company magazine published an article entitled "A Woman's View of the Strike," which argued that walkouts greatly damaged the family and the home.[40]

The overall goal of these programs was to compete with those established by the ATWA. Not only did the Cosmopolitan Club offer an alternative to the YPIL but as soon as the ATWA began its own chorus or band, the American Woolen Company followed suit. And to counter the WCU, the company sold food at cost to workers and announced plans to begin its own cooperative. Thus, in the year following the strike, the ATWA and the American Woolen Company had established two distinct cultural models—one envisioned a worker-controlled society and the other a society in which "a trustee, charged with duties affecting the lives, prosperity and happiness of more than forty thousand workers" looked after each and every one of them.[41]

Wood also tried to win the loyalty of his workers by launching an attack on local store owners. He did this by announcing his intention to open a ten-story department store in Lawrence that would sell food and other necessities at low prices to workers. Wood made his proposal at the time of the December 1919 wage hike so as to give greater credence to his charge that local merchants could be blamed for the high cost of living that had absorbed previous wage increases. And to generate employee support for this plan, Wood headed a motorcade through town that American Woolen mill hands were given time off from work to attend.[42]

The American Woolen Company's plan brought into the open a rift between the local merchants and William Wood that in the past had been kept out of the public eye. Ironically, it was Leonard Bennink, a prime organizer of the For God and Country parade, who now took up the cudgels for the shop owners. Bennink called the company's announcement "an insult to every merchant in Lawrence"—the reaction one might have anticipated from the owner of the city's largest department store. Other merchants now portrayed themselves as defenders of Lawrence's mill hands, questioned why the American Woolen Company did not distribute its excess profits to its employees, and criticized the company's welfare policies for telling workers "how to live." [43] Naturally, the ATWA had nothing but contempt for Wood's effort to appear as a "benevolent philanthropist" and viewed the company's plan as a disguised effort to create a form of "control and despotism" such as existed in company towns. Scornful workers greeted Wood with "hoots and jeers" when he drove through the city and employees boycotted a reception at his estate. But as further evidence of the skewed nature of class relationships in Lawrence, the CLU endorsed Wood's plan since as representatives of non-mill workers, they had no reason to fear the plan's paternalistic aspects and welcomed the competition that would be offered to Lawrence's merchants. [44]

The brief episode revealed much about the relative power of social classes in Lawrence. The merchants vehemently protested Wood's plan but they lacked the will to truly challenge him. After one meeting in which Wood brushed aside the storekeepers' concerns, a leading businessman observed: "In the final analysis, the interests of the Lawrence merchants and the American Woolen Company are identical." Equally revealing is the way in which Wood chose to drop the department store idea. When he abandoned the project, he did not even mention the merchants' objections but instead said he was responding to workers' protests and actually apologized for having given the impression that he wanted to interfere "with our employees cooperative stores." Rather than do this, Wood announced that the company would sell only a limited amount of food at cost to workers. [45]

In developing projects such as the department store, Wood acted independently while the manufacturers continued to set their own labor policies. The one exception came in November 1919 when the mill owners jointly granted Father Milanese $60,000 for the construction of an Italian Roman Catholic community building. As in the case of the prior contribution to Father Milanese, this was a "secret cash transaction" as it was necessary to keep the corporate sponsorship "absolutely confidential." [46] Pacific and Arlington had shown little interest in establishing welfare programs, but the American Woolen Company's initiatives made their managements uneasy since they feared falling too far behind in this area. As a result of the need to at least make the appearance of keeping up with their competitor, both Arlington and Pacific began life insurance programs and Pacific established a welfare department though it did little other than to conduct English classes and sponsor some athletic teams. This mill would come under far more pressure in 1922 when strikers shut the plant down for six months. Immediately upon the conclusion of that walkout, Pacific began an employee representation plan—a step that the American Woolen Company had not taken.[47]

It is difficult to assess how much damage the American Woolen Company's programs did to the ATWA. The Federal Council of Churches report on the 1919 strike claimed that as a result of these changes employees had "greatly modified" their attitudes towards Wood but their own investigator's private correspondence casts doubts on the validity of this conclusion.[48] The ATWA called on workers not to be "deceived" by Wood's "charity" and urged its members to boycott all company functions. According to the union, many workers refused to accept their free copies of *The A. W. Employees Booster* and walked out of the organizing meeting for the Cosmopolitan Club. Other workers reportedly only participated in activities "through fear of the bosses."[49] On the other hand, the numerous photos and the lists of participants in the clubs give an impression of wide-scale participation, and Lawrence leftists in the early 1920s spent an inordinate amount of time attacking "McNulty's League of Nations"—a sure sign it was having an impact.[50]

Wood's megalomania, though, constantly interfered with his efforts to wean workers from unions. "Songs to Our Captain Billy," receptions where workers gathered under signs reading "A Man Without A Stain Upon His Honor," and Cosmopolitan Club statements that Lawrence was "most of the time . . . the most contented industrial city in Massachusetts . . . due to the principles of square dealing established between Mr. Wood . . . and his employees" were all signs that Wood's power, as well as the million dollars per year he earned in salary and commissions, had gone to his head.[51] In fact, many of Wood's pet projects, especially the building of Shawsheen Village, proved foolhardy and cost the company dearly—an aspect not fully revealed until Wood, upset by his son's death in an automobile accident, by plummeting profits, and by his own illness, committed suicide on a deserted Florida road in 1926.[52]

Repression

Both local and federal officials attempted to interfere with the activities of the Lawrence local. As soon as the strike ended, city authorities made it clear that interference with workers' First Amendment rights would not cease. They had permitted one ATWA rally on the common but then revoked permission for future meetings on the grounds that a speaker had predicted that "within four months" the union "would be in control of the mills." The unavailability of the common meant that workers once again had to hold their outdoor meetings on vacant lots. The Lithuanian Social Camp Association at Methuen was the one "sanctuary" available to workers but this was not a readily accessible location. Even when the ATWA local met at that spot, extreme precautions had to be taken. For instance, Giovannitti had to be brought "secretly" to a meeting there because workers remained mindful of the 1916 and 1919 "kidnappings" of Joe Ettor and Anthony Capraro.[53]

City authorities directed much of their attention towards the Sunday School for Workers' Children. At first, police officials, upon receiving a complaint from the director of the YMCA, merely visited the school and warned its staff to cease operations. When school officials refused to obey this order, the police conducted a full-scale raid in which they seized all of the students' records and ordered the seventy-five children in attendance to return to their homes. They followed this action with return "visits" in order to ensure that the school had not resumed operations.[54] Police took other steps to hinder the union's efforts: they raided Ime Kaplan's home and charged him with violating Massachusetts' recently enacted antianarchy statute, they banned ATWA plays on the grounds they contained subversive material, and they fed information about the ATWA to the Bureau of Investigation.[55]

Federal agents hardly needed informants as they had been keeping close tabs on labor activists in Lawrence for the past year. These officials made use of the material they had been compiling when the U.S. Department of Justice carried out the nationwide Palmer Raids on 2 January 1920. Of fifteen persons taken into custody in Lawrence, six (Ime Kaplan, Frank Coco, Frank Szajna, Joseph Salerno, William Blazonis, and Mike Bolis) had served on the ATWA staff and a number of others had been active in the union. Federal agents also seized vast quantities of literature from the homes of the victims and from the headquarters of the Lawrence local. Except for Szajna, who was released immediately, the detainees spent anywhere from a few days to three weeks at the Deer Island prison located off shore from Boston.[56]

Far more than the local crackdown, the Palmer Raids aroused fears that reverberated throughout the entire immigrant community. An ATWA-sponsored protest strike against the raids "fizzled" as only a tiny number of workers dared to walk out of the mills. Census officials reported that following the arrests, many immigrants refused to give their names to government investigators.[57] In response to Capraro's request that Anthony Bimba come to Lawrence, Muste replied that "I've seen Comrade Bimbo [sic] he says it is absolutely out of the question for him to appear in public at this time, for reasons that you may guess and the same holds for all the effective Lithuanian speakers that he knows."[58] When Kaplan visited Lithuanian workers in Nashua who had also been victims of the raids, he had to reassure them "not to lose courage, that things would turn out all right."[59]

In general, little attention has been paid to the repercussions of the Palmer Raids on the labor movement. The Lawrence case suggests that a major purpose of these arrests was to discourage labor activity. By snatching labor organizers, the government hoped to demonstrate to rank and filers the "costs" of militancy. And yet, as is often the case, repression also generated great anger. Large crowds celebrated the release of the detainees and Capraro reported that the arrests had created a "wave of solidarity" and a new opportunity for oganizing in Lawrence. Nashua workers, many of whom had joined the Communist party, appeared concerned only about the legal fees as they were determined to continue with their political work.[60] Whatever their impact, two points need to be stressed. First, the Palmer Raids should be viewed as a continuation of federal efforts throughout 1919 to hinder radical labor activity since they were different only in method rather than in purpose from the actions of the NWLB in Paterson and of the Division of Conciliation and Mediation in Passaic. Second, the greatest source of fear remained the blacklist; without mill employment few workers could remain in Lawrence for long. Governmental repression merely supplemented the "terrorism" of the American Woolen Company, which remained the dominant force in workers' lives.[61]

The 1920–1921 Depression

The 1920–1921 depression that led to widespread unemployment across the country delivered a further blow to the ATWA's hopes in Lawrence. The economic downturn came on the heels of a woolen and worsteds boom that lasted from May 1919 through May 1920 during which large numbers of Italian and Polish immigrants continued to pour into the city. But the prosperous period ended abruptly when the American Woolen Company went on a three-day schedule in June 1920, a step that proved only preliminary to an enormous shock, the closing of all of the American Woolen Company's mills in Lawrence on 9 July 1920. This shutdown— called "the great lockout of 1920" by labor activists—lasted until September 1920 when the company recalled 5,000 employees, though these and most other American Woolen mill hands did not resume working full-time until the spring of 1921. In contrast, the Arlington mills went on four-day weeks but never closed down completely and the Pacific mills pretty much maintained normal schedules through the depression.[62]

The closing of the American Woolen Company's mills served as the bluntest possible assertion of corporate power. Just as workers had used market conditions to their advantage during the war, Wood took advantage of the postwar depression to discipline Lawrence workers.[63] He told his employees that the summer was "the best season for a two month's vacation," but by January 1921 the distress of Lawrence residents surpassed that of the winter of 1914–1915. Many workers could not afford to pay their rent, buy clothing, or properly feed their families and requests for aid overwhelmed private charities and the city's welfare department. The majority of the American Woolen Company employees settled in for a "depressed state of waiting" though many others sought work in other cities or left the country altogether.[64]

The specter of widespread unemployment alarmed Lawrence's mayor William White who had never previously attacked the manufacturers. But now faced with an unfeeling company that refused to give any hint as to its plans, White changed his tune. Citing "pitiable stories" told him by those who had been thrown out of work and expressing concern for the city's ability to pay for soup kitchens and for the additional welfare costs, White declared:

The mills have no right to close without good and sufficient reason. They made millions during the war and should now operate in order to give the people employment even if they had to sell cloth at cost. What's a million dollar loss to the American Woolen Company.[65]

White also questioned whether the company had ulterior motivations for the closings and demanded that Wood personally appear before the city council in order to explain the reasons for the shutdown. When Wood disdainfully dismissed the request, White suggested that Governor Coolidge order a legislative investigation of the company so as to compel Wood to testify.[66]

A number of prominent Lawrence residents supported White's stand and a columnist for the *Lawrence Sun American* agreed with the mayor that the American Woolen Company had "no moral or legal right" to close.[67] But the city council, whose most outspoken member was the director of public safety, Peter Carr, who had been elected on the pledge that he was "just the man to crush the power of Bolshevism in Lawrence," showed no inclination to compel Wood to testify before them. For a while White kept up the fight and threatened to release some "great stuff" on the American Woolen Company if Wood did not reopen the mills, but White soon backed off from this stand when he refused to reach out to the ATWA, the one group in the city that would have given him full backing for his campaign.[68] Instead of calling upon the ATWA for support, White continued to deny the union the right to meet on the common and turned down all invitations to speak at their meetings as he remained fearful of radical labor.[69] As in Paterson and Passaic, this fear of leftism dominated the local scene after 1912 and prevented the type of alliances between the working class and local middle class that had been far more common in small industrial cities in the late nineteenth century when ethnic and ideological cleavages were not as sharp.[70]

As a result of the shutdown, the ATWA local faced a major crisis as the bulk of its members worked at the American Woolen mills. There was a dismal lack of precedents for union resistance to "employer strikes" but the union tried. A "curtailment committee" attempted to build ties to the CLU and to Mayor White and the union asked for a Federal Trade Commission investigation and even considered seeking a court injunction against the closings. But little could be done as over 1,000 of the union's members left the city in the last six months of 1920 and other workers ceased paying dues or attending meetings. As a sign of workers' desperation, the small Plymouth mill in November 1920 slashed wages and yet prospective employees still lined up outside. In such an atmosphere, even another appearance by Arturo Giovannitti evoked little response as worker morale sank.[71]

Before business picked up, the Arlington and Pacific corporations in December 1920 delivered a second jolt to mill workers when they along with most other New England textile manufacturers cut their employees wages by 22.5 percent. Lawrence workers had expected a wage slash but they had not anticipated one that would practically wipe out all of their postwar wage increases.[72] But lacking any semblance of organization, the Pacific and Arlington employees were in no position to fight this round of wage cuts and only a tiny number of mill hands, who were replaced immediately, walked out in protest.[73]

As usual, the American Woolen Company preferred to act on its own and held back from announcing a cut. This actually gave the ATWA time to prepare for a slash, and the union held a New England conference of all the ATWA locals to coordinate a plan of attack in case the textile trust decided to reduce its employees' wages. Muste and other leaders vowed that "hell" would "break loose" if the company tried to take back workers' gains, but when Wood in mid-January 1921 finally announced the same 22.5 percent cut, all attempts to arouse a response failed since, unlike in 1912 and 1919, after six months of massive layoffs and mill closings Lawrence workers were not in a fighting mood.[74]

Subsequent events demonstrated that Lawrence workers had only been temporarily subdued as, angered by a steady deterioration of working conditions and by a second wage cut, Pacific mill employees in 1922 staged a prolonged battle that eventually forced the management to give up its efforts to enact the new slash. The ATWA was not around to lead this battle as the Lawrence local, its treasury empty and its membership dissipated, was no more able than the IWW to survive a depression. However, even before the economic downturn began, an ideological dispute broke out within the Lawrence local that damaged the ATWA but also led to the emergence of a new union and a new leadership that was better prepared to counter the postwar employer onslaught.

Benjamin Legere and the One Big Union

It is quite possible that the Lawrence local could have survived the 1920–1921 slump if workers had warmly embraced its leaders and its program. But as was to be true in Passaic and Paterson as well, many mill hands expressed doubts about the desirability of an ACWA-style union and about the fitness of the intellectuals to lead the organization.

Workers wasted no time in expressing their reservations about the intellectuals and upon the very conclusion of the 48/54 walkout the general strike committee rejected a "victory statement" drafted by Harold Rotzel because it talked about "a willingness to forget and forgive those things which have caused bitterness and ill-feeling" and a desire "to create a world free from the exploitation of workers and do it in a peaceful way."[75] The language of this declaration typified that used by Rotzel and Long, who were less willing than Muste to cast aside their pacifism and adopt the language of workers. Long and Rotzel also indicated that they had joined the ATWA in order to guide workers in the proper direction. For example, Long called upon college-educated persons to join the labor movement to prevent the "lesser intelligence" from gaining control of unions and Rotzel called for an "orderly educated evolution" so as to render revolutionary methods unnecessary.[76]

Workers' distrust of Rotzel and Long became apparent after a Boston newspaper printed an editorial in October 1919 claiming that the intellectual leadership had conferred with William Wood to discuss means of bringing "peace to the mills." The article raised workers' eyebrows as it reminded them of Rotzel's "victory statement," and its publication led members of the Lawrence local to question openly if the ministers still clung to principles that "cannot benefit labor because they promoted church interests."[77] The ATWA moved immediately to minimize the harm done by the controversy. Although Long denied that any such meeting had taken place, Muste penned a special editorial in the *New Textile Worker* in which he disavowed any intention to do "church work" in the ATWA and reiterated his own belief that there could never be peace between "exploiter and exploited, master and slave."[78] Workers remained suspicious. Shortly after the publication of Muste's statement, the Lawrence local obliquely attacked the intellectuals by proposing that only textile workers be allowed to sit on the ATWA's executive board.[79] On a more basic level, Rotzel and Long could not and would not shed their middle-class backgrounds, religious perspectives, or principles. On these grounds alone, they were bound to face hostility from workers whose direct actionist traditions and revolutionary beliefs made them suspicious "of anything connected with the bourgeois."[80]

Members of the Lawrence local also questioned the union's basic principles. These doubts surfaced after the October 1919 ATWA convention adopted a constitution that prohibited the national office from imposing contracts on locals but permitted locals to sign their own agreements. Upon hearing of this action, the Italian branch drafted a strongly worded protest, which the Lawrence central council (the union's governing body) approved. In voicing their objections, Lawrence workers argued that the speeding up of machinery and increases in the cost of living often rendered contracts obsolete before their expiration date, and echoing the Wobblies, the dissidents held that signed agreements gave one local "the legal license to scab on another" and killed any possibility of ever holding "a general strike in the industry." The local further stated they believed that such a provision represented "the first step backward from the original idea of the Amalgamated as a revolutionary industrial union" and ended their statement with these words: "'Workers of the world unite. You have nothing to lose but your chains'. The time contract is one of the chains."[81]

Other disputes cropped up in the contentious local as many workers vehemently objected to proposals that the ATWA merge with the ACWA. So strongly did workers oppose this idea that Muste had to dissuade Capraro from even raising the affiliation issue in Lawrence.[82] Capraro himself became a target for much of the anti-ACWA sentiment as Ime Kaplan accused him of being an "ACWA agent" and of working for a merger in order to increase his own salary. Although the Lawrence central council disavowed Kaplan's charges, Capraro resigned from the local because he considered that the union as a body had failed explicitly to repudiate Kaplan's accusations and "its mean implications."[83] This resignation further diminished the ACWA's influence in Lawrence as Capraro had earned great respect for his contribution to the 48/54 strike and to the YPIL.

Despite these controversies, opposition to the ACWA/ATWA program did not fully crystalize until April 1920 when Benjamin Legere arrived in Lawrence. A charismatic and flamboyant figure, Legere spoke a language that appealed to many workers and his far-flung experiences offered a decided contrast to the intellectual cadre.

Born in Taunton, Massachusetts, Legere had worked as a machinist, playwright, and actor before first coming to Lawrence in 1912. Although he played only a minor part in the Bread and Roses strike, he coordinated the defense effort for Ettor, Giovannitti, and Caruso. As part of this campaign, he conducted a series of highly successful street meetings throughout New England that garnered support for the accused Wobblies. A man of daring, he was the only IWW leader who showed up at the For God and Country parade—a bit of bravado that nearly cost him a beating. From Lawrence, Legere had gone to Little Falls, New York, to aid a textile strike in that town. During the course of the struggle, he was arrested and sentenced to one year in a New York penitentiary. Upon his release from prison, Legere made speaking appearances on behalf of the IWW, performed for small theatre companies and worked at odd jobs until he joined the Bird of Paradise theatre group, which happened to be touring western Canada in the spring of 1919, the precise time that the One Big Union (OBU), which had just been formed, was winning over most of the western Canadian members of the Trades Labour Congress (Canada's equivalent of the AFL). Caught up in this agitation, Legere quickly became an ardent supporter of the OBU.[84]

The OBU appealed to Legere because it had much in common with the IWW and yet appeared to offer a far sounder approach for organizing. Like the Wobblies, the OBU placed great stress on local autonomy, rank-and-file control, low dues, and the need for proletarian solidarity. In the same vein as the IWW, it viewed political activity as being relatively unimportant and did not put great emphasis on winning signed contracts. The greatest difference between the OBU and the IWW related to structural questions as the OBU condemned industrial as well as craft unionism. Instead of grouping workers by industry, the OBU favored organizing them on a territorial basis. In part, the OBU favored this type of organization because it believed that workers changed their jobs so often that they did not identify for long with particular industries. Basically, though, the OBU backed this idea because it believed that workers were far more likely both to develop and practice solidarity along territorial than industrial lines—a concept that, given Canada's vast territorial expanse, appeared to make sense. For instance, the OBU argued that if police tried to break a miner's strike on Vancouver Island, miners in "far away" places could provide little aid for them while the support of local workers could prove to be decisive in such a battle.[85]

The OBU enjoyed extraordinary growth during the first six months of 1919 as workers flocked to its banner and a number of city-wide trades councils voted to affiliate with it. Its greatest success came in the wake of the May 1919 Winnipeg general strike as many of its adherents played leading roles in that struggle. Despite the strike's less than satisfactory outcome, the OBU emerged as the leading union in Winnipeg and won the loyalty of diverse groups of workers such as painters, teamsters, tailors, and railway workers.[86]

Even before the Winnipeg general strike took place, Legere had become greatly enthusiastic about the OBU. Never one to shy away from

159

the action, while he was visiting Calgary, Alberta, with his troupe in April 1919, he actually took the podium at one meeting and urged rank-and-file unionists to revolt against their leadership. The next day Canadian Mounties arrested Legere and jailed him in Lethbridge on the charge of spreading "IWW propaganda." The authorities held him for thirty-three days until local miners who were sympathetic to the OBU secured his release. However, the Mounties promptly rearrested Legere and expelled him from Canada. Upon his return to the United States, Legere resumed his peripatetic ways and made appearances in Baltimore, Pittsburgh, and New York City on behalf of the Workers' Defense Union, a group concerned with the plight of political prisoners. All during this time, Legere continued to agitate for the OBU since he remained "convinced that Canadian labor" was "leading the workers of the western world toward industrial freedom and the new society." [87]

In April 1920, Muste invited Legere to join the ATWA staff in Lawrence. Muste made this offer despite Legere's outspoken support for the OBU and despite the open dissension within the Lawrence local. The ATWA later claimed that Legere obtained the position under "false pretenses," but Muste had to be aware of Legere's views. Unfortunately, it is not clear why Muste made such an egregious error. According to Bert Emsley, who quickly became Legere's protege, "militants" in the Lawrence local demanded that Legere be dispatched to the city. [88] There is no evidence to support this claim and it is quite possible that Muste assigned Legere to Lawrence simply because he knew the former Wobbly was well respected there for his Ettor-Giovannitti-Caruso defense work and appeared to be the ideal person to revive the local at a time when the national was pushing a strike for the forty-four-hour week and 50 percent wage increase. Of French descent and an English speaker, Legere also appeared to be a person who could reach groups that had remained outside the ATWA orbit. Given Muste's naiveté at this point in his life, he may not have realized how much Legere's opinions ran counter to those of the very union that hired him.

Upon arriving in Lawrence, Legere proved to be a lightning rod for the ATWA dissidents and he immediately attracted a number of workers to his side. His supporters succeeded in getting the YPIL to sever its connections with the ATWA and won a number of spots on the union's central council. The division within the local came to a head in June 1920 when Legere defeated Rotzel in a hotly contested election for branch manager, but the national office nullified the election on the grounds that the voters had not been required to show membership cards before casting their ballots. This action only heated up the controversy and Carlo Tresca had to be called to Lawrence to soothe over the bad feelings. In any case, Legere won the second election by an even larger majority and he took office as manager of the Lawrence local in July 1920—a mere four months after arriving in the city.[89]

Legere was the catalyst but he merely tapped preexisting hostility to the ACWA and the ATWA. Indeed, opposition to the ACWA figured prominently when Legere sought the manager's post on a platform that opposed an ATWA/ACWA merger and favored secession if a fusion ever took place. Legere's supporters most clearly stated their objections to the ACWA in a trenchant document entitled "Verses from the Bible of the Amalgamated Clothing Workers of America," which they issued to counter pro-affiliation articles in the *New Textile Worker*. This piece of "counter-propaganda" castigated the ACWA for signing agreements that limited workers' power on the shop floor, that made sympathy strikes illegal, and gave employers the right to fire employees who disobeyed decisions made by a Board of Arbitration.[90] By using clauses taken from its contracts, its critics thus portrayed the ACWA as a union that sought peace with capitalists or as Legere commented: "The Amalgamated members talk like radicals but do not act like them."[91]

The OBU's very name evoked memories of the Wobblies, and Legere's greatest support came from those who remained most loyal to the IWW's principles. This included large numbers of Italian workers and almost all of Lawrence's Franco-Belgians, who roiled at the very mention of contracts and who had remained aloof from the ATWA.[92] The ability to appeal to Wobbly sympathizers would appear to be somewhat contradictory as Legere made no secret of the OBU's critique of the IWW's industrial format. Legere worked around this problem by holding up the 1912 strike rather than the 1919 walkout as his model for action and he even later claimed that "some sections of the One Big Union have been organized since 1912."[93] Significantly, once the OBU established itself in Lawrence, the city's local castigated the national OBU office for carrying its criticisms of the IWW too far and pointedly reminded it that "the only difference between these two One Big Union movements are differences of structure."[94]

Following his election as branch manager, Legere spent most of his time trying to convince workers of the need for a "class union." Many of his attacks on the ATWA focused on what he viewed as the organization's over-centralization, a defect he viewed as inherent in industrial unionism. In contrast to a union "whose expensive, inefficient organizational machine" dissipated workers' per capita tax money in a fruitless effort to organize the textile industry, the OBU offered "local solidarity, local centralization, local autonomy, rank and file control"—a radical version of localism, other variants of which appeared in Passaic and Paterson.[95]

Criticism of the ATWA's "waste" and "extravagance" had great appeal as the Lawrence local continued to deteriorate in the face of the depression. Of course, the union's standing was not helped by the fact that it had a head who favored secession from the national organization. This intolerable situation came to a climax in December 1920 when members of the Lawrence local voted on whether they wished to remain within the ATWA, join the OBU, rejoin the IWW, or reconstitute themselves as a totally independent union. Legere marshaled all of his forces for this contest, but now Muste served as the principal foil: the Lawrence Central Council had just rebuked the ATWA head for sending a letter to William Wood requesting a conference to discuss the rumored pay cuts. The pro-OBU forces promised workers that unlike "Mr. Muste," they would not ask their enemy for "fairness" and that they would present a far more militant opposition to any slash in wages than would the ATWA.[96] To give credence to the OBU pledge to organize community-wide resistance, Legere began to develop ties with Essex County shoe workers who also faced disastrous levels of unemployment.[97]

To counter Legere, the ATWA, led by Joseph Salerno, mounted its own defense of industrial unionism. The ATWA rejected the idea that the primary ties of Lawrence's textile workers were with other city employees rather than with other textile workers and cited Legere's inability to get the local CLU to endorse the OBU concept as proof that his oft-cited Winnipeg example did not apply to Lawrence. The ATWA also warned workers not to be fooled by a "rattle-brained 'revolutionary adventurist'" whose "'mass actionist'" rhetoric obscured the OBU's lack of program and reminded its members that since industrial unions sought to train workers to run industries in the future, any organization that rejected the industrial basis was "misconceived" and "false in theory."[98]

The actual balloting proved to be a disappointment to OBU supporters as Salerno defeated Legere in a new contest for branch manager and Lawrence workers voted 1,181 to 1,106 to remain within the ATWA fold. Of those who voted against the ATWA only 500 voted for the OBU, the remaining ballots being cast for the IWW or for an independent union.[99]

The election results demonstrated that even though many Lawrence workers had preferred Legere's leadership to Rotzel's, they still remained unconvinced that industrial unions represented "evasions of class struggle." Many Sicilians in particular, following the lead of Salerno, most likely decided to stick with the ATWA.[100] The very fact that Lawrence workers, unlike those in Passaic, had often been divided made it difficult to build support for the territorial concept. One also wonders about those workers who did not vote. Had they tired of the ideological wrangling that weakened efforts to oppose wage cuts?

The electoral defeat did not stop Legere from establishing a Lawrence chapter of the OBU, and by the spring of 1921 he had enlisted the help of 48/54 veterans Emile Lemaire, Ime Kaplan, and Samuel Bramhall as well as Bert Emsely, who remained his chief lieutenant.[101] Through street meetings that gave Legere an opportunity to put his theatrical training to good use, through publication of a strictly local paper, *Lawrence Labor*, and through supporting the struggles of other Lawrence workers, the OBU began to expand its base beyond the Franco-Belgian and Italian workers at the American Woolen Company and it became the only Massachusetts union to gain members in 1921. By 1922, Lawrence served as the center of the OBU in eastern North America and the union made a supreme effort during the six-month strike of that year to reach "the Americans and French Canadians" and to break down the "barrier between the American workers and the non-English speaking workers."[102] But by 1923, Legere began to complain about the need to go house to house for dues and about the stubborn allegiance of the city's nationality groups to their own ethnic organizations—problems that had bedeviled the IWW and the ATWA, and these difficulties along with the Pacific mill's company union, another textile depression, and factional fighting eventually wrecked the OBU.[103]

As for the ATWA, large numbers of workers had voiced their confidence in industrial unionism but, battered by nine months of in-fighting that compounded all of the union's other troubles, the Lawrence local had lost the will to fight. In a last ditch effort to spark a revival, Capraro and Muste spoke at meetings and the union voted to reorganize along departmental rather than nationality lines, but by the spring of 1921 the union was doing little other than showing films and it closed its doors that summer.[104] The broad contours would prove to be similar in Passaic; in the New Jersey city the ATWA was also to discover that workers were reluctant to embrace national unions and that corporations could prove resourceful when faced with a new threat. The intellectual cadre would also experience great discomfort in Passaic but there they would be attacked for being too radical whereas in Lawrence they were viewed as being too conservative—an important indicator of the difficulty of spreading the same industrial union message to Poles and Slovaks as well as Lithuanians, Franco-Belgians, and Italians.

Chapter Eight

THE ATWA IN PASSAIC

The ATWA had grounds for both optimism and pessimism as it set out to establish the Passaic local. It had reasons to be hopeful because the 1919 strike showed that the thirst for unionization had accompanied the "settling in" process. The fight for union recognition had also demonstrated that Passaic workers could call upon an interconnecting network of community, church, and fraternal institutions in the challenge to the Wool Council. Now that aid had been received from the ACWA and the ATWA had been formed, the 9,000 woolen and worsted workers who had enrolled in the union could also expect that additional resources would be made available to them.

But the decision to call upon outsiders also portended difficulties since not all workers agreed that a national union should be brought into the city. Those who opposed outside "interference" could rightfully claim that the turn to the ACWA had violated the original union's constitution, while the disappointing outcome of the second strike had damaged the credibility of those who had been the most ardent advocates of the ACWA's entry. Lacking the socialist cadre of Lawrence and Paterson, a disproportionate share of the leadership fell upon Pluhar, who as a Czech could not command the loyalties of any important segment of the city's mill population. The ATWA's close relationship with the ACWA also presented a problem in Passaic because many Polish workers viewed the ACWA as pro-Bolshevik and Jewish-dominated—at a time when the Polish national cause was taking on an anti-Bolshevik and anti-Jewish cast.

What Can a Union Do?

As soon as the second strike ended in April 1919, the ATWA moved to establish itself on a permanent basis. Over 5,000 workers paid the first month's dues and the union planned to enroll 10,000 members by the fall. As a result of the ACWA's financial assistance, the Passaic branch had an ample treasury with which to begin its work. Pluhar remained head of the local in addition to serving as treasurer of the national union, and three full-time organizers were placed on the payroll. The very existence of a well-financed organizing campaign had no precedent as never before in the city's history had a textile union embarked upon such a drive as the ATWA mapped out.[1]

In keeping with the preferences of Passaic workers, the local initially organized branches according to place of employment rather than by nationality. Despite the use of this structure, the ATWA had only slightly more success in Passaic than in Lawrence in redressing workplace grievances. At the Botany plant, the ATWA established a minimum scale of $24 per week for male and female weavers and exacted a form of recognition. These workers displayed their power in July 1919 when the Botany weavers shut off their looms while their representatives presented new demands for increased pay for idle looms, an equal distribution of work, and an end to discrimination against union members. Soon thereafter, mule spinners at the Garfield plant of the Forstmann & Huffmann Company staged a successful strike for the abolishment of piecework and for a minimum weekly pay of $33.[2]

These limited victories were not duplicated in any other departments or in any of the other mills. Given the lack of clout on the shop floor, the union, as in Lawrence, had no choice but to try to establish viable activities in the community in order to retain workers' support. With the exception of the Magyars, Passaic's immigrant groups had established nothing like the Lithuanian Social Camp Association or the Italian,

Franco-Belgian, and Lithuanian cooperatives, and the union did not even attempt to create the type of radical cultural programs that it put into place in Lawrence. Instead, the ATWA put its greatest stress on the teaching of what it called "union, workingmen's English" because a large percentage of Passaic's workers spoke only their native tongue and thus could not fully participate in the union. Upon his arrival in Passaic, Robert W. Dunn took charge of these classes, which a U.S. Department of Education investigator found to be the finest in the city and the only ones in which adult "students" were treated with dignity and respect.[3]

Even the most successful English classes could perform only an ancillary function, and the Passaic local still had to figure out what a union without a contract or any form of recognition could do. The one option appeared to be to prepare for the "big battle" that could effectively mobilize Passaic's workers into the ATWA's ranks. Dunn favored this strategy and believed that the ATWA had lost a "golden opportunity" by failing to lead another strike when workers had become restless in the summer of 1919. But with workers still paying debts that they had accumulated during the walkout, locally based leaders at that point discouraged talk of starting the "battle royal" that Dunn considered inevitable.[4]

Once the national organization in February 1920 launched its campaign for the forty-four-hour week and 50 percent pay hike the local began to make preparations for a strike. In addition to the two major demands, the local declared that it also sought union recognition, "absolute elimination of the blacklist and the espionage system," and the abolition of all night work for women workers. This agitation gave the intellectual leadership a splendid opportunity to show their mettle since Cedric Long had been reassigned to Passaic while Dunn remained in the city and Muste traveled regularly from New York City to give advice and to speak at the numerous meetings the union sponsored to drum up support for its goals. By the end of April, Muste reported that Passaic was "ready to walk out at any time." But he hesitated to call a strike because he believed a textile slump to be on the horizon and thought that the manufacturers might actually welcome a walkout.[5]

In the meantime, the mill owners stole some of the ATWA's thunder when they granted all of their adult employees a three-dollar-per-week pay hike. The Wool Council intentionally bestowed the increase in the form of a bonus so they could easily revoke it at some point in the future, but in an immediate sense, the move did blunt the strike talk.[6]

Following the manufacturers' announcement, the intellectuals made a series of vacillating moves that illustrated their lack of preparation for leadership and effectively ruined the union's Passaic local. Though the Wool Council had hardly addressed their key demands, the union decided to postpone the strike call on the grounds that the ATWA would be in a far more powerful position in the near future. To bolster this argument, Muste deliberately distorted the results of the recently concluded ACWA convention to make it appear as if the ACWA had sanctioned a merger with the textile workers. He told one mass gathering that "once we get one big union we can get everything we want" and implied that a strike would occur once the two Amalgamateds had joined together.[7]

The very next day the ATWA changed its mind and sent a letter to the manufacturers stating that since the three-dollar-pay increase came in the form of a bonus, "in reality" it gave "no actual increase" to the workers. The union resubmitted its demands and warned the Wool Council that the "spirit of rebellion" was "spreading rapidly" and that a walkout was "not far distant" unless the manufacturers made some concessions. The union gave the mill owners three days to reply to this note before the ATWA took further action. Naturally, the Wool Council did not respond, so the ATWA had no choice but to live up to its threats or to risk losing face. Although Muste still hesitated to urge workers to walk out, those who attended a raucous gathering in Garfield finally voted to strike. Muste pledged that the ACWA's resources would be made available to the Passaic workers and Long promised that Passaic would have a "big strike" that would rid the city of the Wool Council's spy system.[8]

Remarkably, the ATWA at the last moment once again grew skittish and called off the planned walkout. In justification of this move, the leadership cited the Wool Council's "extensive" strike preparations and expressed fears that the manufacturers would turn any work stoppage into a lockout that would keep workers on the streets for three months. Muste tried to put the latest reversal in the most favorable light by telling workers that the union had actually outmaneuvered the manufacturers:

They have been putting things over on us for a long time. Now we'll put one over on them. They are all ready to have you on strike tomorrow morning. Well it will be a healthy surprise for them when you go to work tomorrow morning leaving it to your Executive Board to call you out when it sees fit. When the Board gives you the word you will all come out on strike and give them another healthy surprise.[9]

In actuality, the Passaic local had once again changed its mind because of concern that its small membership made it impossible to carry out an effective walkout and because Muste and Long proved unwilling to take the risks that could have built a mass base for the ATWA. Having initiated a movement for a strike, they preferred to postpone action rather than follow through on their plans.

The last-minute loss of nerve damaged Long's reputation and in July he abruptly left Passaic and severed his connection with the ATWA. Pluhar remained in Passaic but he also soon ceased to play an active role in the local. In an effort to recapture its lost membership, the ATWA reorganized along nationality lines.[10] This move was akin to that of the Lawrence local when it moved to a shop form of organization in January 1921. In each case, the ATWA locals sought structural solutions for problems that went far beyond the particular format that the union adopted.

Ironically, for all of Muste's fears the 1920–1921 economic downturn did not hit Passaic as severely as Lawrence and the city witnessed nothing close to the devastating American Woolen shutdown. In fact, Forstmann & Huffmann, whose creative designers and dyers allowed it to retain much of the market for fine women's goods, ran on full schedules right through the depression. In June 1920, Botany did begin to run on four-day-per-week schedules but it maintained its night shift for women workers, which had been a prime ATWA target. But the union's weakened position did not allow it to attack Botany's policy of running at night while cutting down day workers' schedules and as a sign of the ATWA's diminished strength, in January 1921 the Wool Council rescinded the three-dollar bonus that it had granted in May 1920 and imposed an additional 7.5 percent cut without facing any overt resistance from workers.[11]

On the surface, the scenario appears similar to the one in Lawrence but there were significant differences between the two cities. Even before the May 1920 fiasco and far more than in Lawrence, the Passaic branch had difficulty in holding its ranks. While the Passaic local in September 1919 claimed to have over 5,000 adherents, Robert W. Dunn reported that the branch had a "dependable membership of not more than nine hundred."[12] The suddenness of the drop and the failure (unlike in Lawrence and Paterson) of another union to step into the breach left by the ATWA, indicate that a number of special factors inhibited the unionization of the city's work force. The rest of this chapter will be devoted to explaining why, despite the obvious militancy of Passaic's textile workers, it became so difficult to build a union in that city during the immediate postwar period.

The Ethnic Factor

Although localist in orientation, Passaic workers also responded to international currents. Thus, despite Pluhar's hopes that workers would submerge their own ethnic identifications, nationality disputes could interfere with organizing efforts. This was especially true in 1919 and 1920, when political battles, revolutions, and wars involving Poles, Jews, Ukrainians, and Magyars reverberated through the streets of Dundee. In some cases, as with the Magyars, revolutionary fervor in Europe steeled workers in their radicalism. But within Passaic's large Polish community, battles overseas between Jews and Poles and between Poland and the Soviet Union had a deleterious effect upon the union.

Clashes between Jews and Poles broke out in a number of American mill towns and cities beginning in December 1918. Normally, tensions between these two groups just simmered, but they boiled over when American Jews learned that a number of pogroms had occurred in the new state of Poland. Some of the worst violence took place in Galicia, where the Polish army joined civilians in murdering Jews and seizing their property. Upon hearing of these atrocities, Jewish organizations in the United States issued stern protests and convinced the Allied powers to support their demand that Poland agree to a special minorities treaty guaranteeing protection for Jews and other minorities before it could be formally granted independence. To Polish leaders on both sides of the ocean, such a treaty represented an infringement on Polish sovereignty and they denied that any attacks against Jews had occurred. Polish anti-Bolshevism entered into the controversy since by virtue of the prominent role that some Jews had played in the Russian Revolution, it had become common in the Polish community to refer to Bolshevism as if it were a Jewish movement.[13]

Overt conflict in Passaic began in December 1918 when the Polish Merchants and Tradesmen's Association called for a boycott of Jewish-owned stores. This was the first time that any group in Passaic had ever called for a boycott of Jewish enterprises though such a tactic had been used by Poles overseas on a number of occasions. The appeal made note of events in Poland by linking support for the newly independent Polish state with the need to rid Poland of Jewish enterprises and by summoning Passaic's Polish residents to spend their money with merchants who supported their national aspirations rather than with those who used their money "as a weapon" against them. Members of Passaic's Jewish community became further aroused when a leaflet distributed by a Polish shopkeeper asked Poles to avoid Jewish store owners who had "sucked your blood for centuries" and claimed that money spent in Jewish stores ended up in Moscow.[14]

Tensions between Passaic's Poles and Jews subsided during the walkout but they surfaced again in May and June 1919 at the precise time that the ATWA first tried to establish itself in the city. During these two months, Jews in Passaic staged protests against the pogroms and representatives of Jewish and Polish community organizations traded angry charges and denunciations. While no actual street fighting between Poles and Jews took place, violence almost occurred when a rumor was spread that a Polish woman had been found dead in a Jewish-owned shop.[15]

The Polish petit bourgeoisie who claimed that Poles did 90 percent of their "purchasing in Jewish owned stores" certainly had the most to gain from the conflict and in an effort to win the patronage of Polish workers they charged that Jewish control of business meant that Poles could only get "dangerous work" and criticized "big Jewish capitalists."[16] Of most consequence for the ATWA, Stephen Novack and Louis Kymack, both of whom held office in the Independent Union, joined the anti-Jewish agitation and both coupled their attacks on the Passaic local with references to "New York Bolsheviki" and to "Rubenstein of Paterson." At one point, the Independent Union, whose entire leadership was Polish, even claimed that "Eastside merchants" bankrolled the new union so as to create the same strife in Passaic "as has already happened in Russia and Hungary."[17] Many of these charges aimed at identifying the ATWA as a Jewish, pro-Bolshevik union whose very supporters were enemies of the Polish people.

Other leaders in the Polish community did their best to undermine the union. Glita's, Kowal's and Maciag's, the three largest Polish halls where workers had met during the 1919 strike all shut their doors to the ATWA. Likewise, just a few weeks after the walkout ended, the Polish priests cordially welcomed top officials of the Wool Council to a week-long church bazaar that practically every Polish organization in the city co-sponsored.[18] This was a seal of approval that the church and the benefit societies would never have granted to the ATWA, which challenged their own hegemony within the Polish community.

Anti-Bolshevism reached a peak in August 1920 as Russian armies approached Warsaw in a counterattack upon Polish forces that had invaded the Soviet Union in an ill-fated effort to regain Poland's 1772 boundaries. The Soviet advance led the priests to invoke Poland's historic role as the "bulwark of Christianity . . . against the barbarians of the

East" and they sponsored a number of meetings that intertwined the Polish national cause with that of Roman Catholicism. Though Father Monteuffel spoke at these gatherings, Father Kruczek, the popular Galician-born priest, engaged in the most strident assaults on the Bolsheviks, calling them "vandals" and "oriental fanatics" and declaring the war to be one "between the social order as built up during the past 2,000 years and the principles of anarchy." A rally of 10,000 Passaic Poles one day after "the Miracle of the Vistula," in which Polish armies repulsed the Soviets, capped the frenzied activity. At this mammoth demonstration, Polish women dressed in the costumes of their native regions, church choirs sang traditional Polish folk songs, and Fathers Monteuffel and Kruczek once again coupled Polish and Polish-American nationalism by thanking the U. S. government for its anti-Soviet stance.[19]

Just as Lawrence's *prominenti* used the Fiume issue, Passaic's ethnic elite took advantage of the events in Poland to enhance their own status in Polonia. But one should not necessarily assume that Passaic's Polish residents had to have anti-Bolshevism forced upon them since only a small number of Polish workers gave their support to a movement that espoused atheism. The hostility of Polish mill hands to the left had been evident in Passaic during the 1919 strikes when the leadership of the Polish handkerchief workers, unlike that of the woolen and worsted workers, continuously denounced Bolshevism. And as soon as the ATWA, whose founding convention had endorsed Bolshevism, arrived in Passaic, the handkerchief workers broke from the union.[20]

In an effort to minimize ethnic differences, the Passaic local held up the trade union as "the only place where the Jew and the Pole, the German and the Italian, the Catholic, Protestant, Jew and infidel sit together in harmony" but it did not win the support of many Polish workers.[21] That these divisions could be overcome became apparent in 1926 when Albert Weisbord, a Jew and a member of the Communist party assumed leadership of the walkout. During that strike, Weisbord pioneered a new approach to "the national question" by appealing to Slavs' anti-German prejudices through attacks on the "Kaisers," "Prussians" and "Junkers" who owned the mills. He defused the "Jewish question" by bombarding Passaic's Jewish commissioner of public safety, Abraham Preiskel, with criticism. These tactics proved so successful that Polish workers even took to calling Weisbord "Jecusko," meaning "Little Jesus." But unfortunately for the ATWA, the tensions between Jews and Poles and the Soviet Union and Poland crested in 1919 and 1920 and even the few fainthearted efforts to make use of anti-Germanism fell on deaf ears.[22]

In marked contrast to the Poles, Magyars and German-Hungarians played a prominent role in the union's affairs. Hungarian and German-Hungarian halls such as Zukers and Neubauers hosted the ATWA, and Garfield's Belmont Park, which was operated by the Magyar Ladies and Gentlemen's Association, served as the site for outdoor gatherings. A number of Hungarians spoke at meetings and Herman Virang, who edited the Passaic local's newsletter, also published *Szabad Szajto*.[23] In general, Magyars and German-Hungarians had a more cosmopolitan perspective than Poles. As an important indication of the more outward-looking viewpoint, Margaret Haray served in a leadership position during the 1919 strike and another Hungarian woman, Margaret Teller, became very active in the ATWA whereas Polish women did not even play a leadership role in the handkerchief strike, not to mention the ATWA.[24] The differing levels of participation in union affairs is partly attributable to the fact that Magyar women were far more likely to learn English than Polish women who, according to a government survey, "clung most tenaciously to their own language . . . and to their own national life and customs."[25]

European events also had a far different impact on Magyar workers than on Poles as Hungary was the only country outside of the Soviet Union in which communists gained power during the upheavals of 1919. During its brief reign, the Hungarian Soviet Republic nationalized industry, seized rural estates, and enacted a number of reforms that benefited workers. These changes received extensive publicity in *Elöre*, which was avidly read by Hungarian workers, and large gatherings in Passaic heard accounts of the revolution's progress from representatives of the newspaper. When Rumanian forces overthrew the Béla Kun government and the "white terror" commenced, a number of refugees—in what could be called a chain migration of leftists—came to Passaic.[26]

Besides the Magyars and the German-Hungarians, Passaic's Ukrainians continued to give considerable support to the left. Much like the Jews and Lithuanians, many Ukrainians viewed the Poles rather than the Soviets as their principal enemy because Poland had staked out a claim to eastern Galicia, the area from which most Ukrainians in the United States originated, while the Soviet Union had pledged to grant the Ukraine considerable autonomy. Federal authorities certainly considered Ukrainians a threat since this community bore the brunt of the Palmer raids. The Ukrainians, for reasons that are not altogether clear, did not participate much in the ATWA's affairs, but they played an extremely important role in the 1926 strike since that walkout came before

Stalin liquidated the Ukrainian communist leadership and snuffed out Ukrainian autonomy—moves that lessened support for the left among Ukrainian workers in the United States.[27]

For the most part, though, Hungarians remained the cutting edge of the labor movement in Passaic. When the OBU made a brief foray into the city in 1921, it used the Hungarian Workingmen's Home as its base. In 1926, a Hungarian workers' group instigated the strike; Gus Deak, a Hungarian, headed the strike committee; Neubauer's served as strike headquarters.[28] On the other hand, compared to Lawrence, there were fewer groups in Passaic with such a radical perspective. In fact, Hungarian participation may have hindered the recruitment of Slovaks who continued to bear great resentment against Magyars and who do not appear to have participated in the union at all.

The Independent Union and Other Sources of Opposition

As in Lawrence, the ACWA/ATWA version of industrial unionism failed to win acceptance among certain elements of the Passaic working class. In contrast with Lawrence, almost all of the opposition came from those who criticized the union for being too radical rather than for being too conservative. The ATWA lost support in Lawrence because workers compared it unfavorably to the OBU, but in Passaic, the union encountered difficulties because of the unfavorable contrast with the original Independent Union, which continued in existence. Although this organization had only a small membership and may have been secretly subsidized by the Wool Council, its pronouncements put the new union on the defensive and provide a good guide to the ATWA's vulnerability in Passaic.

Every time the ATWA planned an action, the Independent Union attacked it. Essentially, these assaults stressed three themes: that the ATWA lacked Americanism/patriotism; that outsiders controlled the union; and that it misappropriated or misused workers' dues payments. The last charge resembled accusations made by Legere since the Independent Union also accused the ATWA of being a "money grubbing machine" that paid exorbitant salaries to organizers who held "soft jobs."[29] As in Lawrence, the intellectuals' involvement in the ATWA lent a certain credibility to these charges. For example, a leaflet circulated at the time of the May 1920 strike agitation attacked the newcomers in a strikingly effective manner:

Workers, wake up. Those who are trying to make you go on strike do not work for a living. Some are preachers. What do they know about labor? Why do they stop preaching and become labor agitators? Because they could get more money out of your union dues. Where do the dues come from. Out of your pocket.

You work with your hands, forty-eight hours a week. The union leaders work with their mouths, one hour a day. Your toil supports these men in a life of ease. Can't you see these men are fooling you? Workers wake up.[30]

To further its cause, the Independent Union adopted a constitution that forbade "salaried positions" so that the union's services would be provided in a "clean and unselfish manner."[31] This same constitution kept the clause that provided for the expulsion of anyone working for an "outside union," and the independent organization constantly ridiculed Pluhar for going to New York for consultations with the ATWA's national leadership.[32]

Charges that the ATWA took "an apathetic stand on patriotism" had been used ever since Gus Roth and Louis Kymack had tried to create a split during the 1919 strike. This theme became closely linked with anti-Bolshevism and the founding meeting of the Independent Union called upon all those who opposed the Soviet Union to join forces with it. On May Day 1920, the UTW joined in these attacks when it placed advertisements in the Passaic newspapers accusing the ATWA of favoring the Soviet form of government as well as one big union, sabotage, and the general strike to take control of industry. The UTW's statement concluded with this query: "How can any textile worker . . . either join or hold membership in the Amalgamated Textile Workers of America and at the same time be loyal to our flag and American institutions."[33] Shortly thereafter, in Passaic's newspapers anonymously written notices appeared that reprinted excerpts from a Cedric Long article under the heading "The Gospel of Lenin and Trotsky—preached by Rev. Cedric Long, organizer." The culmination of the defamatory campaign came in May 1920 when the union's enemies hung effigies of Long and Pluhar at a strategic Dundee location so that mill employees would have to pass them on the way to work. Stuffed in the dummies' coat pockets were copies of *Elöre* and messages reading "Greetings to Russia sent by Pluhar" and "Lenin's friend."[34]

Confronted by these charges, the ATWA tried to present a more moderate image in Passaic than in Lawrence. Pluhar disavowed the founding convention's pro-Bolshevik resolutions and went to great lengths to portray the ATWA as a "responsible union." Unlike the Lawrence branch, the Passaic local publicized the signing of a collective-bargaining agreement between a New York City ATWA local and silk manufacturers that established a board of arbitration and talked about the need for the "suppression of the militant spirit." In keeping with this posture, literature distributed by the Passaic local stressed that the ATWA sought to win signed contracts that could realize practical gains for workers.[35] Significantly, the UTW advertisements did not even appear in Lawrence since workers there, who believed Long was more a friend of William Wood than of Lenin, would have laughed at the accusation that the ATWA stood for the IWW's principles.

Even within the ATWA staff, dissension developed as organizers criticized Pluhar for failing to give a complete accounting of his trips to New York City and protested when they discovered that members of the national union's staff were paid more than those employed by the local. In general, members of the Passaic local appeared more concerned about questions relating to finances than general principles and their votes on national-referendum questions were unanimous whereas the ballots of the Lawrence local were often split. The lack of either solid unionist or secularist traditions made it difficult to build a union based on mass participation among workers who were "less sophisticated and less experienced" than those in Lawrence.[36] As a result, Pluhar continued to carry a heavy burden of the leadership and it is not surprising that the attacks on the union often focused on him and led to his premature departure from the organization.

The Civil Liberties Controversy

As in Lawrence, Passaic city authorities made an all-out effort to impede the ATWA's efforts to organize textile workers. Active suppression had begun as soon as workers had moved away from the protective aegis of Turner and Kehoe, but intimidation of union officials and interference with the day-to-day conduct of the union reached new heights with the election of Abraham Preiskel to the city council and with his subsequent appointment as director of public safety in May 1919.

Preiskel, who was the son of Russian-Jewish parents, was the first east side resident to be elected to the city council since the switch from a ward to an at-large system of voting. A man on the make, Preiskel had promised to give eastsiders a greater voice in city affairs; however, Charles F. H. Johnson, who had deservedly earned a reputation for being the "kingmaker" of Passaic politics, served as his political mentor. Johnson

had wielded considerable influence in the city ever since he had successfully campaigned for the commission form of government and his standing had been enhanced when the Botany company in an effort to lessen
the stigma of its German ownership had appointed him to its board of
directors in 1918.[37]

As soon as he became public safety director, Preiskel moved against
the ATWA: city police arrested "outsiders," broke up meetings, seized
union literature, banned foreign-language speakers, and required the
union to obtain a permit for each meeting. Meanwhile, Preiskel continued Kehoe's policy of assigning detectives to all gatherings in order to
obtain stenographic reports of the speeches and to monitor those who
attended the meetings. Police interference proved most damaging in July
1919 when the ATWA tried to turn a brief Botany weavers' work stoppage into a full-scale walkout. At that time, Preiskel stationed himself at
the mill's gates, accused Pluhar of stealing workers' funds, and treated
Passaic as if it were a "closed city" to which organizers needed special
permission to enter.[38]

Much of the intelligence gathered by Turner and Preiskel served as a
basis for selecting the sixty Passaic residents whom detectives seized
during the Palmer raids and during two follow-up raids in the first week
of January. Police made their "greatest catches" at Ukrainian clubrooms,
but they also entered forty homes and took men and women from their
beds. Those arrested included Frank Latawiec, the ATWA's Polish organizer, and Alex Burlak and Wasil Kowilenko, whom Turner identified
as being "active" and "prominent" in the recent strike. Accepting the
congratulations of Frank Stone, chief of the Northern New Jersey Bureau
of Investigation, Turner pronounced himself "well satisfied" with the
raids but warned "we have not stopped yet." He meant what he said.
For on the night of February 1, in the style of the "slacker raids," members of the United American War Veterans and local police descended on
a Ukrainian dance hall and took thirty-five more suspected radicals into
custody. Forsaking his former "nice guy" approach, Turner refused to
give relatives any information on the detainees and one of those held, an
army veteran named Michael Marcinak, died while in custody at Ellis
Island.[39]

To workers who had turned to an outside organization because they
wished to break free of local authorities, the ATWA's inability to halt
police repression called into question the union's claim that it could bring
new resources to the fight against the Wool Council. Another sign of its
weakness was that the ATWA had not even been able to get Postmaster

Cowley to turn over $9,000 of the original union's dues money that had been given to city officials for safekeeping. Finally, in February 1920, the ATWA decided to challenge police interference with its affairs. This was one battle the union was prepared to fight since the ATWA leadership had close ties with the recently organized American Civil Liberties Union, which desired to aid workers in their fight to exercise First Amendment rights.[40]

The opening salvo in this campaign came when the ATWA and the ACLU co-sponsored a meeting for which they refused to apply for a permit. At this gathering, police dragged the recently released Frank Latawiec, who had been banned from speaking in Passaic, from the podium each time he attempted to address the crowd. When police in exasperation at Latawiec's persistence turned the lights off in the auditorium, the ATWA organizer dramatically read the New Jersey Constitution by candlelight. Preiskel responded to this act of defiance by requesting the city council to pass a new ordinance which forbade "all street parades, processions, street assemblies and public meetings" unless organizations obtained a permit twenty-four hours in advance. He claimed that the regulation was modeled on a similar one that had been enacted in Duquesne, Pennsylvania, during the recent steel strike, even though the Passaic statute actually covered a wider range of activities. Despite opposition from the Passaic Trades and Labor Council (PTLC), the *Passaic Daily News*, and the Associated Fraternities (which represented numerous civic and ethnic groups), it received unanimous support from city council members.

Soon after the passage of the ordinance, the ATWA and the ACLU again met without giving the police prior notification. City officials took no action but vowed to stop all gatherings once the edict took legal effect. But, a short time later, the ATWA and the ACLU held a third meeting without having secured written permission. Soon after this occasion, the ATWA arrived at an agreement with Preiskel by which he agreed to waive the requirement for the written permit so long as the ATWA informed police of all scheduled meetings. Though the ordinance remained on the books, the ATWA and the ACLU considered this to be a victory for their position and released a joint statement that declared Passaic to be "opened for free speech" and that pledged the city would "not be allowed to relapse into its former dark and closed condition."[41]

Preiskel backed away from his hard-line position partly because the PTLC threatened to call "a three-day strike" if the ordinance went into effect. Preiskel had tried to cultivate the support of the city's AFL unionists by assuring them that the ordinance was aimed exclusively at the ATWA. This offer of "personal immunity" failed to sway the PTLC because the Duquesne edict itself had been aimed at an AFL union. By citing this precedent, Preiskel aroused the suspicions of Passaic's craft unionists who, unlike Lawrence's CLU members,were not closely tied to the city administration.[42]

From an organizational standpoint, the free-speech fight revealed the strengths as well as the weaknesses of the Passaic local. Certainly, this type of encounter was ideally suited for Long's talents as he was far more effective in leading civil-liberties struggles than workplace battles. The controversy had the further advantage of allowing Muste and Long to make extensive use of their New York City contacts; leading civil libertarians such as Dr. Henry F. Ward of the Union Theological Seminary, Professor Underhill Moore of the Columbia University Law School, Albert de Silver and Louis Budenz of the ACLU, John Haynes Holmes of the Community Church, and Norman Thomas visited Passaic to participate in the joint ACLU/ATWA meetings, which received considerable national publicity. On the other hand, it is questionable whether the "liberal Protestant language," to borrow Henry F. May's phrase, made sense to the immigrant workers. The barriers were both cultural and linguistic as Budenz, who spoke Hungarian, was the only outside speaker who could communicate with workers in their native languages. Aware of its dilemma, the ATWA tried to involve the labor priest Father Kazincy of Braddock, Pennsylvania, in the campaign. But not only was Father Kazincy unable to go to the city, many of the free-speech meetings had to be held at the headquarters of the Workmen's Circle as police intimidation scared off proprietors of other auditoriums from letting the ATWA use their facilities. So effectively did authorities exert pressure that when Long decided to call off the battle, he cited the need to get hall owners "unloose again" as a major reason for ceasing to confront police.[43]

Although the ACLU wished to press the issue until the city actually repealed the repressive ordinance, Long preferred to "let the test of all this wait until we get the organization matters and our demands to the bosses settled in some way."[44] Long's position indicated he knew that having gained breathing space, the ATWA had once again to focus its attention on its principal enemy, the Wool Council. And ultimately, far more than anything done by the city administration, the manufacturers' ability to augment their already considerable power sealed the union's fate in Passaic.

Welfarism—Passaic Style

Except for Julius Forstmann's installation of a cafeteria and a few other minor changes, the manufacturers had shown little interest in welfare work prior to the 1919 strike. After the walkout, some of the mill owners altered their labor policies considerably though, as in Lawrence, their interests in welfarism varied greatly. Christian Bahnsen, a Passaic resident and president of the Gera company, took the lead. In the months following the walkout, this firm established an athletic association, a day nursery and child welfare center, an Americanization club, a stock subscription plan, and a new monthly magazine, the *Gera Mill Booster*.[45]

Bahnsen also tried to exploit the mill workers' resentment of shopkeepers. As in Lawrence, this effort came at the time of a December 1919 pay hike. At this time, Bahnsen personally addressed his entire work force and told his employees that the manufacturers had received reports from the clergy that storekeepers had "mulcted" their employees. And just like William Wood, Bahnsen threatened to "put up the biggest store in the city" if such "profiteering" continued. Of course, Bahnsen had no more intention than Wood of building such a store but by pandering to mill employees' resentments of Dundee's shopkeepers, he hoped further to demonstrate that he was genuinely concerned about his workers' welfare.[46]

Of all the mill owners, Julius Forstmann once again proved the most resourceful. Following the 1916 walkouts, Forstmann had originated the idea for the Wool Council and in the aftermath of the 1919 strike, he demonstrated a similar inclination to adjust his labor policies. His plant adopted all of the Gera's programs and added a Sick and Death Benefit Association. Under its operation, a deceased employee's family received death benefits and an ill employee received one-half of his or her pay up to twenty-six weeks if he or she had worked under two years and two-thirds of his or her weekly pay if he or she had been employed for over two years. Never one to miss an opportunity to increase the surveillance of his employees, Forstmann's plan guaranteed that a doctor would visit a worker in his or her home the day after having been reported as sick. Forstmann allowed his employees to vote on the participating doctors but he chose the names that appeared on the ballot—a method of selection that led the Passaic Practitioners' Club to protest loudly that Forstmann handpicked the doctors so they could become part of the Wool Council spy system.[47]

An employee-representation plan stood as the true centerpiece of

Forstmann's welfare programs. Under the provisions of its "joint agreement," elected representatives from the plant's fifty-three wards met with an equal number of company-appointed delegates four times per year. In addition, rules, amusement, housing, general welfare, and restaurant committees gave workers a sense of participation in planning the company's welfare activities and provided an outlet for grievances. As was often the case, management introduced the "reform" in order to encourage workers to develop shop-centered loyalties rather than industry-wide bonds.[48]

According to Robert W. Dunn, the company union's immediate goal was to "break" the ATWA local and though it did not accomplish this objective by itself, it proved quite effective. Run by Robert Reinhold, a New York City labor expert brought in by Forstmann to direct the company's welfare programs, the employee-representation plan initially aroused enthusiasm among Forstmann's workers. By 1926, many of them changed their minds and demanded that the company union be abolished but the damage had already been done to the ATWA.[49]

Lacking local ownership and always slower to make adjustments, Botany lagged behind in welfare work. Its only major initiative in 1919 involved the establishment of a life insurance program for employees. The company finally installed a lunchroom in 1920 because its board of directors had become concerned that without a "fully equipped cafeteria" the firm would only obtain "such employees as cannot secure positions at the other mills."[50] But the board turned down suggestions that it spend money on such minor improvements as chairs for female employees, metal lockers, and new dressing rooms or restrooms and the mill continued to be "conspicuously lacking in anything that might contribute to the health . . . of its workers."[51]

Botany of course maintained its membership in the Wool Council, which sponsored a series of new athletic programs, including baseball and basketball leagues and a "miniature Olympiad" for male and female workers held in the summer of 1920. Athletics provided workers with a healthy form of recreation that lessened some of the burdens of work and served as an important vehicle for the Americanization of immigrants who had rarely had an opportunity to participate in team sports. Wool Council secretary J. Frank Andres noted the socialization goals of these activities when he commented that many workers had been "educated along athletic lines" in 1920.[52] Athletic events also built loyalties to a particular company. At basketball games each team had its own cheerleaders and "rival" workers sat on opposite sides of the hall. As Andres also observed: "Every employee should become an athletic booster and support the team carrying the color of his mills."[53]

Even more so than in Lawrence, the new initiatives presented the ATWA with a quandary as it had to convince workers not to be fooled by the companies' largesse. When the Botany weavers struck in July 1919, the management announced that all those who participated in the walkout would lose their "bounty rights," which guaranteed them Christmas bonuses and inclusion in the life insurance plan. Pluhar called this "a rope around your neck to keep you in the mills" and "a trick to keep the workers disorganized," but these enticements may have limited the scope of the walkout.[54] At other times, the ATWA tried to discourage participation in mill dances and in athletic contests, and at one point an ATWA member complained that "some of the workers don't stop to consider that they could play baseball to their heart's content without any assistance from the bosses."[55] Perhaps this ATWA organizer did not understand that participation in an organized league with uniforms, umpires, trophies, and a decent playing field offered many advantages over sandlot baseball. This was a minor misconception but it mirrored the ATWA's dilemma in Passaic since the union had difficulty holding members when the manufacturers could provide more tangible "benefits" than the labor organization.[56]

The Wool Council and the Expanded Spy Network

Although welfare work helped to combat the ATWA, the Wool Council continued to believe that repressive techniques provided the best means to defeat unions. As in 1912 and 1916, extensive blacklisting followed the walkout and the partial nature of the second strike aided in the identification of militants. Most of the strike's organizers, including Pluhar and his two sons, never worked in the mills again. Naturally, the strike did not lead to any change in the mills' policy of requiring prospective employees to obtain a card from the central employment bureau. By 1921, an investigator for the National Association of Wool Manufacturers (NAWM) reported that the council had records covering over 50,000 workers. An additional "looseleaf book record" describing the work history of each employee supplemented the information contained on the card files. The NAWM agent considered the blacklisting operation to be so thorough that no "radicals" or "undesirables" escaped detection "no matter how often they change[d] their names."[57]

In the wake of the strike, the Wool Council buttressed its control over the work force through the use of clandestine agents, most of whom worked in the mills. One of the watchdogs' jobs was to help boost output; the Wool Council instructed them to keep a close tab on "any and everything that will tend to increase economy, decrease expense and stimulate production." The spies' primary task was to keep an eye out for "agitators" and they were expected to report "any person who complained about his wages or working conditions" or who expressed interest in joining a union. The agents also learned how to counter the arguments of radicals. Their instructions read in part:

An Americanization movement is going on throughout the United States. Americanization, when brewed down, is nothing more than the ability to speak some English and use common, ordinary, everyday horse sense. When a fellow worker spouts a lot of silly propaganda, you should put up a sensible argument based on the facts that will make a monkey of this would be trouble maker. Eventually he or she will see his or her fault and become sensibly American.

Intelligence gathering also extended outside of the mills as the operatives were told to "attend meetings, say where they are held. Give names of speakers and write up what they say. Mention number of men and women present. Furnish complete particulars and details concerning all meetings." In addition, the mill owners asked the informants to report all conversations that they had with employees on the way to and from work as well as all other incidental information that they obtained.[58]

Wool Council operatives actually secured places within the "innermost circles" of the Passaic local. Calling themselves the Workers Intelligence Committee, these agents periodically distributed leaflets that accused Pluhar of stealing funds from the local's treasury and that revealed damaging information about internal union affairs such as staff grievances and the drop-off in dues payments. At the time, the ATWA proved unable to identify the person or persons responsible for the leaks, which meant that a sense of distrust affected the top ranks of the organization. So effective was this Wool Council tactic that the ATWA considered the Workers Intelligence Committee to be a far greater threat than the Independent Union, whose pronouncements grew more and more palpably pro-company.[59]

While spying on workers became so pervasive in the 1920s that the decade could be properly termed "the age of industrial espionage," the Wool Council's network proved particularly fearsome and Robert W.

Dunn, who became an expert on such matters, thought that the Passaic manufacturers had created "the most efficient labor espionage system" that he had "ever known."[60] The impact on workers greatly concerned the ATWA leadership and at a July 1919 meeting, Pluhar almost had to plead with those present to take a strike vote: "Go ahead and raise your hands, don't be afraid. How do you expect to get anywhere if you are afraid to go after what you want."[61] By 1920, the labor writer Marion Dutton Savage, who visited a number of the ATWA locals, believed that the Passaic workers, unlike those in Lawrence, had become "so cowed" that they had "little initiative."[62]

Committed to open organizing, the ATWA really did not know how to combat the Wool Council's expanded apparatus. The union's best opportunity to expose the violation of "American ideals" came in November 1919 when the Wool Council overreached itself and spied on Alice Barrows Fernandez, a representative of the Federal Bureau of Education who had come to Passaic to investigate why so few immigrant workers attended public schools. In the course of her inquiry, she stopped at the ATWA headquarters where she had a long conversation with Pluhar and Dunn. A Wool Council agent who happened to be present gave Passaic's superintendent of education, Dr. Frederick Shepherd, a detailed typewritten account of Fernandez's meeting with the ATWA leadership. To the Wool Council's surprise, Shepherd told Fernandez that she had been spied upon, though Fernandez did not make this fact public until the Wool Council further angered her by denying the accusations and by claiming that "a corporation worth $20,000,000 ought to have some control over the public schools."

Outraged by the Wool Council's arrogance, Fernandez, who was the niece of former Speaker of the House Thomas Brackett Reed, took two steps that called attention to the damaging impact of the spy system. First, her final report held that a successful adult education program could not be created in Passaic "so long as an espionage system, so subversive of mutual trust and social confidence" remained in place. Second, she told the Passaic press about the Wool Council's spying and about her conversations with the Wool Council's representatives. Fernandez's revelations led a number of Passaic residents to call for the abolition of the spy system. And a progressive Republican state representative from Passaic, Grover Heinzmann, introduced a bill in the New Jersey state legislature to outlaw industrial espionage. A statement attached to the proposed bill specifically condemned the Wool Council's spy network for holding workers "in a virtual state of industrial enslavement."

The ATWA did its best to capitalize on the publicity but the organization proved too weak to mount a truly effective campaign against the Wool Council. Once Fernandez left the city, the publicity died down and while Preiskel and Mayor McGuire, who upheld the Wool Council at every turn, remained in office the local Republican party at the urging of Charles F. H. Johnson denied Grover Heinzmann renomination to the New Jersey Assembly.[63]

As a result of the Wool Council's surveillance, workers became so hesitant to enroll openly in the ATWA that the Passaic local in its dying days had to apply to the union's national office for special permission "to recruit local Passaic secretly" due to "the control exercised by the five large woolen manufacturers over the workers."[64] As it turned out, a clandestine organization of Hungarian workers at the Botany company eventually provided the spark that set off the tumultuous year-long 1926 strike. The extraordinary militancy of this walkout also suggests that in the long run, the spying and blacklisting bred resentments that resulted in the "big battle" that Dunn had been sure would come some day. But the ATWA, weakened by ethnic divisions and faced with workers' distrust of its leaders, lacked the know-how or the staying power to combat as formidable a foe as the Wool Council.[65] On the surface, the prospects appeared much better in Paterson, a city where workers were never "cowed" and where disgruntled UTW members were thirsting for a new, more militant organization.

Chapter Nine

THE ATWA IN PATERSON

The ATWA had good reason to be confident as it entered Paterson. The city's small shops resembled those in the garment industry that the ACWA and the ILGWU had organized with such great success. Silk workers, whether they be English, Jewish, Italian, or German very often had belonged to unions even before they had arrived in America and the Paterson local would not be required to convince workers of the need for a permanent organization. Given their class-based loyalties and secular orientation, workers were not likely to be deterred from joining a socialist-oriented union. Moreover, unlike the situations in Lawrence and Passaic, the walkout which had begun on 3 February 1919 had lasted only a few weeks—this increased the likelihood that the ATWA would be able to get workers out of the shops again if a strike movement developed.

Silk workers' disgust with the UTW's sleight of hand that had resulted in their receiving a mere two-hour reduction in hours in April 1919 further enhanced the ATWA's chances. The UTW's weakened position stood in marked contrast to its status in May 1916. At that time, the UTW had emerged with much of the credit for winning the nine-hour day. By 1919, the UTW appeared to be once again more concerned with countering the left-wing unions than with aggressively challenging the manufacturers.

A remarkable silk boom that actually led to some labor shortages gave the ATWA even more reason for optimism. So great was the speculative surge that during 1919 manufacturers had to bid against one another in order to purchase looms, and aspiring mill owners filed incorporation papers on a weekly basis. The growth came on top of the steady gains registered during the war and allowed the city to reverse some of the inroads that had been made by Pennsylvania firms.[1]

Sectorial divisions and sectarianism stood as the foremost obstacles to the ATWA's goal of building a single industrial union in Paterson. Not only did ribbon, broad-silk, and dyeing compose three distinct sectors, workers who labored in these branches had their own unique traditions. Ribbon weavers had developed a shop-centered work culture and looked to a past when they had exercised considerable job control. The organization of dyehouse employees had come in bursts and these workers had forged their solidarity during violent battles in the city's streets. Broad-silk weavers defy easy description since their work places varied from the cockroach shop to the thousand-loom Doherty mill, but Jewish weavers influenced by Bundist traditions remained the dominant element in this sector. Further complicating the ATWA's task, the IWW and the remnant of the WIIU were sure to oppose the new union; the IWW's objection to the ACWA's participation in the February 1919 walkout had already shown the harm that could be done by divisions on the left.

Establishing the New Local

To head the Paterson local, the ATWA had turned to Evan Thomas even though he had no experience in negotiating silk-price lists, which could be extremely complicated. The choice of Thomas was especially unusual in that the city had a number of labor veterans with considerable savoir faire in dealing with the manufacturers. This much could be said for Thomas, he threw himself into the job with the same intensity that he had approached nonresistance. A friend who visited him in August 1919 reported that he worked daily from 7:00 AM to 11:30 PM and expressed "hope" that he would "take a little time to eat in the near future."[2]

The Paterson local started out with a considerable membership; practically all of the Jewish members of the WIIU joined the ATWA while the Jewish branch of the Socialist Party, the Paole Zion, and the various chapters of the Workmen's Circle all encouraged their members to join the new union.³ A number of Socialist party activists also enlisted in the ATWA. SP adherents had been instrumental in putting together the coalition that had won the nine-hour day in 1916, and in 1919 party members had chaired meetings of the radicals' Eight Hour Day Conferences. It had always been their hope that a single industrial union could bring together all of Paterson's labor radicals. Those who joined the ATWA included frequent party candidates Frank Hubschmidt and William Derrick, Fred Harwood, who had also served briefly on the UTW's staff, and Charles J. Hendley, who had been on the executive committee of the People's Council for Peace and Democracy.⁴

Hendley headed one of the ATWA's major projects, the Amalgamated Textile Workers School whose declared purpose was "to educate the ATWA members so they could in turn educate our fellow workers." The school, which opened its doors in September 1919, conducted classes in English, citizenship, economics, and public speaking and instructed workers on how to run shop committees. The school also sponsored a lecture series in conjunction with the Young People's Socialist League, in which nationally known speakers gave presentations on a wide range of topics, including the black liberation movement in the United States, English imperialism in India, and political developments in such countries as Mexico and the Soviet Union.⁵ The school reflected the ATWA's own interest in education as well as the Bundist and Socialist party influences in the Paterson local, but these efforts at what might be described as "uplift unionism" did not necessarily interest those who did not share the same background as the ATWA leaders.

The Second Forty-Four Hour Fight

Upon coming to Paterson, the ATWA announced that its first objective would be to win the forty-four-hour week for silk workers. Manufacturers claimed that no action could be taken to alter the NWLB's forty-eight-hour edict as the text of the decision said it was to remain in force for the "duration of the war." According to the mill owners, this meant until a peace treaty had been ratified. Many workers, on the other hand, argued that since the ruling actually came in the form of a recommendation, it could be altered at any time.[6] Regardless of these fine distinctions, Paterson's silk workers chafed at the restrictions imposed by the NWLB and they directed much of their anger at the UTW for its role in the short-hours ploy.

Seven hundred hat-band weavers became the first workers to take action when they staged a successful two-week strike for the forty-four-hour week in July 1919.[7] Known as an "independent lot," the highly skilled weavers had often been the most aggressive of all of Paterson's workers since the hat-band branch faced little outside competition. Threats by the UTW to take disciplinary action against them only spurred them on as they relished their reputation for militancy. In 1916, they had been in the forefront of the nine-hour agitation and they had conducted a successful one-week strike for a pay increase in 1918. Proud of their separate craft identity, they had only joined the UTW's Ribbon Weavers Local 980 in 1918 and they expressed little regret about taking an action that so directly defied UTW president John Golden.

The ease with which the hat-band weavers won the forty-four-hour week forced the Paterson UTW to repudiate its support for the NWLB settlement, and the union announced that it intended to establish the shorter workweek for all silk workers on 4 August 1919. This just happened to be the date that the ATWA had already set for its own forty-four-hour walkout and the UTW's goal was to undermine the Amalgamated's strike movement. However, the mill owners now took the position that the NWLB forbade any alteration of the agreement for at least six months from the date of the decision. John Golden agreed with this interpretation and he convinced (or forced) the Paterson UTW to go along with his views. Consequently, the manufacturers and the UTW jointly declared that the forty-four-hour week would begin on 10 October 1919, an agreement that the UTW hailed as further proof of its ability to win gains "without strife and struggle."[8]

Naturally, this arrangement provoked an outcry from many segments of Paterson's labor movement. Ribbon weavers in particular expressed outrage over the "secret" manner in which the UTW and the manufacturers negotiated the accord and over the news that the national office had ordered Local 980 to expel the rebellious hat-band weavers. The UTW justified the expulsion edict on the grounds that all locals had to live up to written agreements if harmonious relations were to be maintained between manufacturers and the union. Although one member predicted that Golden would soon have "to expel the entire membership" of the ribbon-weavers' branch, the UTW, which often took an almost perverse pride in its willingness to oust dissident locals, professed to be fully prepared to do so if workers insisted on violating "solemn agreements."

This intraunion quarrel gave the ATWA a golden opportunity when over 7,000 silk workers walked out of the shops on August 4. Strikers included members of the ATWA and the IWW as well as disgruntled members of the UTW broad-silk and ribbon weavers' locals. Indeed, many UTW rank and filers viewed this as a "grudge" strike against their leadership and as a protest against the lack of democracy in the union.

Over the course of the next two weeks, most silk workers won the forty-four-hour week as well as a 12 percent wage increase to make up for the lost hours. The small broad-silk mill owners became the first manufacturers to give in as they could not afford a shutdown while they were backed up with orders. Since they were also prospering in the boom period and hours were to be reduced in two months in any case, larger manufacturers saw little point to holding out. By mid-August 1919, practically all broad-silk and ribbon shops had granted the eight-hour day and the forty-four-hour week. At last, with little national publicity, workers had won one of the chief objectives of the 1913 strike and brought the fight they had begun in the wake of the Armistice to a successful close.[9]

The ATWA won many members by virtue of its leadership of the walkout and the UTW had little choice but to squirm out of its commitment to the October 10 date. Claiming that one of the manufacturers who had signed the NWLB accord had granted the forty-four-hour week, the UTW on August 9 announced that the entire agreement had been abrogated and that UTW members now had authorization to strike. The latest in a long line of maneuvers, this tactical retreat was forced on the UTW if it was to have any hope of recouping its standing among Paterson silk workers. As it was, the UTW leadership remained badly shaken by the ATWA's ability "to put over the forty-four hour week."[10]

The Limits to the ATWA's Growth

Despite its impressive beginning, the ATWA proved incapable of expanding its base in Paterson. Unlike in Passaic and Lawrence, the union's difficulties could not be attributed to police interference though in June and July 1919, local authorities did make a concerted effort to destroy the ATWA when they banned all of the union's meetings, arrested

Thomas, charged him with "inciting opposition and hostility to the United States government by advocating the Soviet form of government in its stead," and conducted a raid on the ATWA headquarters in which they seized all of the union's files, membership lists, bank accounts, and correspondence.[11]

Police Chief Tracey suddenly halted the repressive campaign in mid-July. Evidently, local authorities had become concerned that the ATWA was about to launch a civil liberties campaign that would have proven a major embarrassment to the city. Upon his arrest, Thomas had declared that "if the police interfere, we shall gladly go to jail to vindicate these rights," and the Civil Liberties Bureau had already instituted a law suit against the city's police department.[12] The ATWA also received support from the Sons of Italy, which offered the union its hall for meetings, a sign that the union could count on considerably more community support than in Passaic. Though a Bureau of Investigation operative expressed puzzlement that Tracey had ceased the crackdown after having been so firm in "his desire to beat these people," the ATWA never again had any serious confrontation with local authorities.[13]

For the most part, internal rather than external factors account for the union's stagnation. The limits to the union's growth first became evident when efforts to recruit the dyehouse employees ended in failure. These workers, inspired by the weavers' success, had left thousands of dollars of goods to spoil in the vats and walked out of the plants in mid-August. These were precisely the type of unorganized and unskilled employees that the ATWA believed ripe for its industrial union message, and the new union quickly assumed direction of the strike. The Paterson local sponsored a number of mass meetings and parades, aided in the picketing of the dyehouses, and opened three stores to provide workers with food and other provisions. The ATWA also issued a national appeal for aid entitled "Oppressed Workers Call for Help"; it stressed the dyehouse employees' status as the most exploited group of Paterson workers. Since they were due to begin working on a forty-four-hour schedule on October 10, at the ATWA's urging, dyehouse employees demanded a 25 percent wage increase as well as shorter hours.

Taking on the dyehouses was more akin to tackling Botany and Forstmann & Huffmann than organizing the small silk shops since these plants had the wherewithal to hold out against the workers. Neither the National nor the Weidmann companies, which were the two dominant firms in Paterson, had ever dealt with unions, and a pledge by Evan Thomas that workers would never again leave the tubs without giving seven-days notice had no appreciable effect on their hard-line stance. By the end of September, the strike began to peter out and a rush back to the plants occurred on October 10 when the forty-four-hour week went into effect. The strike had not accomplished anything and the ATWA had lost its one opportunity to add this group of workers to its ranks.[14]

To a certain extent, the dyehouse employees' walkout failed because they received little support from the silk workers. Though the *New York Call* had expressed "absolute certainty" that there would be a sympathy strike, no such action materialized. The ATWA assessed its own Paterson shops for aid but otherwise the dyehouse employees' request for help went unheeded.[15]

The very nature of the ATWA leadership also hampered the strike movement as Evan Thomas remained deeply committed to pacifism while dyehouse employees had become accustomed to employing militant tactics. During the 1894, 1902, and 1913 strikes, the largely Italian labor force that lived and worked in the Riverside district had often assaulted strikebreakers. And unsurprisingly, though fairly restrained compared to earlier years, dyehouse employees in August and September 1919 once again attacked scabs and fought with police.[16]

Ever since they had arrived in Lawrence, the intellectuals had been troubled by workers' readiness to use force. At the time of the 48/54 walkout, Cedric Long had credited the ministers with exerting a "restraining and law abiding influence on the workers" and had refused to defend certain participants in the strike lest the union appear to be "countenancing" violence—a position that shocked Anthony Capraro.[17] During the dyers' helpers strike, the intellectuals continued to adhere to this stance and Thomas stated that the union's policy was to "hold the men back from rioting."[18] When the police arrested an Italian member of the union for carrying a concealed weapon (a broken broom handle with an iron roller attached), Thomas read the individual out of the union and commented that the ATWA was "not in favor of such actions and did not care to have persons responsible for them as members."[19] Norman Thomas, who became involved in the walkout, claimed that the ATWA had shown workers "the folly of violent tactics and given outlet to their spirit by carefully organizing picketing. They have aroused the social sense," he continued, "and restrained the man who will 'fix heem' with a brick by showing him how he will not only hurt himself but the good name of his comrades." Like his brother Evan, he viewed the ATWA as an organization that would set an example of "responsible industrial unionism" as opposed to "bitter and irresponsible 'mass action.'"[20] Unfortunately for the ATWA, such opinions did little to win the support of the militant dyehouse workers whose strikes continued to be marked by violence right through the 1930s.

The ATWA's lack of Italian cadre also hampered its efforts to recruit the dyehouse employees. One Italian organizer, Frank Falatio, served on the Paterson local's staff, but it is a sign of the union's weakness that Frank Coco had to be sent down from Lawrence to help with the organizing effort. Joseph Yannarelli, the one person who could have made a difference, remained outside of the ATWA orbit. Yannarelli was a long-time associate of Carlo Tresca and had served as an organizer for the Detroit IWW/WIIU between 1908 and 1918. Beloved by many of Paterson's silk workers, Yannarelli was later active in the 1924 strike and in 1933 spearheaded the organization of the AFL Dyers' Union.[21] In 1919, unlike his comrades, he remained loyal to the WIIU. Without his aid, the ATWA was further limited in its efforts to reach out to this group of workers.

Even with the loss of the dyers' helpers strike, the ATWA maintained its base in the broad-silk sector, where large numbers of Jewish weavers labored. During November 1919, the union led a number of shop strikes in which over 2,000 workers won pay increases ranging from 15 to 20 percent despite efforts by the UTW to sabotage the walkouts by instructing its members to cross the ATWA's picket lines. The ATWA also used the occasion to propagandize for the abolition of piecework and for the establishment of a uniform wage scale, two long sought-after goals of Paterson's unionists. Following the work stoppages, the ATWA claimed to have fifty-six shops under its control though the UTW retained the loyalty of many workers because it continued to receive concessions from manufacturers who preferred "to have their workers join the AFL rather than see them become members of the Amalgamated."[22] The ATWA even charged that the mill owners paid workers' initiation fees in the UTW—hardly an outrageous claim given the manufacturers' and the UTW's habit of working together in order to defeat radical unions.[23]

The UTW's ability to hold on to its broad-silk membership meant that by January 1920, workers in this sector had become divided into three groups. Approximately 1,500 broad-silk weavers belonged to the UTW. Most of these workers were of British backgrounds since the UTW continued to harbor resentments towards "foreign" workers and directed its organizing drives specifically at English-speaking workers.[24] The ATWA had enlisted about 2,000 predominantly Jewish silk weavers while thousands of Italian and Syrian and Armenian broad-silk weavers, who had arrived in the city just before the war, did not belong to a union.[25]

After January 1920, the ATWA's broad-silk membership remained stagnant. This was mainly because the ATWA's greatest source of strength—its large Jewish membership—also proved to be a source of weakness. The problems the ATWA encountered in this sector are particularly instructive as they illustrate how purely local considerations could determine the union's fate.

An explosive growth of the cockroach shop caused the union's dilemma. While over 175 of these shops were founded between 1915 and 1918, in 1919 alone over 170 more shops opened as Paterson was seized by a georgette crepe fever such as it had never seen before. By 1920, there were over 555 broad-silk shops in Paterson as manufacturers even converted abandoned churches into mills.[26] As in coal mining, the wartime expansion had been spurred by tremendous demand and by the industry's low start-up costs. That an army of small producers emerged in Paterson is also attributable to the entrepreneurial ambitions of Jewish workers as practically all of these "mushroom manufacturers" were Jewish weavers who jumped at the opportunity to go into business for themselves.[27]

Much as in the garment industry's subcontracting sector, these tiny shops often had the worst working conditions. The owners had a reputation for continually nagging their employees and for enforcing the pettiest rules and regulations—patterns that grew out of their own precarious financial condition. Weavers often had to work alongside the owners' relatives as well as the boss weaver himself. These family members often refused to strike when other workers walked out of the mills. The substandard conditions in the cockroach shops threatened to undermine the standards of all weavers in Paterson, a point made by Edward Zuerscher and Lewis Magnet as early as 1914 when they testified before the Commission on Industrial Relations.[28]

The vast expansion in the number of cockroach shops disturbed some members of Paterson's older and wealthier German-Jewish community who complained that even "butchers" and "cobblers" were going into the silk business and engaging in business practices such as Paterson's "curb exchange" that embarrassed the more established Jewish population.[29] The ease with which workers could buy their own looms on credit caused the most conflict within the Workmen's Circle, to which most Jewish weavers belonged. The controversy within the Workmen's Circle peaked in 1924 when some members who had become bosses kept their mills open during the strike—a development that stirred great controversy within the entire national organization.[30] But even by 1920, a branch had to be dissolved because most of its members had become "small bosses."[31]

The ATWA became concerned that it was losing members who were being lured away from the union by dreams of becoming rich. An article in the *New Textile Worker* ridiculed those who left the working class in order to become "a Guggenheim" and who instead ended up exploiting their own families in sweatshops. The desire of Jewish workers to become manufacturers also created problems for the ILGWU in the 1920s as many of their members moved in and out of the business world.[32] In the long run, efforts to build a permanent Jewish labor movement in the United States suffered from these trends. In the context of Paterson, the desire of many Jews to open their own shops restricted the ATWA's growth in the very sector where it had the most strength. This helps explain why, despite such a promising start, the ATWA local had reached its maximum membership by January 1920.

Sectarianism on the Left

A nasty fight between the ATWA and the remnant of the IWW also damaged the new union's efforts. Despite their dwindling membership, the Wobblies remained grimly determined to hold on to the approximately twenty-five small broad-silk shops still under their control. In August 1919, Frederick Blossom succeeded Adolph Lessig as head of the Paterson local. Trained as a medical doctor, Blossom had a most unusual background for a Wobbly; he had worked for the Associated Charities of Cleveland and been active in the New York Birth Control League. A member of the Socialist party, he had no prior experience as a labor organizer. Under Blossom's direction, the Paterson IWW enjoyed a brief revival when it established a new lecture series, a German Propaganda Group, and a Women's Education Committee. To aid these endeavors, the Wobblies began to publish *The Paterson Textile Worker* edited by Blossom, who had previous journalistic experience with *The Birth Control Review*.[33]

For all of these positive efforts, the Wobblies spent an inordinate amount of time attacking the ATWA. A front-page cartoon in one issue of their newspaper showed a textile worker portrayed as a fish going for bait that had the ATWA's name on it, and over half of the copy was devoted to criticism of the ATWA. At other times, the Wobblies made Legere's assaults on the intellectuals look tepid by comparison as they accused the ATWA leaders of being "sentimental college boys," "sky pilots" and "clerical gentry" who believed in "working class dependency on other than working class elements." Naturally, the ATWA's connection to the ACWA also brought forth abuse as the Wobblies claimed that the ATWA served as a "front" for the clothing workers union, which wished to absorb the textile workers in their "machine."[34]

Many of these accusations seemed designed to discredit the ATWA rather than to initiate a debate on the relative merits of the two types of industrial unionism. Already in 1916, the Wobblies' bitterness over their own decline interfered with efforts to build left unity in Paterson. Now, their hopes shattered by the nationwide wartime repression, the IWW engaged in far less principled criticism of the new union than the WIIU, which had lost the bulk of its membership to the ATWA.[35] Blossom's comments were particularly uncalled for as he came from the same type of background as the ATWA intellectuals and he appears to have been motivated by a desire to ingratiate himself with the Wobbly rank and file.[36]

This is not to say that the IWW's criticism lacked merit since the ACWA and the ATWA had taken actions that seemed almost designed to irk a union that had suffered so grievously at the hands of the Wilson administration. For instance, in a vain effort to curry favor with city officials when the ACWA came to Paterson in February 1919, it boasted about its efforts on behalf of the Liberty Loan drives and pointed with pride to Secretary of War Newton D. Baker's praise of the union's abstention from strikes during the conflict. The Wobblies also objected that the Paterson ATWA local, for what it viewed as opportunistic reasons, had billed itself as an "American Union for the Textile Workers of America" and had hung American flags in its office. The ATWA local had also expended a large sum in renting a hall, in hiring a paid staff, and in distributing literature—a further reproach to a union that had sustained itself in almost penurious fashion.[37]

On a more practical level, the IWW often took actions that harmed the ATWA. For example, during the dyers' helpers' strike, the IWW refused to hand over relief funds to Thomas because they claimed there was no guarantee that the money would not be used to pay the ATWA staff members. According to the ATWA, at the time of the November 1919 broad-silk strike, the IWW shops deliberately settled for a price list below that of the ATWA's in order to "sabotage" the walkout. The most bitter confrontation between the two unions occurred during a series of strikes against the Blake Company. This firm operated two shops; the ATWA controlled one of them and the IWW controlled the other. During the work stoppage, each union accused the other of scabbing, and a number of confrontations between the ATWA and IWW members occurred on the picket lines. In the midst of the conflict, the IWW denounced Thomas as a "socialist divinity student" and as an "outsider," which led the beleaguered Thomas to observe that "the IWW under Blossom exists only to sabotage the Amalgamated."[38]

Sectarian infighting became really fierce after federal agents seized seventeen members of Paterson's anarchist community along with "the richest storehouse of anarchist literature in the United States" in a raid on 17 February 1920.[39] Most of those taken into custody, including Ludovico Caminata, had resided in Paterson since the turn of the century. Caminata had at one time been the editor of *La Questione Sociale* until it was suppressed by federal authorities. When the officials arrested Caminata they accused him of continuing his propagandistic activities by clandestinely publishing another newspaper, *La Jacquerie* (The uprising). The Bureau of Investigation claimed that it had discovered Caminata's editorship of *La Jacquerie* through reading *La Folla*, the organ of the Italian Socialist Federation that had been exchanging recriminations with the anarchists. In actuality, an undercover agent had infiltrated Paterson's anarchist community and the government had known for some time that Caminata was putting out *La Jacquerie*.[40] The agents disguised their source of information in hope of furthering the division between the two groups of leftists. From their perspective, the strategy worked splendidly as the anarchists, who should have known better, accepted the Bureau of Investigation's account and accused the socialists of betraying them while the socialists replied that Caminata had previously acted in cowardly fashion by subjecting them to anonymously authored attacks.[41]

These raids affected the Paterson IWW since they had always had close ties with the anarchists and a number of their members had been seized by the federal agents. The alleged responsibility of the socialists for these arrests also gave the Wobblies one more reason to attack Carlo Tresca, Joe Ettor, and Arturo Giovannitti. Tresca and Ettor along with Elizabeth Gurley Flynn had been expelled by the IWW in 1916 for disobeying the union's instructions during the Messabi iron ore strike, and Flynn, Tresca, and Giovannitti had further aroused the Wobblies' wrath when they separated their cases from the IWW leaders who had been indicted in September 1917.[42] It is no surprise then that the IWW upon hearing of the latest "treachery" ran a front page headline in its national organ *New Solidarity* that read: "Rivals of the IWW Instigate Federal Raid at Paterson" and continued "Amalgamated and Political Groups play role of police informers against Italian workers." This dispute also gave Blossom and other Wobblies an opportunity to resume their criticism of the "ACWA machine" when they claimed Tresca and Giovannitti had been out to get Caminata ever since he had refused an offer to join the ACWA on the grounds that it was "a reactionary union masquerading under the cloak of a false radicalism."[43]

The attacks on the ATWA could not mask the IWW's own weakness. Further damaged by the arrests, in the spring of 1920, the IWW gave up all efforts to hold on to its organization. The ATWA also suffered as the constant bickering revealed the continued inability of the radical unions to cooperate. In this sense, the ATWA's hope that silk workers would "forget old factions and unite under a new banner" was bound to founder as one could hardly expect that the IWW would give its support to a union with which it had so many differences.[44]

The Silk Depression of 1920–1921 and the Open Shop Campaign

The prosperous period for silk ended abruptly in March 1920 when the "most disastrous" slump in the industry's history hit the trade. Of all manufacturers, those who produced georgette crepe were hit hardest. Production of these goods had been stimulated by the great consumer demand of 1916–1919 and small manufacturers had gone deeply into debt in order to purchase looms. By the summer of 1920, a number of these mill owners became hard-pressed as banks called in loans and other creditors demanded payment for goods or for services that had been rendered. These small manufacturers, in turn, became the first to impose wage cuts, and a number of mills reduced their workers' wages 15 to 30 percent during the summer of 1920. In those mills where workers staged strikes in protest against the cuts, bosses fired the old employees and hired replacements. Because unemployment in the broad-silk sector had reached the 40 percent mark by July, employers had little trouble finding other weavers to fill these positions.[45] Along with the cuts, many mill owners took advantage of the depression to impose stricter work rules, welcoming the opportunity to remind workers that they were "the virtual owners of the mills and not simply tolerated by the employees who work there."[46]

Though the ATWA suspended those who accepted the cuts for having "betrayed themselves, their union and their class," the union could do little to stem the wage reductions.[47] By mid-July, it became clear to the ATWA that workers faced losing all of their postwar gains. The ATWA also believed that only by acting in conjunction with the UTW—a union it had previously denounced as "reactionary"—could workers have any hope of holding back the employer offensive. For this reason, the ATWA put aside past organizational differences and along with the UTW co-sponsored a series of mass meetings. These gatherings sought to allow silk workers themselves to decide what action should be taken in the face of the manufacturers' onslaught.

At these assemblies, Evan Thomas displayed the same vacillation that characterized the intellectual leadership in Lawrence and Passaic. At the very first gathering, he told workers that he was "not sure" if a general silk strike was the "proper remedy" for the cuts. Rather than support a walkout, Thomas endorsed a UTW proposal that a tripartite conference including workers, mill owners, and city officials be convened in order to discuss the crisis. Paterson's Mayor Van Noort responded positively to this idea but the larger broad-silk manufacturers rejected the arbitration plan. The mill owners' refusal to meet with the unions led the ATWA and UTW members to vote jointly in favor of a strike that was scheduled to begin on 26 July 1920—a date set at a spirited mass meeting attended by 4,000 silk workers that served as a notable demonstration of how drastic wage cutting had brought members of rival unions together.

Quite predictably, at the very last moment, John Golden informed the Paterson UTW that the national union's executive board refused to sanction the strike call. Accordingly, the UTW broad-silk local withdrew its support for the walkout. Although the UTW continued to endorse shop strikes against wage cuts, this meant that the union would not give its approval to a general strike. The UTW's decision left the ATWA with the choice of either conducting the strike by itself or cancelling the planned walkout. While the ATWA leadership expressed "regret" and "surprise" at the UTW's edict, it once again chose the cautious course and called off the strike on the basis that it was "impossible for one union to do any-thing alone" as "the whole plan had been based on the principle of united action by all of the unions involved."[48]

To a greater extent than in the other cities, the denouement revealed the intellectuals' failings since in Paterson, the ATWA found its actions controlled by the very union it had condemned for lacking militancy. Indeed, much of the ATWA's campaign against the UTW had been based on the accusation that the craft union always sold workers out at crucial moments. There was certainly no reason to be caught by "surprise" by the UTW's decision as Lewis Magnet, the head of the broad-silk local, had been arguing all along against a general silk strike. And since John Golden had often accused the ATWA of being a "Bolshevik" organization, there was almost no basis for the belief that he would approve of a joint effort with them. To compound matters, the ATWA called off the planned walkout in the face of firm evidence that a majority of the organized broad-silk workers would respond to a strike call.

Naturally, the collapse of the general strike movement encouraged the bosses to continue with their wage cuts. By August 1920, large manufacturers as well as small mill owners had reduced workers' pay as much as 40 percent. In many cases, the installation of a new class of work became an excuse for additional wage slashes and union workers continued to be fired and replaced with non-union help.[49] Along with the wage reductions, Paterson employers joined manufacturers across the country in an open-shop campaign that public relations-minded businessmen, taking advantage of war-induced patriotism, had labeled as the American Plan. The Associated Industries of Paterson—the old Employers Association under a new name—took charge of this antiunion offensive. In a series of newspaper advertisements, the Associated Industries announced that henceforth it would oppose "any limitation upon the amount of work which may be accomplished in a given time"—a veiled reference to the enforcement of the one- and two-loom system of ribbon and broad-silk weavers. Echoing themes being heard from coast to coast, Paterson's silk manufacturers also declared their opposition to restrictions on the training of apprentices and to the participation of "outside" union representatives in the settlement of grievances. The ads praised "scabs" as "red blooded, independent American citizens" and manufacturers once again stated their intention to put a halt to the constant shop strikes in Paterson. As part of its campaign, the Associated Industries opened its own "free employment bureau," which aimed at ending all union control over the hiring of workers.[50]

The open-shop offensive signalled that the employers had decided to cease all forms of cooperation with the UTW. The Associated Industries took this step partly because the diminished strength of the left-wing unions meant that the manufacturers no longer needed the UTW's help in fending off the radical challenge. In June 1919, the ribbon twisters and loom fixers had signed a one-year contract that the employers hailed for guaranteeing labor peace. In the changed circumstances of August 1920, the mill owners refused to renew this agreement and would not meet with UTW shop committees that it had dealt with previously. The ribbon twisters and loom fixers, in turn, would no longer even reveal the names of their officers for fear that they would be fired.[51]

The manufacturers' moves discredited the strategy that the UTW had followed since 1916. Although James Starr, the head of the horizontal warpers local, now condemned the mill owners for conducting an "industrial war" against workers, a few years before he had praised Paterson's manufacturers for being "about as good a bunch of employers as I know anywhere."[52] Cooperation with the bosses had bred complacency within the UTW's ranks and its preoccupation with battling dissidents had cost the union the support of the very militants it needed at a time like this. Already, the wage slashes had led most of the broad-silk weavers to desert the UTW. In the midst of the open-shop campaign, it lost whatever ribbon weavers remained in the organization.[53] Only the horizontal warpers and the ribbon twisters and loom fixers locals remained from the UTW's highly successful wartime recruiting drive and the union never again played a leading role in Paterson.

Despite the ATWA's and the UTW's weakness, the Associated Industries only partially accomplished its goals. To employers, the hours issue became the central concern as the manufacturers claimed that Paterson was "the only important industrial city in the United States" that continued to operate on the forty-four-hour-per-week schedule. Consequently, the Associated Industries recommended that all Paterson silk firms begin the forty-eight-hour week on 17 January 1921. From the perspective of workers, the attempt to lengthen the working day represented the boldest attack yet on their postwar gains.

Mill owners had no difficulty in reimposing the forty-eight-hour week in the dyehouses as workers there lacked organization. In the broad-silk sector, so many mills were operating on partial schedules that it was impossible to reinstitute the forty-eight-hour week simultaneously. The crucial test came in the ribbon industry, especially since the ribbon manufacturers division of the Associated Industries had ardently backed this movement. In this sector, employees beat back the attempt to reimpose the longer work week. When the mill owners announced that workers had to report at 7:20 AM on 17 January 1921, the weavers and other ribbon mill employees continued to come to the shops at 8:00 AM.

Confronted with their workers' determination to hold on to the August 1919 gains, ribbon employers did not even try to lock workers out and hours remained set at forty-four.[54]

The ribbon weavers' success indicates that of all Paterson employees they were the best positioned to combat the employers' offensive that would come increasingly to center on the loom-assignment issue.[55] In addition, a new union, the Associated Silk Workers (ASW) emerged from the campaign as the only effective silk-workers organization in Paterson. The very success of this union helps explain why the Paterson ATWA local failed and for this reason, the early history of the ASW merits closer examination.

The Associated Silk Workers

The hat-band weavers, who had been expelled from the UTW, took the initial steps that led to the formation of the ASW. These workers, who were Paterson's foremost practitioners of "artisanal democracy," met together with a number of other ribbon weavers on 5 August 1919—in the midst of the renewed forty-four-hour fight—to found the new organization.[56] The ATWA had expressed great optimism that these workers would join its ranks since representatives of the UTW's Ribbon Weavers Local 980 had participated in the meetings of the radicals' Eight-Hour Work Day Conference in February 1919. Moreover, UTW ribbon weavers in New York City and Long Island who had also rejected the NWLB settlement were in the process of joining the ATWA and the union expected that the Paterson employees would follow suit.[57] The ATWA's failure to attract these workers dealt a severe blow to its hopes of building an industrial union in Paterson. If the ribbon weavers had joined the broad-silk weavers, the ATWA's membership would have exceeded the UTW's and the accession of these employees would have added large numbers of workers who had solid unionist traditions to the ATWA's ranks.[58]

The ribbon weavers did not scorn the ATWA because they opposed industrial unionism; in fact, the ASW's constitution called for an industrial-type of structure. Rather, the ribbon weavers rejected the ATWA primarily because they wished to belong to a local rather than to a national organization. An early ASW pronouncement stated: "What we propose to do is organize a silk union right here in Paterson that will be independent of outside organizations, we will run it ourselves," and almost all of the union's statements that followed stressed its desire to concentrate on "the problems at hand in the city with strictly local officers."[59] Although this localism had deep roots, it also grew out of the string of conflicts between ribbon weavers and the UTW's national office. Many of the ASW's founders had been especially upset by the UTW's policy of requiring central office approval for all strikes. Unfortunately for the ATWA, this experience had bred a distrust of all national unions. As one of the ASW's founders, Leon Chevalier, put it:

The silk workers don't have any paid leaders. The silk workers have brains enough to run their own labor organizations. . . . The only thing a labor leader can do is live on the fat of the land and sell the workers out when he gets his price. No labor leader is going to sell me out. That is why I belong to the Associated Silk Workers. We have no leaders to sell us out. . . .[60]

In the eyes of the ASW, a belief in local autonomy and democratic control went hand in hand. At a 1921 conference of independent textile unions, the ASW's official statement noted that "ours is a local organization, very democratic. There is no one in authority."[61]

Protective and defensive in orientation, ribbon weavers' own work experiences led them to frown upon the ATWA style of unionism. Their consciousness was forged in shop struggles against dilution and the stretch-out, and when ribbon weavers discussed their plight, they talked of the need to return to the 1894 price list. A union headed by a man who had never run a loom had no appeal to them and when they searched for leaders (they had them despite their disclaimers) they turned to men like Thomas Bottomley, Fred Hoeschler, and William Westerfield who had years of experience in the silk industry.[62] Ever ready to be convinced that their own interests could not be met by national unions, they had defied both the IWW and the UTW when these organizations had shown a lack of sensitivity to their needs and traditions.

As one might suspect, the ASW's ideological orientation differed sharply from the ATWA's. In contrast to the ATWA's sponsorship of a wide-ranging educational program that dealt with national and international affairs, the ASW concentrated on exclusively shop-level issues. Significantly, Jewish workers who never shed the Talmudic habit of disputation even when they moved into a more secular world played little role in its affairs.[63] In its world view, the ASW actually had much in common with nineteenth-century unions such as the Knights of Labor, which divided the world into producers and non-producers, and the

ASW's constitution spoke of the "inevitable conflict between those who do the work of the world and those who live in ease and idleness from their labor."[64] In style and content, the ASW most closely resembled the independent shoe workers' organizations founded in the early 1920s in Lynn and Haverhill, Massachusetts. In both cases, workers rebelled against the attempts of national unions to impose settlements on locals with a strong sense of craft and local autonomy.[65]

Following its founding, the ASW experienced a slow but steady growth. It first concentrated on winning over those ribbon weavers who remained within the UTW—a task that it had accomplished by the fall of 1920. The ASW did not actually conduct a walkout until spring 1922 when 500 ribbon weavers at the Johnson-Cowdin plant fought a fourteen-week strike that prevented a return to the forty-eight-hour week. During the next few years, the ASW concentrated on preventing any further deterioration of working conditions and on organizing the broadsilk weavers. Its shop-level success attracted IWW veterans such as Adolph Lessig and Ewald Koetggen as well as Joseph Yannarelli to its ranks. This steady determination to build an organization on sound footing allowed the ASW to lead a four-month strike in 1924 that prevented some of the broad-silk mill owners from imposing the four-loom system. Notably, workers in 1924, as in 1913, fought against the stretchout. Only unions solidly grounded in the workplace could hope to lead the gritty battles of silk weavers who by 1923 had taken to referring to themselves as "The Martyred Workers of Paterson."[66]

Unlike the ASW, the Paterson local of the ATWA could not survive the 1920–1921 depression. It participated in the January 1921 effort to preserve the forty-four-hour week and tried to woo the UTW's disaffected broad-silk weavers but nothing could stem the branch's decline. Of the union's activities, only the educational work remained in place and in September 1921 the ATWA admitted its failure and surrendered its Paterson charter to the ASW.[67] In contrast, silk locals in Allentown, in Norwalk, Connecticut, and in Northampton, Massachusetts, maintained themselves until the ATWA's demise in 1925. But the victim of weak leadership, ideological rivalries, sectorial divisions, business ambitions of Jewish workers as well as of the 1920–1921 depression, the Paterson local proved no more successful than those in Passaic and Lawrence and thus the three branches in which the ATWA had placed its greatest hopes were essentially finished a mere two years after their founding.

Chapter Ten

CONCLUSION:
THE LOCALS' FAILURE

Those who attempted to establish unions in mass-production industries such as textiles faced an imposing set of barriers. Companies granted wage increases at strategic times, welfare programs weaned workers away from unions, the blacklist effectively eliminated labor organizers, and corporations used economic downturns to reassert their power over the work force. Notably, in Passaic and Lawrence some of the employers made effective use of a carrot-and-stick approach when the Forstmann & Huffmann and the American Woolen companies both spied on workers and engaged in other repressive activities while at the same time they founded welfare programs that met many of the workers' needs. This successful linkage of paternalism and repression explains in part why during the next round of strikes in Lawrence and Passaic, the work stoppages focused on the Pacific and the Botany mills—two firms that made little effort at welfarism. And in Paterson's silk industry, where employers' need for skilled labor rendered the blacklist ineffective and where companies lacked the surplus capital to spend on welfare, strife remained continuous through the 1920s.

External factors alone do not account for the failure of the three locals since the union suffered grievously from a number of internally generated problems. Three in particular stand out: (1) the difficulty of uniting workers with widely varying political and cultural traditions; (2) workers' lack of faith in national unions; and (3) the inability of the intellectual cadre to win the trust of workers.

Ethnicity and Religion

In examining the cultural and ethnic barriers that separated workers, the categories "old" and "new" are of little use as groups such as the Irish and the Poles though arriving in America at different time periods shared a common perspective. The role the church played in particular communities is of far more importance than date of arrival in determining whether a group had a radical/conservative, inward/outward looking, or cosmopolitan/particularistic perspective. While mill owners benefited from these cultural divisions they did not create them and did not even have to work very hard to exploit them as church-connected groups and those with an anticlerical orientation had basically incompatible worldviews.

In the Irish, French-Canadian, Polish, and Slovak communities, the Roman Catholic Church had become identified with the struggles of an oppressed group rather than with the ruling class.[1] For these ethnic groups, the church served as the social glue that bound people together since workers' children attended parochial schools, priests defended the national cause, and the church structured much of the communities' social life. Even though the U.S. Roman Catholic Church in the fall of 1919, at Father John Ryan's behest, had adopted a liberal program of social reconstruction, formal positions such as this had little immediate impact on the local level where ardent Catholics remained hostile to socialistically inclined unions.[2] One could argue that religious Catholics were bound to have been particularly opposed to a union headed by former Protestant ministers, but they had also remained aloof from the IWW as all radical unions, regardless of their leadership, drew opposition because they challenged church-based loyalties.

It is more difficult to generalize about groups that gave significant support to socialist unions. To a certain extent, left-wing organizations drew their membership from those such as the Germans, German-Hungarians, Franco-Belgians, northern Italians, and Jews who had prior industrial experience. But the radical sympathies of many Lithuanians, Hungarians, and southern Italians demonstrate that the real connecting link is the extent to which groups had developed an anticlerical perspective or had organized their community life outside of the church.

Each nationality had its own unique viewpoint on religion. Franco-Belgians hated the church and took pride in their identity as freethinkers. Many Lithuanians had rejected the Roman Catholic Church but still belonged to an independent parish. Southern Italians often ridiculed their priests and yet participated in religious pageants and festivals. Jews had rejected orthodoxy but still respected the Jewish tradition. Hungarians might have attended church regularly but exhibited a lack of religious fervor compared to Slovaks and Poles.[3]

In each case, regardless of whether members of these nationalities attended church or not, unlike the religiously based groups, they had founded a wide range of secular-oriented organizations such as singing societies, drama groups, cooperatives, and mutual aid societies that lacked any connection to the church. These organizations served as a training ground for future labor leaders and often encouraged a secular or anticlerical perspective. To the most active members and especially to socialists, opposition to church authority, hierarchy, and ritual was an essential component of their radicalism. And yet, they had to recruit workers who remained devoted to a church that viewed socialism as a form of heresy and who often believed that socialists lacked sufficient concern for their own national causes.

By the 1930s, these divisions proved to be of less importance. At that point, labor activists developed a common language that united the sons and daughters of immigrants under the twin banners of the CIO and the New Deal. For this to occur, socialists and communists had to abandon or disguise their radical backgrounds while others had to alter traditional beliefs in order to embrace liberalism and social unionism.

Localism and the Local Context

The variation in the local settings also made it difficult to build a single national industrial union. That workers in the neighboring cities of Passaic and Paterson had little contact with one another is the most obvious example of the fact that workers did not necessarily develop bonds even when they shared a common history of militancy. And of course, the ATWA quickly learned how even woolen and worsted centers such as

Lawrence and Passaic that appeared on the surface to be similar could differ.[4]

Of most significance, in each city the ATWA faced a challenge from a rival union that appealed to workers' distrust of national organizations. In Lawrence, the OBU found a receptive audience among former Wobblies with direct actionist traditions; in Passaic, the Independent Union retained a base among the inward-looking Polish and Slovak workers; and in Paterson, the ASW gained adherents among ribbon weavers whose vision did not extend much beyond the immediate work place. Interestingly, although the three varieties of localism had different roots and varied greatly in terms of ideology, they made use of a common language as the OBU, Independent Union, and the ASW all questioned the need for dues to be sent to a national headquarters, criticized the employment of a paid staff, and challenged the very concept of centralized unions. Indeed, the very power of these appeals suggests that perhaps historians have been overly preoccupied by the battle between advocates of craft and industrial unionism and have ignored the extent to which workers disagreed on questions related to centralization versus decentralization and national versus local unions.

To the ATWA leadership, the extent to which workers directed criticism at the union because of its connection to the ACWA proved to be the most unexpected development. In Lawrence, direct actionists wanted nothing to do with a union that signed contracts; in Passaic, Polish workers distrusted a New York-based, Jewish-led union, and in Paterson, ribbon weavers evinced little desire to affiliate with other textile workers, not to mention the clothing workers. Although advocates of local control employed the language of democracy, they at times made demagogic appeals to the rank and file that made light of the need to develop ties with those in other communities. Rhetoric of this type still resonated through mill towns in the 1930s but by then far more workers were willing to accept a degree of centralization even if this meant surrendering control over their own affairs.

The Intellectuals' Leadership

Weak leadership provided by men who were thrust into positions for which they were not prepared hurt all three locals. The result of inexperience, their own naiveté, and an overintensity they brought to their work, the intellectuals' shortcomings became obvious on both a day-to-day basis and especially at the moment of crisis in each city when their reluctance to take decisive action became most evident. None of the locals proved able to recover from the debacles of the spring and the summer of 1920 and after that point their memberships rapidly declined. By way of contrast, the ATWA branches in localities such as Webster, Massachusetts, the Pawtuxent Valley of Rhode Island, and Rockville, Connecticut, remained viable until the union's death in 1925.[5]

Although all of the intellectuals had left the ATWA by 1921, they did not draw the same conclusions from their experiences. Three of them, Evan Thomas, Harold Rotzel, and Cedric Long, withdrew completely from the labor movement after 1920. Thomas, who was especially ill prepared for the maelstrom of Paterson, became a medical doctor and never again played an active role in labor affairs. Rotzel, who later admitted that his talents "were not well suited to the work of the labor movement," turned to farming to make a living. Embittered by the virulent opposition he faced, Rotzel warned potential "C.O. Knights" about the pitfalls of becoming involved in the labor movement because, in his view, workers would eagerly embrace pacifism when it was a "wise and helpful strategy" but would abandon it as soon as "the proletarian revolution were upon them."[6]

Cedric Long, who became active in the cooperative field—a movement better suited to his talents and which absorbed his energies until his death—best expressed the viewpoint of those intellectuals who left the labor movement. In an article he wrote in 1921, Long said that he had come to understand why workers had developed a distrust for the college-educated cadre since any outsider "pretending to voice the same grievances" as workers would always be in an "artificial position." According to Long, he now realized that the willingness of workers to accept help during a strike from almost any outside source had obscured the difficulties that the intellectuals would eventually face. As a result of his own personal reevaluation, Long had embraced the cooperative cause because it appealed "to all men of good will on the basis of their common humanity rather than as members of a fixed class or group."[7] Although Long failed to make this point, the rejection of a class perspective stemmed in part from his own inability to guide workers in the direction he wished them to follow.

The withdrawal of Thomas, Rotzel, and Long from labor affairs confirmed the IWW's prediction that the "philanthropic clergymen and sentimental college boys" would "get tired of their present jobs and look around for a new toy to play with."[8] But other intellectuals who entered labor's ranks via the 1919 strikes and the ATWA stuck with the labor movement and made significant contributions in the field of labor education—an interest they had begun to cultivate in the textile union and in which they truly found their metier. In 1921, Paul Blanshard left the ATWA's Utica local and became director of the ACWA's highly successful educational program in Rochester, New York. He later wrote a number of educational pamphlets on labor issues before embarking on his own personal crusade against the Roman Catholic Church. Robert Dunn, who enhanced his own education through his confrontation with the Wool Council, became an expert on labor spying and company unionism and later returned to Passaic during the 1926 strike. Muste became director of Brookwood Labor College, a training school for union organizers that was probably the most successful institution of this type in the history of the American labor movement.[9]

Muste typified those who remained within the labor fold as he demonstrated an ability to learn on the job and to bend his principles to fit the situation. He took such actions when on spurious grounds he nullified Legere's first election as head of the Lawrence local and when he deliberately distorted the ACWA's May 1920 decision not to absorb the ATWA in order to make it appear as if the opposite result had been achieved. At one point, Muste even asked Anthony Capraro if it were possible to get the Lawrence local to "spontaneously" pass a resolution supporting an ATWA merger with the ACWA.[10] These were of course the types of maneuvers that successful labor leaders had to engage in, and Muste's ability to make this adjustment enabled him to remain within the labor field until his return to peace work in 1936.

As an indication of his disappointment with the ATWA, Muste said little in his autobiographical account about his two-year stint as head of the union although he devoted considerable space to the 1919 Lawrence strike.[11] But when the labor writer George Soule in 1923 conducted a study of the relationship between intellectuals and the labor movement, Muste told him that an aspiring leader should first "actually work in some industrial establishment and serve as a plain member of a union." Soule agreed with this position—a conclusion he arrived at after having interviewed a number of the ATWA veterans.[12] Interestingly, Alice and Louisa Kimball, who decided on their own to go to Paterson, followed precisely this course. These two sisters, who came from a socially prominent family arrived in Paterson after having studied to be social workers at Smith College. Both took jobs in a mill; Alice worked as a ribbon weaver and Louisa as a winder. According to Alice Kimball, her employment gave her a "new and surprising respect" for workers:

As a winder, you're "inside" with a vengeance. You face the same sense of wearing monotony. You have to swallow your injured pride when you have to kow-tow to the boss. You rage like the others at any attempt to overthrow the precious eight-hour day. And just like the rest you sit around when unemployed and watch your savings ooze away and wonder why industry runs on such a stupid basis when you want work and can't get it.[13]

While the Kimballs held the mistaken notion that intellectuals could be "just like" other workers, their mill experience allowed them to gain workers' trust. Louisa eventually served as an officer in the ASW and both women remained active in the Paterson labor movement through the difficult days of the 1920s.[14] Mill employment was less of an option in Lawrence and Passaic, but the Kimballs' determination contrasts with the ATWA cadre's tendency to give up the fight as soon as the union's fortunes began to decline. Psychologically unprepared for the long-term battle and lacking the ideological commitment that later carried the Communist party labor organizers through defeat after defeat, those intellectuals who remained within the labor movement preferred settings that made more direct use of their talents.

The ATWA Locals and the Course of Industrial Unionism

In a 1921 article, William Z. Foster warned labor leaders about the dangers of "sterile utopian unionism." According to Foster, radical industrial unions had failed because they had been "built around certain ideas not held by the great masses" and had compounded their error by needlessly pulling militants out of the AFL.[15] Although he specifically exempted the ACWA from his critique, the ATWA was precisely the type of union that Foster had in mind when he wrote this piece. While Foster later reversed his own position, his critique provides a good framework for a final assessment of the three locals and by implication of the ATWA's efforts to organize the textile industry.

In some ways, Foster was correct. In particular, the ATWA's very founding reflected a form of utopianism since it was foolhardy to think a new union could organize the entire textile industry. After he left the

ATWA, Muste realized that it would have been far more sensible to build a bridgehead in a specialty branch such as hosiery or carpet weaving before even thinking of tackling the giant firms.[16] This tendency to set out impossible goals also led to the ATWA's 1920 campaign aimed at winning a 50 percent pay increase for textile workers. By asking for such a large increase, Muste and the other leaders hoped to dramatize the low level of wages in the textile industry. On the other hand, by making a demand that the union could not win, the ATWA exposed its own weakness and lack of workplace focus.

Ultimately, though, one has to consider that unions such as the ATWA resulted from mass action far more than from the efforts of radical leaders. Without the three 1919 textile strikes, the ATWA would never have been created. Whatever the faults of the union, they stemmed from the hopes that had been generated during the world war rather than from the mistaken notions of a few labor radicals. In this sense, the ATWA locals were very much part of an era during which workers bravely but unsuccessfully challenged capitalists' control over their working lives.

Notes

1. Introduction

1. J.B.S. Hardmann, ed., *American Labor Dynamics in the Light of Post-War Developments* (New York, 1928), 10.
2. For the ACWA's founding, see Matthew Josephson, *Sidney Hillman, Statesman of American Labor* (New York, 1952), 86–110; for the "new unionism," see J. M. Budish and George Soule, *The New Unionism in the Clothing Industry* (New York, 1920).
3. The best account of the ATWA is in Marion Dutton Savage, *Industrial Unionism in America* (New York, 1922), 250–276.
4. Two studies that use the IWW era as an end point are J. D. Osborne, "Industrialization and the Politics of Disorder: Paterson Silkworkers, 1880–1913" (Ph.D. diss., University of Warwick, 1980) and Donald Cole, *Immigrant City, Lawrence, Mass., 1845–1921* (Chapel Hill, 1963). Cole's title is extremely deceptive as the book contains only a small amount of post-1912 material.
5. For this periodization, see David Montgomery, *Workers' Control in America* (Cambridge, 1979), chap. 4.

6. For the history of the UTW, see Robert R. R. Brooks, "The United Textile Workers of America" (Ph.D. diss., Yale University, 1935). After the UTW's 1919 organizational gains, the union had enrolled 19.1 percent of all cotton workers, 15 percent of all silk workers, and only 1.8 percent of all woolen and worsted workers. See Brooks, "The United Textile Workers of America," 59.

7. Marc Karson, *American Labor Unions and Politics* (Boston, 1958), 253–254.

8. For the appeal of the one big union idea in a number of countries, see Larry Peterson, "The One Big Union in International Perspective: Revolutionary Industrial Unionism, 1900–1925," in *Work, Community and Power: The Experience of Labor in Europe and America*, ed. James Cronin and Carmen Sirianni (Philadelphia, 1975), 49–87.

9. For the IWW-led strikes in Lawrence and Paterson, see Melvyn Dubofsky, *We Shall Be All* (Chicago, 1969), chaps. 10, 11. For IWW activity in the other cities, see Michael Ebner, "The Passaic Strike of 1912 and the Two IWW's," *Labor History* 11 (Fall 1970): 452–466; Mary T. Mulligan, "The 1912 Strike," in *Surviving Hard Times: The Working People of Lowell*, ed. Mary Blewitt (Lowell, 1982), 79–103; Robert E. Snyder, "Women, Wobblies and Workers' Rights: The 1912 Textile Strike in Little Falls, New York," in *At the Point of Production: The Local History of the IWW*, ed. Joseph Conlin (Westport, Ct., 1981), 27–48.

10. In 1920, the populations of Paterson, Passaic, and Lawrence were 135,875, 63,841, and 94,270 respectively. See U.S. Department of Commerce, *Fourteenth Census of the United States Taken in the Year 1920* (Washington, D.C.), 1:229, 258.

11. Gerald Rosenblum, *Immigrant Workers: Their Impact on American Labor Radicalism* (New York, 1973).

12. Although I recognize that one can always cite exceptions, I believe it is possible to make overall generalizations about ethnic groups.

13. John Bodnar, *Immigration and Industrialization: Ethnicity in an American Mill Town, 1870–1940* (Pittsburgh, 1977); John Bodnar, *Workers' World: Kinship, Community and Protest in an Industrial Society, 1900–!940* (Baltimore, 1982).

14. For a historian who has written perceptively about the World War I era, see David Brody, *Steelworkers in America: The Nonunion Era* (1969, rpt. New York, 1960).

15. Bruce Laurie, *Working People of Philadelphia, 1800–1850* (Philadelphia, 1980); Peter Friedlander, *The Emergence of a UAW Local: A Study in Class and Culture* (Pittsburgh, 1975).

16. There are a number of fine studies that deal with the attitudes of specific immigrant groups towards unions and radicalism. See Victor R. Greene, *The Slavic Community on Strike: Immigrant Labor in Pennsylvania Anthracite* (Notre Dame, Ind., 1968); Edwin Fenton, *Immigrants and Unions, A Case Study, Italians and American Labor* (New York, 1975); Arthur Liebman, *Jews and the Left* (New York, 1979); Michael Karni, Matti E. Kaups, and Douglas

J. Quilla, eds. *The Finnish Experience in the Great Lakes Region: New Perspectives* (St. Paul, Minn., 1975).

2. The War and the Textile Worker

1. *American Silk Journal*, 35 (March 1916): 30; National Archives, Washington, D.C., Record Group (RG) 2, Records of the National War Labor Board, Docket #1123, "United Textile Workers of America vs. Silk Manufacturers Conference Committee, March 13, 1919," 75, 130–131.
2. Grosvenor B. Clarkson, *Industrial America in the World War* (Boston, 1923), 442; National Archives, RG 131, Records of the Alien Property Custodian, Report of Thomas Prehn, President, Botany, Oct. 22, 1918, Box 44; James Bruce McPherson, "The American Woolen Company's Quarter-Century Record," *Bulletin of the National Association of Wool Manufacturers* (hereafter cited as *Bulletin of the NAWM*), 54 (October 1924): 473–485; *Lawrence Sun American* (hereafter cited as *LSA*), Feb. 3, 1916.
3. National Archives, RG 131, Minutes of the Botany Board of Directors, June 18, 1917, Box 48, and Weekly Letter of the Gera Board of Directors, Aug. 17, 1918, Box 124. For the steady operations of the Passaic mills even during the 1913–1915 downturn, see New Jersey Bureau of Industrial Statistics, *37th Annual Report* (1914), 23, *38th Annual Report* (1915), 21.
4. Phillip B. Scranton, "An Exceedingly Irregular Business: Structure and Process in the Paterson Silk Industry, 1885–1910," in Phillip B. Scranton, ed. *Silk City: Studies on the Paterson Silk Industry, 1860–1940* (Newark, N.J., 1985), 35–72; McPherson, "The American Woolen Company's Quarter Century Record," 477–479.
5. New Jersey Bureau of Industrial Statistics, *40th Annual Report* (1917), 22; *Paterson Press Guardian* (hereafter cited as *PPG*), Aug. 8, 1918. Information on average yearly earnings on woolen and worsted workers is not available after 1916.
6. Federal Council of Churches, *Report on the Strike in the Textile Mills of Lawrence, Massachusetts, February–June 1919* (New York, 1920), 19.
7. *Lawrence Evening Tribune* (hereafter cited as *LET*), Dec. 4, 22, 1914, Jan. 9, 11, 26, 1915.
8. One way by which mill workers could supplement their incomes was through mill thefts. In one year alone, there were 500 arrests in Passaic for the theft of wool, yarn, or cloth, which was usually hidden in workers' clothes or placed in lunch buckets. That this is the figure merely for arrests indicates that the practice was quite widespread. See *Passaic Daily News* (hereafter cited as *PDN*), Feb. 7, 1920.
9. For historians who emphasize immigrants' achievement orientation, see Josef Barton, *Peasants and Strangers; Italians, Rumanians and Slovaks in an American City, 1890–1950* (Cambridge, 1975) and John W. Briggs, *An Italian*

Passage: Immigrants to Three American Cities, 1890–1930 (New Haven, 1978). For a historian who emphasizes the search for security, see John Bodnar, "Immigration and Modernization: The Case of Slavic Peasants in Industrial America," in Milton Cantor, ed. *American Working Class Culture; Explorations in American Labor and Social History* (Westport, Ct., 1979), 332–360; *Worker's World,* 165–191. For a recent work that takes a middle ground, see Ewa Morawska, *For Bread with Butter, The Life-Worlds of East Central Europeans in Johnstown, Pennsylvania* (New York, 1985).

10. Because these strikes played a crucial role in the revival of the labor movement in each city, they are discussed in chapters 3–5.

11. For the American Woolen Company's wartime wage increases, see *Bulletin of the NAWM,* 50 (July 1920): 333. For a similar policy in the steel industry, see Brody, *Steelworkers in America,* 183–184.

12. *Daily News Record,* April 27, 1917, May 4, 1918.

13. National Industrial Conference Board, *The Cost of Living Among Wage Earners—Lawrence, Massachusetts, November 1919,* Research Report #24 (Boston, 1919), 21.

14. "Average Cost of Food in 91 Localities for Families of Varying Incomes," *Monthly Labor Review* 9 (Aug. 1919): 4–5.

15. One also wonders if investigators measured the cost of items such as olive oil, whose price jumped 191 percent between 1914 and 1919. See *Textile Worker* (Lawrence), April 23, 1919. For the importance of food in working-class budgets, see Peter R. Shergold, *The "American Standard of Living" in Comparative Perspective, 1889–1913* (Pittsburgh, 1982), chap. 5.

16. *Paterson Evening News* (hereafter cited as *PEN*), Aug. 27, Sept. 13, 24, 1918.

17. Agnes de Lima, *Night Working Mothers in Textile Mills: Passaic, New Jersey* (New York, 1920), 23; U.S. Department of Labor, Women's Bureau, *The Family Status of Breadwinning Women in Four Selected Cities,* Bulletin #23 (Washington, D.C., 1922), 23.

18. This estimate is based on the finding of the Massachusetts Bureau of Labor Statistics that real wages of industrial workers in that state increased by 9.3 percent between 1913 and 1919. See Massachusetts Department of Labor and Industries, *Thirty-Fourth Annual Report of the Statistics of Manufacture for the Year 1919* (Boston, 1921), xii–xiii.

19. David Jay Bercuson, *Confrontation at Winnipeg: Labor, Industrial Relations and the General Strike* (Montreal, 1974), 34.

20. Anthony Capraro Papers, Immigration History Research Center, University of Minnesota, St. Paul, Minn., Interview with Rose and Grace Santora, Box 8; National Industrial Conference Board, *Hours of Work as Related to the Output and Health of Workers—Wool Manufacturing,* Research Report #12 (Boston, 1918), 15.

21. National Archives, RG 131, Minutes of the Botany Board of Directors, Report by Willibald Franz, Oct. 13, 1921, Box 49.

22. Ibid., Weekly Letter to the Gera Board of Directors, June 8, Sept. 7, Oct. 5, 1918, Box 124.

23. N.J. Bureau of Industrial Statistics, *39th Annual Report* (1916), 32; *Bulletin of the NAWM*, 48 (July 1917): 238.

24. *Lawrence Labor* (hereafter cited as *LL*), Jan. 20, 1923; "The Arlington Mills: Their Growth in Sixty Years," *Bulletin of the NAWM*, 55 (July 1925): 381.

25. *Daily News Record*, April 26, 1917; *PEN*, May 3, 1917.

26. Interviews with Rose and Grace Santora and Mary Glinka, Capraro Papers, Box 8.

27. Elizabeth Glendower Evans, *How Bolshevism is Being Planted in the United States: A True Story, and a Parable* (Boston, 1919), no p. number.

28. Interview with Mollie Pluhar (in author's possession). For the change in the quality of the goods, see also National Archives, RG 131, Julius Forstmann to the Wool Trade Board, June 7, 1918, Box 113.

29. National Archives, RG 131, James Stoddart, Supervisor of Labor, Forstmann & Huffmann Company, to Secretary of Labor Wilson, June 26, 1918, Box 113.

30. *PEN*, July 30, 1918; Interview with Rose and Grace Santora, Capraro Papers, Box 8; *PDN*, Jan. 5, 7, 14, 17, 19, 30, Feb. 9, 1918; for workers' annoyance at the "enormous profits during the war," see Archives of the Archdiocese of Boston, P. G. Waters to Rev. R. J. Haberlin, Report on the Lawrence Strike (hereafter cited as Waters Report), April 10, 1919, p. 12, St. John's Seminary file.

31. George Lyman, *The Story of the Massachusetts Committee on Public Safety* (Boston 1919), 134–138; *LET*, July 5–10, 1918; *LSA*, July 5–10, 1918.

32. *PEN*, May 6, 1918.

33. *Daily News Record*, May 4, 1918.

34. Ibid., April 18, 22, 24, May 3–8, 1918; *PPG*, Aug. 1–3, 1918.

35. Botany had temporarily gone on a nine-hour day due to a shortage of wool. *PDN*, June 17–27, 1918.

36. National Archives, RG 65, Records of the Department of Justice, Bureau of Investigation, File #118448, James Stoddart to A. Bruce Bielaski, June 26, 1918; also RG 131, Stoddart to Wilson, June 20, 1918, Box 113; *PDN*, June 17–27, 1918.

37. Capraro Papers, Interview with Annie Trina, Box 8.

38. Ibid., Interview with Rose and Grace Santora.

39. *PDH*, Oct. 14, 1918. Gera Mill officials became so bothered by the constant fund-raising campaigns that they donated an extra $10,000 to the United War Work campaign so that their employees would no longer be constantly disturbed by solicitations. See National Archives, RG 131, Minutes of the Gera Board of Directors, n.d., Box 122.

40. Throughout this study, the term Magyar will be used interchangeably with Hungarian.

41. For an account of this dispute, see National Archives, RG 65, File #34689, Special Report in re. Czecho-Slovak Propaganda—Passaic, Sept. 20, 1918. For an historical novel that contains an account of this incident, see Fjeril Hess, *Handkerchief Holiday* (New York, 1942), 172–176.

42. For this point, see Robert E. Park, *The Immigrant Press and its Control* (New York, 1922), 195, 207, 441.

43. My comments here are restricted to the ethnic groups that resided in the three cities. For a collection of essays that deals with these issues, see Joseph P. O'Grady, ed., *The Immigrants' Influence on Wilson's Peace Policies* (Lexington, Ky., 1967).

44. *PDN,* March 11, 1918.

45. *PDH,* June 20, Nov. 1, 1918. For the impact of the war upon Polish-Americans, see Stanley R. Pliszka, "The Polish-American Community and the Rebirth of Poland," *Polish-American Studies* 16 (January–June 1969): 40–60; Joseph John Parot, *Polish Catholics in Chicago, 1850–1920* (DeKalb, Ill., 1981), 161–164.

46. Valerie Conner, *The National War Labor Board* (Chapel Hill, N.C., 1983); Alexander M. Bing, *War Time Strikes and Their Adjustment* (New York, 1921), 161–165; Brody, *Steelworkers in America*, 199–213. For the attitude of the Wilson Administration towards labor, see Melvyn Dubofsky, "Abortive Reform: The Wilson Administration and Organized Labor, 1913–1920," in Cronin and Sirianni, eds. *Work, Community and Power*, 197–220.

47. Conner, *National War Labor Board*, 50–67.

48. Arnold Hanko, "Passaic, The Passing of an Idyll," *The American Mercury* 20 (June, 1930): 229; *PEN,* Feb. 15, July 7, Nov. 30, 1917, May 4, Sept. 12, 1918; *LET,* June 6, Aug. 20, 1917; *PDN,* June 25, 1917.

49. National Archives, RG 165, Records of the War Department, General Staff, Military Intelligence Division, File #10110-404, Intelligence Officer, Camp Merritt, N.J. to Intelligence Officer, Hoboken, N.J., n.d.; also RG 65, File #118448, Report of E. T. Drew, April 11, 1918. For the Bureau of Investigation, see David Williams, "The Bureau of Investigation and its Critics, 1919–1921: The Origins of Federal Political Surveillance," *Journal of American History* 58 (December 1981): 560–579.

50. *PDH,* Sept. 3, 5, 1918; *PEN,* Sept. 3, 4, 1918; National Archives, RG 131, Gera Weekly Letter for Sept. 7, 1918, Box 124. For similar raids in Lawrence during which the city's police force "ransacked industrial plants" and seized over 500 workers, see *LET,* June 26, 1918.

51. See e.g. *LET,* Aug. 29, 1917, June 26, 1918; *PEN,* Aug. 28, 1918.

52. Interview with Gus Deak (in author's possession); Papers of the Textile Workers Union of America (hereafter cited as TWUA Papers), State Historical Society of Wisconsin, Madison, Wis., Henry Hunt to Thomas McMahon, 2 October 1926, File 7A, Box 1.

53. *LSA,* May 16, 1917; *Daily News Record,* May 18, 1917.

54. *Daily News Record,* Jan. 9, April 29, 1917; Natonal Archives, RG 2, Docket #1123, Hearing of April 9, 1919.
55. *Textile Worker,* 6 (December 1918): 319; *New York Call,* Jan. 28, 1919.
56. Brooks, "The United Textile Workers," 53, 80.
57. "A Forty-Eight Hour Week," *Bulletin of the NAWM* 49 (April 1919): 146; *LSA,* Nov. 26, 1918; *Daily News Record,* Jan. 27, 1919.
58. For the UTW's position, see *LSA,* Jan. 25, 1919; National Archives, RG 2, Docket #1123, Hearing of April 9, 1919.
59. Brooks, "United Textile Workers," 311; J. M. Budish and George Soule, *The New Unionism in the Clothing Industry,* 257–258.
60. National Archives, RG 65, File #343501, Report of John J. Lyons for Jan. 16, 1919; *PDN,* Feb. 21, 1919; *PDH,* March 3, 1919.
61. *PDH,* Feb. 5, 1919.
62. For the UTW-led strikes, see *Daily News Record,* February–March 1919.

3. Paterson: In the Silk

1. Morris William Garber, "The Silk Industry of Paterson, New Jersey, 1840–1913: Technology and the Origins, Development and Changes in an Industry" (Ph.D. diss., Rutgers University, 1968); Osborne, "Industrialization and the Politics of Disorder," 1–30.
2. Rowland Tappan Berthoff, *British Immigrants in Industrial America* (Cambridge, Mass., 1953), 41–45; Richard D. Margrave, "Technology Diffusion and the Transfer of Skills; Nineteenth Century Silk Migration to Paterson," in Scranton, ed. *Silk City,* 9–34.
3. Margrave, "Technology Diffusion," 13–19; Osborne, "Industrialization and the Politics of Disorder," 13–26; Henry E. Knight, "The Handloom Period in Domestic Silk Making," *American Silk Journal* 38 (April 1918): 50.
4. William Nelson and Charles A. Shriner, *History of Paterson* (Paterson, 1970), 1: 147–148, 344; Steve Golin, "The Unity and Strategy of the Paterson Silk Manufacturers during the 1913 Strike," in Scranton, ed. *Silk City,* 78–81; Garber, "Silk Industry of Paterson," 117–118; Senior Class of the State Normal School, Paterson, New Jersey, *A History of Paterson and its Relations with the World* (Union City, N.J.), 38.
5. Scranton, "An Exceedingly Irregular Business," in Scranton, ed. *Silk City,* 35–72.
6. William A. Poz, "Commission Weaving," *American Silk Journal* 38 (December 1919): 55–58; James E. Wood, "History of Labor in the Broad Silk Industry of Paterson, New Jersey, 1872–1940," (Ph.D. diss., U. of California, 1941), 33; Nelson and Shriner, *History of Paterson,* 1:348.
7. For a government report that contains an abundance of material on the runaway shop and the silk industry in Pennsylvania, see U.S. Senate,

Report on Condition of Women and Child Wage Earners in the United States, Vol. 2, The Silk Industry, 2d Sess. S. Document 645. A summary of the report's findings appears in Florence L. Sanville, "Silk Workers in Pennsylvania and New Jersey," *The Survey* 37 (May 18, 1912): 307–312.

8. *Report on Condition of Women and Child Wage Earners*, 226–230; Shichiro Matsui, *The History of the Silk Industry in the United States* (New York, 1930), 49–54.

9. *Industrial Union News*, February–April 1912; *Solidarity*, March 1–3, April 19, 1912. That the unionist traditions of the area's coal miners did not necessarily carry over to the female silk workers is an interesting question but one that is beyond the purview of this study.

10. See, e.g., U.S. Commission on Industrial Relations, *Industrial Relations, Final Report*, Senate Doc. no. 415, 64th Cong., 1st Sess., 3: 2436, 2616–2617 (hereafter cited as *CIR*); National Archives, RG 2, Docket #1123, March Hearing, 86, 98, 102–103.

11. U.S. Department of Commerce, Bureau of the Census, *Thirteenth Census of the United States Taken in the Year 1910*, (Washington, D.C., 1913), 8:249.

12. U.S. Department of Commerce, *Fourteenth Census of the U.S. Taken in the Year 1920* (Washington, D.C., 1923), 9:952–955.

13. See Scranton, "An Exceedingly Irregular Business," 53.

14. Albert H. Heusser, ed. *The History of the Silk Dyeing Industry in the United States* (Paterson, 1927), 179–294; National Archives, RG 2, Docket #1123, March Hearing, 104.

15. Because so little throwing was done in Paterson, it will not be discussed here.

16. *Report on Condition of Women and Child Wage Earners*, 200.

17. Ibid., 201–203; Scranton, *Silk City*, Plate 14.

18. Wood, "History of Labor in Broad Silk," 186–194, 212–224.

19. Ibid., xviii; Scranton, "An Exceedingly Irregular Business," 46; *CIR*, 3:2429.

20. Figures for Paterson are unavailable, but in New Jersey in 1919 there were 8,528 male and 6,765 female broad-silk weavers. See *1920 Census*, 8:219.

21. Matsui, *History of the Silk Industry*, 50, 206; *Report on Condition of Women and Child Wage Earners*, 206; *CIR*, 3:2427, 2489.

22. Again, one must rely on New Jersey figures that show 1,849 broad-silk and 1,283 ribbon weavers in the state in 1919. See *1920 Census*, 8:219. These figures for broad-silk and ribbon weavers may not be totally accurate as some shops produced both types of goods.

23. For the ribbon weavers, see *PEN*, March 8, 1913; *CIR*, 3:2492, 2589, 2596; *PPG*, March 25, 1916; *Daily News Record*, Aug. 24, 1919; Matsui, *History of the Silk Industry*, 50, 140.

24. See, e.g., Dubofsky, *We Shall Be All*, 281. For Flynn's comments see Elizabeth Gurley Flynn, "The Truth About the Paterson Strike," in Joyce L. Kornbluh, ed. *Rebel Voices: An IWW Anthology*, (Ann Arbor, 1964), 223.

25. *CIR*, 3:2469, 2574, 2586–2588, 2595, 2605, 2618; *PEN*, Sept. 27, 28, 1916; National Archives, RG 2, Docket #1123, March Hearing, 16–17, 128.
26. Wood, "History of Labor in the Broad Silk Industry," 160; see also *Daily News Record*, Aug. 29, 1918.
27. Works Progress Administration, *New Jersey: A Guide to its Present and Past* (New York, 1939), 351.
28. New Jersey Bureau of Industrial Statistics, *36th Annual Report* (1914), 188.
29. Heusser, ed. *The History of the Silk Dyeing Industry*, 218–245.
30. David Saposs Papers, State Historical Society of Wisconsin, Madison, Wis., "Occupations of Immigrants Before and After Coming to the United States," Box 21. See also Montgomery, *Workers' Control in America*, 34.
31. Margrave, "Technology Diffusion," 9–34; Senior Class, *History of Paterson*, 34.
32. This is the figure for Paterson residents who listed German as their mother tongue. See *1920 Census* 2:1024.
33. *PEN*, Nov. 16, 1918; *Paterson Directory for 1914*, 913–916; Delight W. Dodyk, "Winders, Warpers, and Girls on the Loom: A Study of Women in the Paterson Silk Industry and Their Participation in the General Strike of 1913" (Masters' Thesis, Sarah Lawrence College), 38.
34. For early German involvement in the IWW, see *Solidarity*, Oct. 1, 1910. Lessig was an exception as his experience came in the broad-silk sector.
35. Significantly, the IWW's first Paterson strike occurred at the Graef Hat Band Company. See Wood, "History of Labor in the Broad Silk Industry," 201.
36. Osborne, "Industrialization and the Politics of Disorder," 178–186.
37. Rudolph Vecoli, *The People of New Jersey* (New York, 1965), 191.
38. This discussion is largely based on two excellent papers by George Carey, "*La Questione Sociale*, An Anarchist Newspaper in Paterson, N.J. (1895–1908)" and "The Vessel, The Deed and The Idea: Anarchists in Paterson, 1895–1908." Both are on file at the American Labor Museum, Haledon, N.J. See also Osborne, "Industrialization and the Politics of Disorder," 119–135.
39. Carey, "The Vessel, The Deed and the Idea," 8.
40. These events are discussed in chap. 9.
41. *1920 Census*, 2:1024. I am indebted to Caesarina Earl for information concerning the origins of the southern Italians.
42. For a work that explores the cultural and political divisions separating northern and southern Italians, as well as the forces that eventually led to greater unity, see Dino Cinel, *From Italy to San Francisco: The Immigrant Experience* (Palo Alto, 1982).
43. Carlo A. Altarelli, "History and Present Condition of the Italian Colony of Paterson" (Masters' Essay, Columbia University, 1911).
44. For working class residential districts in the Paterson area, see John A.

Fitch, "The I.W.W., An Outlaw Organization," *The Survey* 30 (June 7, 1913); John A. Herbst, "A Slice of the Earth. The Story of the American Labor Museum Botto House Historic Site, Haledon, New Jersey." Booklet on file at the American Labor Museum.

45. Jewish life in Lodz has been best depicted in I. J. Singer, *The Brothers Ashkenazi* (1936; rpt. New York, 1980). The 8,000 figure is based on the fact that 11,709 Paterson residents listed Yiddish as their mother tongue in 1920. Some of these persons had most likely been born in the United States. See *1920 Census*, 2:1024.

46. For the Bund in this era, see Ezra Mendelsohn, *Class Struggles in the Pale* (Cambridge, England, 1970); Henry Jack Tobias, *The Jewish Bund in Russia: From its Origins to 1905* (Stanford, 1972).

47. Henrietta Szold, *The American Jewish Yearbook 5667* (Philadelphia, 1907), 46–47; Richard D. Lewis, "Labor-Management Conflict in Russian Poland: The Lodz Lockout of 1906–1907," *East European Quarterly* 2 (January 1974): 413–434.

48. Those who came to Paterson from Lodz had previously worked in cotton and woolen mills. Evidently, they chose to come to Paterson as it was a city of small shops.

49. Quoted in Vecoli, *The People of New Jersey*, 251.

50. Melech Epstein, *Jewish Labor in America* (1950; rpt. New York, 1969) 1:xix.

51. For Patersons's Workmen's Circles branches, see YIVO Institute for Jewish Research, New York City, Minutes of the Meetings, National Executive, Workmen's Circle. For the influence of former Bundists, see Irving Howe, *World of Our Fathers* (New York, 1976), 292–295.

52. Of all groups, the anarchists appear to have made the most effort to challenge patriarchal notions.

53. The annual reports of the Bureau of Industrial Statistics for the years between 1907 and 1912 are filled with reports of male and female weavers striking together.

54. *CIR*, 3:2492–2493.

55. Scranton, "An Exceedingly Irregular Business," 64; Osborne, "Industrialization and the Politics of Disorder," 68; *Report on Condition of Women and Child Wage Earners*, 331; Dodyk, "Warpers, Winders and Girls on the Loom," 38.

56. Wood, "History of Labor in the Broad Silk Industry," 191–221; *CIR*, 3: 2413–2415, 2424–2425.

57. New Jersey Bureau of Industrial Relations, *36th Annual Report* (1914), 187; *CIR*, 3:2417, 2428–2429, 2480, 2589.

58. *CIR*, 3:2417, 2428–2429, 2480, 2589.

59. The Detroit IWW took its name from the location of its national headquarters. In 1916, the organization changed its name to the Workers' International Industrial Union. Hereafter, the terms Detroit IWW and WIIU will be used depending on the date involved.

60. Osborne, "Industrialization and the Politics of Disorder," 281–282; Wood,

"History of Labor in the Broad Silk Industry," 232–234; Paul Brissenden, *The IWW; A Study of American Syndicalism* (1919, rpt. New York, 1957), 243–247.

61. *Industrial Union News*, January–July 1912; Wood, "History of Labor in the Broad Silk Industry," 234–244; New Jersey Bureau of Industrial Statistics, *35th Annual Report* (1913), 229-230.
62. *Solidarity*, March 30, April 6, 1912.
63. For early efforts to raise the eight-hour issue, see ibid., Dec. 29, 1911.
64. The course of events is best followed in *PEN*, January–March 1913. For the demands of workers in each sector see *PEN*, March 13, 1913. For other accounts of the strike, see Dubofsky, *We Shall Be All*, chap. 10; Philip Foner, *The Industrial Workers of the World, 1905–17* (New York, 1965), 351–372; Alice Huber Tripp, *The I.W.W. and the Paterson Silk Strike* (Urbana, 1987) appeared too late to be used.
65. For these points, see *PEN*, March 8, 10, 1913.
66. For a trenchant, after-the-fact critique, see *The Syndicalist*, Sept. 1–15, 1913. See also Golin, "The Unity and Strategy of the Paterson Silk Manufacturers" in Scranton, ed. *Silk City*, 73–97.
67. *Industrial Union News*, March 1912.
68. For the members of Paterson's WIIU executive committee, see National Archives, RG 165, File #10110-406, Report of Ted Vella to Major Biddle, May 8, 1918. For Paterson's Jewish SLP Federation, see SLP Papers, Accession, Wisconsin State Historical Society, Madison, Wis., Box 64, Folder 10.
69. For this point, see Paul Buhle, "Italian-American Radicals and Labor in Rhode Island, 1905–1930," *Radical History Review* 17 (Spring 1978): 121–151; James D. Osborne, "Paterson: Immigrant Strikers and the War of 1913," in Joseph R. Conlin, ed. *At the Point of Production: The Local History of the IWW*, (Westport, Ct., 1981), 61–78.
70. Mary Brown Sumner, "Broad Silk Weavers of Paterson," *The Survey* 27 (March 16, 1912): 1932–1935.
71. New Jersey Bureau of Industrial Statistics, *35th Annual Report* (1913), 230.
72. *Industrial Union News*, March, April, 1912, April 1913.
73. *CIR*, 3:2467.
74. *Industrial Union News*, October 1918.
75. Ibid., October 1912, August, December 1917, August 1918. Yannarelli represented an important exception to the Jewish leadership of the WIIU and his role is discussed in chap. 9.
76. Though he fails to note that the Paterson IWW local survived beyond 1914, James D. Osborne is one of the few historians who has recognized that the ribbon weavers remained their strongest supporters through the end of that year. See James D. Osborne, "The Paterson Silk Strike of 1913— Immigrant Silk Workers and the IWW (Masters' Thesis, U. of Warwick, 1973), 128–145.
77. Elizabeth Gurley Flynn, *The Rebel Girl* (1955; rpt., New York, 1986),

170–173; *PEN*, Sept. 4, 9, 17, 24, 30, 1915, Jan. 20, 1916; *New York Times*, Oct. 11, 18, Nov. 12, 26, Dec. 1, 1915, Jan. 21, 1916.

78. *PEN*, Aug. 18, Sept. 9, 14, 18, 1916; *Solidarity*, Oct. 21, 1916. For the IWW's success in the small broad-silk shops, see also National Archives, RG 2, Docket #1123, March Hearing, 60.

79. National Archives, RG 65, File #127191, Report of E. T. Drew for Jan. 23, 1918, and File #118448, Report of Drew for May 3, 1918; RG 165, File #10110-406, Reports of Intelligence Officer, Camp Merritt, June 5, 26, 1918.

80. Albert Wyman, head of the Paterson Employers Association, failed in his efforts to get federal authorities to round up the Wobblies, though they did conduct a raid on IWW headquarters. See National Archives, RG 165, File #10110-406, Statement of Albert Wyman.

81. National Archives, RG 65, File #200813, Report of E. T. Drew for May 6, 1918.

82. *PEN*, Feb. 5, 7, 1916.

83. For the 1913 campaign, see Patrick L. Quinlan, "The Paterson Strike and After," *New Review* 2 (January 1914): 26–33.

84. Matsui, *History of the Silk Industry*, 219; *PEN*, Sept. 11, 1915, Sept. 18, 1916.

85. Flynn, "The Truth About the Paterson Strike," in Kornbluh, ed. *Rebel Voices*, 223; *CIR*, 3:2572; National Archives, RG 2, Docket #1123, March Hearing, 148–150.

86. *PEN*, March 17–25, April 6, 1916; *PPG*, March 25, 1916. The silk workers' victory forced almost all of Paterson's other employers, including the dyehouses, to grant the nine-hour day. See New Jersey Bureau of Industrial Statistics, *39th Annual Report* (1917), 190–193.

87. *PPG*, March 27, 28, 1916; *PEN*, April 3, 5, 12, 15, 1916.

88. *PEN*, April 29, 1916.

89. *PEN*, Sept. 13, 1917, Sept. 13, 1918; *Daily News Record*, June 28, 1918; National Archives, RG 2, Docket #1123, March Hearing, 33; Dubofsky, *We Shall Be All*, 276.

90. For the UTW's new opposition to the four-loom system, see *CIR*, 3:2417, 2428–2429.

91. *Daily News Record*, April 17, 1918.

92. Brooks, "History of the UTW," 84–87. Notably, upon organizing its Textile Council, the Paterson UTW said it hoped that it would put an end to the city's "small disturbances." See *PEN*, April 17, 1916.

93. *PEN*, March 21, 1916, Sept. 13, 1917.

94. This group appeared to be modeled on an Eight-Hour League that had been set up in 1912. See Quinlan, "The Paterson Strike and After," 26–28.

95. National Archives, RG 2, Docket #1123, March Hearing, 46.

96. Altarelli, "History and Present Condition of the Italian Colony," 20; Osborne, "Immigrant Strikers and the War of 1913," 71; *PEN*, March 17, 1913.

97. *Industrial Union News*, June 1917, Aug. 9, 1919; National Archives, RG 65, File #118448, Report of E. T. Drew for April 11, 1918.

98. *PPG*, Dec. 6, 9, 1918, Jan. 6, 1919.

99. *Daily News Record*, Aug. 29, Sept. 8, Oct. 22, 1917; *Industrial Union News*, Aug. 9, 1919.

100. *Rebel Worker*, Feb. 15, 1919.

101. *New York Call*, Jan. 13, 1919.

102. *Paterson Morning Call*, Jan. 17, 1919.

103. Ibid., Dec. 31, 1918, Jan. 23, 1919; *PPG*, Jan. 23, 28, 1919; *PEN*, Jan. 31, 1919. The Textile Council was made up of all of the local unions.

104. The forty-seven-hour figure was evidently chosen in order to convince silk workers that the Paterson locals had not totally caved in to the national.

105. *PEN*, Feb. 3, 4, 1919; National Archives, RG 2, Docket #1123, March Hearing, 92.

106. Brody, *Steelworkers in America*, 234.

107. John A. Fitch, "The Paterson Silk Mill Strike A Year After," *The Survey* 32 (June 27, 1914): 339–340; National Archives, RG 2, Docket #1123, February Hearing, 30.

108. *New York Call*, Feb. 3, 11, 1919; *PPG*, Feb. 7, 8, 1919; *Paterson Sunday Chronicle*, Feb. 9, 1919.

109. National Archives, RG 2, Docket #1123, February Hearing, 19 ff.

110. Ibid., February Hearing, 57–59; National Archives, RG 2, Records of the Federal Mediation and Conciliation Service, File #170/125, Report by James Hughes, Feb. 15, 1919.

111. *Paterson Morning Call*, Feb. 15–20, 1919; *Rebel Worker*, March 15, 1919.

112. *New York Call*, Feb. 4, 15, 1919.

113. *PEN*, Feb. 17–21, 1919; *PPG*, Feb. 17–21, 1919.

114. *PEN*, Feb. 17, 1919; *Paterson Morning Call*, Feb. 18, 1919.

115. During the first few days that the mills were reopened, over twenty workers had been arrested for disobeying the "order." See *Paterson Morning Call*, Feb. 18–20, 1919.

116. The most objective description of this dispute is in *PEN*, Feb. 20, 1919. See also *New York Call*, Feb. 4–7, 1919; *New Textile Worker* (hereafter cited as *NTW*), April 10, 1920.

117. *PPG*, Feb. 8, 1919.

118. The dispute between the ACWA and the IWW is discussed in chap. 6.

119. *New York Call*, Feb. 9, 10, 1919; *Paterson Sunday Chronicle*, Feb. 9, 1919; *PEN*, March 3, 1919; *Rebel Worker*, March 15, 1919; *New York Call*, Feb. 9, 1919.

120. *New York Call*, Feb. 16, 1919; *Rebel Worker*, Feb. 15, 1919.

121. National Archives, RG 2, Docket #1123, March Hearing, 50 ff.

122. The war was not technically over until a peace treaty had been signed. See *PPG*, April 10, 1919.

123. *Rebel Worker*, May 1, 1919; *PPG*, April 1, 10, 12, 15, 1919; *PEN*, April 11, 14, 1919. Manufacturers' announcement of a 4 percent pay hike to make up for the lost hours only slightly allayed workers' anger. See *PPG*, April 21, 1919.

124. For this point see the comments of Lewis Magnet in National Archives, RG 2, Docket #1123, March Hearing, 118–119.

4. Passaic:
Foreign Manufacturers and
Foreign Workers

1. Michael Ebner, "Passaic, New Jersey, 1855–1912, City-Building in Post Civil War America" (Ph.D. diss., U. of Virginia, 1974), 47–49; Jay Michael Hollander, "Prelude to a Strike," *Proceedings of the New Jersey Historial Society* 79 (July 1961): 161–162; William W. Scott, *History of Passaic and its Environs* (New York, 1922) 2: 185–186.

2. *Skilled Hands* (privately printed by the Forstmann Woolen Company, 1944), 10–15; Arthur Harrison Cole, *American Wool Manufacture* (Cambridge, Mass, 1976), 2: 163; *Bulletin of the NAWM* 41 (September 1911): 414–417; National Archives, RG 65, File #17936, Report of E. T. Drew for March 3, 1918. Though the mill for a long time kept the Huffmann name, only the Forstmann family was involved in its operation.

3. Hollander, "Prelude to a Strike," 162; *PDN*, Nov. 25, 26, 1918, Feb. 1, March 12, 1919; N.J. Bureau of Statistics, *The Industrial Directory of New Jersey*, 210–211, 461–464.

4. Cole, *American Wool Manufacture*, 2: 157–158, 186, 213–220; Victor S. Clark, *History of Manufactures in the United States* (New York, 1929) 2: 197–199; *Bulletin of the NAWM*, 45 (July 1915), 286; Eloise Shellabarger, "The Shawled Women of Passaic," *The Survey* 44 (July 3, 1920), 463.

5. *PDN*, Dec. 11, 1918, March 10, 1919; *PDH*, April 21, 1919; *New York Times*, Sept. 22, 1920; National Archives, RG 65, File #17936, Reports for May 18, July 23, 1918. For Forstmann's libel suit against Palmer, see *Bulletin of the NAWM*, 50 (October 1920), 457.

6. For a listing of the mills by size see the untitled document in National Archives, RG 131, Box 123.

7. *1920 Census*, 9: 952–953; *Industrial Directory of New Jersey*, 211.

8. From here on, all references to Passaic mills are meant to include those in Garfield and Clifton as well.

9. U.S. Immigration Commission, Reports of the Immigration Commission, *Representative Community "D"*, (Washington, D.C., 1911) 61st Cong., 2nd Sess., 79: 303–307.

10. These figures are based on the mother tongue of residents of Passaic and Clifton in 1920. No such figures are available for Garfield although the census does give the country of birth of the foreign-born in Garfield. In 1920 this included Czechoslovakia, 880; Hungary, 1,337; Italy, 2,536; Poland, 1,231. See *1920 Census*, 2: 1034–1035, 3: 652.

11. Sister M. Gaudentia, "The Polish People of Passaic," *Polish-American Studies* 5 (July–December 1948): 76–77.
12. Information on the origins of Passaic's Slovaks is based on an examination of an insurance log at Passaic's Slovak Catholic Sokol. In general, the assistance of Daniel Tanzone, assistant editor of the *Katolicky Sokol*, has proven indispensable in sorting out Passaic's complex ethnic history.
13. For the economies of Galicia and eastern Slovakia, see Ivan L. Rudnytsky, "The Ukrainians in Galicia Under Austrian Rule," in Adrei S. Markovits and Frank Sysyn, eds. *Nationalism and the Politics of Nationalism—Essays on Austrian Galicia* (Cambridge, 1982), 52–53; M. Mark Stolarik, "Immigration and Urbanization: The Slovak Experience, 1870–1918" (Ph.D. diss., U. of Minnesota, 1974), chaps. 1, 2.
14. See John E. Bodnar, *Immigration and Industrialization*; Morawska, *For Bread with Butter.*
15. U.S. Immigration Commission, *Representative Community "D"*, 334; William M. Leiserson, *Adjusting Immigrant and Industry*, (1924, rpt. New York, 1969), 326–329; Hanko, "The Passing of an Idyll," 230.
16. For biographical sketches of Slovak saloon owners in Passaic, see *Slovenskenovy—Slovak News—60th Anniversay of the Slovak Pioneers in Passaic and Vicinity*, April 1942, Passaic Catholic Slovak Sokol. For suggestive comments on physical abuse of wives, see Frank Marquart, *An Auto Worker's Journal* (University Park, Pa, 1975), 5; Karel D. Bicha, "Hunkies: Stereotyping the Slavic Immigrants, 1890–1920," *Journal of American Ethnic History* 2 (Fall 1982), 26–28.
17. Stolarik, "The Slovak Experience," 77–79.
18. *PDN*, May 14, 1917; *PDH*, April 4, 1919; Shellabarger, "The Shawled Women of Passaic," 466; Bessie Olga Pehotsky, *The Slavic Immigrant Woman* (Cincinnati, 1925), 55–56. For the role of the Roman Catholic Church in the Polish community, see also Parot, *Polish Catholics in Chicago, 1850–1920.*
19. Rev. Raymond J. Kupke, "The Slovak National Church—Passaic, New Jersey and the Jeczusko Affair (seminar paper, Catholic University of America), Diocese of Paterson Archives, Clifton, N.J. This was the only independent Slovak church in the United States and it affiliated with the Polish National Catholic Church.
20. Father Monteuffel denied that he was a German. According to his account, he had grown up in Posen when it was under Prussian rule and the Prussian authorities had forced the Monteuffel name upon him at the time of his father's death. See *PDH*, Feb. 28, 1912.
21. *PDH*, Feb. 27–29, March 1–25, April 16, 23, 24, 1912; *PDN*, March 13, 1918; *The Issue* (Passaic), April 1912, microfilm copy in Miscellaneous newspaper file, Wisconsin Historical Society, Madison, Wis.; Archives of the Diocese of Paterson, File of Reverend Stanislaus Kruczek. For the Polish National Catholic Church, see Victor Greene, *For God and Country; The Rise of Polish and Lithuanian Ethnic Consciousness in America, 1860–1910* (Madison, Wis.,

1975); Lawrence Orzell, "A Minority Within a Minority: The Polish National Catholic Church, 1896–1907," *Polish American Studies* 26 (Spring 1979): 5–32.

22. Kupke, "The Slovak National Church," 15; *A History of the Origins, Growth and Development of SS Peter and Paul Polish National Catholic Church of Passaic, New Jersey*, booklet in Passaic Public Library. For other church fights in Passaic, see *PDH*, May 5, 1914, July 25, 1916, Aug. 14, 1916; *PDN*, May 21, 1920.

23. *PDN*, Dec. 29, 1917, May 1, 15, 1918; *PDH*, May 17, 1918.

24. *PDN*, Jan. 24, 1917; National Archives, RG 131, Weekly Letter to the Gera Board of Directors, June 8, 1918, Box 124; RG 65, File #171190, Memorandum for Mr. Bielaski, April 11, 1918.

25. For an account of a fund-raiser in which Passaic's Ukrainian "socialist workers" and "church people" raised relatively equal amounts, see *PDN*, April 3, 1917. For Ukrainians, see also Franz Borkenau, *World Communism* (Ann Arbor, 1962), 100–101; Jaroslav Petryshyn, *Peasants in the Promised Land: Canada and the Ukrainians 1891–1914* (Toronto, 1985), chap. 3.

26. For the enforcement of this policy in Passaic, see *PDN*, Feb. 27, 1919.

27. *1920 Census*, 2: 1034–1035, 3: 652–653; Interview with Gus Deak (in author's possession); *PDH*, May 14, 18, 1919; *PDN*, May 1, 1918; *Passaic Directory for 1919*, 66–67; Paula Kaye Benkart, "Religion, Family and Community Among Hungarians Migrating to American Cities, 1880–1963," (Ph.D. diss., Johns Hopkins University, 1975), 61–75. Origins of Passaic's Magyar residents is derived from an examination of the marriage records at St. Stephen's Roman Catholic Church in Passaic.

28. Andrew C. Janos, *The Politics of Backwardness in Hungary, 1825–1949* (Princeton, 1982), 10, 49; Archives of the Diocese of Paterson, Holy Trinity File, Box 13; *Passaic City Directory for 1919*, 66–67. See also Juliana Puskas, *From Hungary to the United States* (Budapest, 1982).

29. *PDN*, April 6, 8, May 25, June 22, 1914; Count Michael Károlyi, *Fighting the World* (New York, 1925), 87–91; Béla Vassady, Jr., "The 'Homeland Cause' as Stimulant to Ethnic Unity; The Hungarian American Response to Károlyi's 1914 Tour," *Journal of American Ethnic History* 2 (Fall 1982): 39–64.

30. *1920 Census*, 3: 652; U.S. Immigration Commission, *Representative Community "D"*, 304; Ebner, "Passaic, New Jersey," 83.

31. *Jewish Roots—A History of the Jewish Community of Passaic and Environs* (Clifton, N.J., 1959); U.S. Immigration Commission, *Representative Community "D"*, 304; Jessie Davis, "My Vacation in a Woolen Mill," *The Survey* 30 (Aug. 10, 1918), 541.

32. Udetta Brown, *A Survey of Housing Conditions in Passaic* (Passaic, 1915), 13–14.

33. Morton Siegal, "The Passaic Textile Strike of 1926," (Ph.D. diss., Columbia University, 1952), 85–94; *PDN*, Sept. 30, Oct. 1, Nov. 10, 11, 24, 1919.

34. Michael H. Ebner, "Socialism and Progressive Political Reform: The 1911 Change of Government in Passaic," in Bruce Stave, ed. *Socialism and the*

Cities (Port Washington, NY, 1975), 117–140; *PDN*, April 18, May 15, 1916; *PDH*, May 17, 1918.

35. *1920 Census*, 2: 652; Scott, *History of Passaic*, 2: 693, 765–768; Interview with Mollie Pluhar.

36. These job descriptions apply to the Lawrence as well as the Passaic mills.

37. The division of labor in a worsted mill was actually far more intricate than indicated by the table since most of the machine processes had a number of subcategories.

38. Weavers were not supposed to stop the machine to repair all imperfections and they had to make snap decisions as to which damages they should repair themselves and which should be passed on to the burlers.

39. These job descriptions are largely based on U.S. House of Representatives, *Wool and Manufacturers of Wool—Report of the Tariff Board on Schedule K of the Tariff Board*, 2d. Sess., House Document 342, 954–1077. See also Davis, "My Vacation in a Woolen Mill," 538–541; Shellabarger, "The Shawled Women of Passaic," 463–468; Florence Kelley, "Wage Earning Women in War Time: The Textile Industry," *Journal of Industrial Hygiene* 1 (Oct. 1919): 261–273; Massachusetts Board of Labor and Industries, *Fifth Annual Report* (Boston, 1918), 40–41; National Archives, RG 131, Gera Weekly Letter for Aug. 24, 1918, Box 124; *PDH*, March 2, 1916; *LET*, Aug. 1, 1917.

40. See Joseph White, *The Limits of Trade Union Militancy—The Lancashire Textile Workers, 1910–1914* (Westport, CT, 1978).

41. For wage rates in the Passaic mills, see Records of the NAWM, Museum of American Textile History, North Andover, Mass., New Wage Rates in Passaic Woolen and Worsted Mills, March 15, 1918, Box 86, Folder 3.

42. Shellabarger, "The Shawled Women of Passaic," 467; U.S. Department of Labor, Women's Bureau, Bulletin No. 23, *The Family Status of Breadwinning Women in Four Selected Cities* (Washington, D.C., 1922), 26; *Daily News Record*, March 8, 1917.

43. Cf. Tamara K. Hareven and Randolph Langebach, *Amoskeag—Life and Work in an American Factory City* (New York, 1978), part 4.

44. De Lima, *Night Working Mothers in Textile Mills*, 6–17.

45. *New York Sunday Call Magazine*, June 25, 1916; *PDN*, July 16, 1919.

46. Shellabarger, "The Shawled Women of Passaic," 464; Davis, "My Vacation in a Woolen Mill," 541.

47. For the Consumers' League's efforts, see Consumers' League of New Jersey, *16th Annual Report, July 1, 1916–June 30, 1917*, 8. See also *Daily News Record*, March 8, 1917.

48. Kelley, "Wage-Earning Women in War Time," 266.

49. Hanko, "Passaic, The Passing of an Idyll," 231; New Jersey Bureau of Industrial Statistics, *39th Annual Report* (1917), 342.

50. New Jersey Bureau of Industrial Statistics, *35th Annual Report (1912)*, 235–289; "A New Jersey Weaver, A Budget and A Gospel of Revolution," *The Survey* 28 (May 18, 1912): 289–291; *New York Call*, March 27, 1912.

51. SLP Papers, Accession, Henry Kuhn to Paul Augustine, April 9, 1912, Box 37, Folder 11.
52. Ebner, "The Passaic Strike of 1912 and the Two IWW's," 452–466; *New York Call*, March 28, April 3, 8, 9, 10, 1912; *Solidarity*, April 6, 20, 1917.
53. *PDN*, March 30, April 1, 15, 18, 1917.
54. *The Issue*, April 1912.
55. For the SP's role in opposing the commission form of government, see Ebner, "Socialism and Progressive Political Reform," 116–140. See also, Charles Leinenweber, "The American Socialist Party and the 'New' Immigrants," *Science and Society*, 32 (Winter 1968): 1–25; Paul Buhle, "Debsian Socialism and the 'New Immigrant' Worker" in William O'Neil, ed. *Insights and Parallels* (Minneapolis, 1973), 249–303.
56. *PDH*, March 11, 1916.
57. This account of the 1916 strikes is primarily based on *PDH*, March 1–May 1, 1916. See also New Jersey Bureau of Industries, *39th Annual Report* (1916), 239–243; Records of the NAWM, Minutes of the Second Meeting, Passaic Local Conference held at the office of the Forstmann & Huffmann Company, June 21, 1916, Box 31.
58. Records of the NAWM, Minutes of the Second Meeting of the Passaic Local Conference, Box 31.
59. Hanko, "Passaic, The Passing of an Idyll," 233. See also National Archives, RG 65, File #17936, Report of E. T. Drew for March 3, 1918.
60. Records of the NAWM, Minutes of the Second Meeting of the Passaic Local Conference, Box 31.
61. By allocating votes according to the number of employees in each mill, the council's constitution guaranteed that Botany and Forstmann & Huffmann would dominate decision making. For the constitution and a statement of the Council's purposes see *Bulletin of the NAWM*, 67 (July 1917): 232–239.
62. National Archives, RG 131, Weekly Letter to the Gera Mill, June 8, 15, 1918, Box 131.
63. Evidently this goal was not immediately achieved as in 1918 some employees continued to leave the mills in the summer to work on nearby farms. See ibid., Weekly Letters to the Gera Board of Directors, April 27, May 18, 1918, Box 124, Thomas Prehn to John Quinn, 21 May 1918, Box 131.
64. Siegal, "Passaic Textile Strike of 1926," 109–110.
65. *Bulletin of the NAWM*, 67 (July 1917): 232–239.
66. *PDH*, April 24, 1918.
67. Ibid., June 15, 1918; *Daily News Record*, June 18, 1918.
68. Ebner, "Passaic, New Jersey," 142–147; *PDH*, May 27, 1914.
69. National Archives, RG 131, Weekly Letter to the Director of the Gera Mills, Jan. 11, 1919, Box 124.
70. Before this date, Passaic workers received an overtime premium of 25 percent after sixty hours. See *PDN*, Feb. 3, 1919.

71. National Archives, RG 131, Minutes of the Botany Board of Directors, Jan. 30, 1919, Box 148. The reasons for the American Woolen Company's decision is discussed in chap. 5.
72. *PDN*, Feb. 3–7, 1919; *PDH*, Feb. 3–7, 1919. Passaic Worsted employees did not walk out until the next week.
73. For the ethnic composition of Passaic's boiler firemen, see National Archives, RG 65, File #34689, Representative Drucker to Bielaski, 19 Dec. 1917.
74. *PDN*, Feb. 5, 8, 10, 13, 17, 1919.
75. Ibid., Feb. 7, 1919.
76. See ibid., Feb. 5–7, 1919; *PDH*, Feb. 5–7, 1919.
77. *PDH*, Feb. 17, 20, May 15, 1919.
78. Most likely Pluhar was a mule spinner although firm evidence is lacking on this point.
79. Pluhar's perspective shares much with Austro-Marxists such as Otto Bauer and Max Adler. See Tom Bottomore and Patrick Goode, eds. *Austro-Marxism* (Oxford, 1978).
80. This account is primarily based on an interview with Mollie Pluhar. See also *PDH*, Feb. 20, 1919, *PDN*, Feb. 21, 22, 1919. For the CIO leadership in the 1930s, see Friedlander, *The Emergence of a UAW Local*, and Ronald W. Schatz, *The Electrical Workers: A History of Labor at General Electric and Westinghouse, 1923–1960* (Urbana, Ill., 1983), chap. 4.
81. *PDN*, Feb. 19, 1919.
82. Ibid., Feb. 7, 21, 1919.
83. Ibid., Feb. 4, 1919.
84. For the "settling in" concept, see Daniel J. Walkowitz, *Worker City, Company Town: Iron and Cotton-Worker Protest in Troy and Cohoes, New York, 1855–1884* (Urbana, Ill., 1978), chap. 4.
85. *PDH*, Feb. 11, 1919.
86. Ibid., Feb. 11, 22, 1919.
87. For the 1916 and 1917 strikes, see ibid., May 26, 27, June 3, 5, 1916; *PDN*, Jan. 17–19, 24, 30, 1917.
88. *PDN*, Feb. 7–20, 1919. For a listing of the twelve branches, see *PDH*, Feb. 20, 1919.
89. *PDN*, Feb. 24, March 6, 11, 12, 14, 18, 19, 1919; *PDH*, March 5, 10, 13, 14, April 29, 1919. Mary Heaton Vorse Papers, Archives of Labor History and Urban Affairs, Wayne State University, Detroit, Mich., Some Information on the 1919 Strike Not for Publication, Box 123.
90. *PDH*, March 17, 18, 1919.
91. Ibid., Feb. 25, 27–28, March 3, 1919.
92. Ibid., Feb. 12, 17, 25, 1919; *PDN*, Feb. 22, 1919.
93. *PDN*, March 3, 4, 22, 1919.
94. Ibid., March 3, 4, 22, 1919.

95. The first public report of the possibility of the ACWA's involvement came on March 14. See ibid., March 14, 1919.
96. Ibid., March 17, 1919.
97. It is even possible that Roth and Kymack had all along been "in the pay of the mill owners" because upon the walkout's conclusion they assumed leadership of the Independent Union whose only function appeared to be to attack the ATWA local. For this claim see Hanko, "Passaic, the Passing of an Idyll," 235.
98. *PDN*, March 17, 1919; *PDH*, March 17, 1919. For late nineteenth-century labor activity see Martin Shefter, "Trade Unions and Political Machines: The Organization and Disorganization of the American Working Class in the Late Nineteenth Century," in Ira Katznelson and Aristide R. Zolberg, eds. *Working-Class Formation: Nineteenth Century Patterns in Western Europe and the United States* (Princeton, 1986), 218–219. For the role played by parades during immigrant strikes see Charles Leinenweber, "Socialists in the Streets: The New York City Socialist Party in Working Class Neighborhoods, 1908–1918," *Science and Society* 41 (Summer 1977): 152–171.
99. For the names of the central committee members, see *PDN*, Feb. 10, 12, 19, 1919; *PDH*, Feb. 15, 1919.
100. *PDN*, March 18, 19, 1919; *PDH*, March 17–19, 1919.
101. *PDH*, Feb. 11, 1919.
102. *PDN*, Feb. 13, 1919.
103. *PDN*, March 21, 1919; National Archives, RG 280, Records of the Federal Mediation and Conciliation Service, File #170/158.
104. *PDN*, March 21, 1919; *PDH*, March 21, 1919.
105. For the text that appeared in the Passaic newspapers, see *PDH*, March 24, 1919. A version that was printed in the wool manufacturers' journal omitted any mention of the nondiscrimination clause. The significance of this will become clear later. See "A Forty-Eight Hour Week," *Bulletin of the NAWM*, 49 (April 1919): 149–150.
106. *PDH*, March 22, 1919.
107. Ibid., March 24, 1919.
108. *PDN*, March 18–22, 1919; *New York Call*, March 20, 23, 1919; Montgomery, *Workers' Control in America*, 105.
109. Saposs Papers, Interview with Matthew Pluhar, President Independent Textile Workers Union, April 3, 1919, Box 21.
110. *PDH*, March 26, 1919.
111. Ibid., March 27, 1919.
112. It was probably no coincidence that the firings occurred at the Garfield Worsted Company whose president, Gustav Schmid, also headed the Wool Council.
113. *PDN*, Feb. 10, 15, 1919; *PDH*, March 8, 26, 27, 1919; Saposs Papers, Interview with Matthew Pluhar, Box 21.
114. *PDH*, March 27–29, 1919.

115. Records of the NAWM, Minutes of the Second Meeting of the Passaic Local Conference, June 21, 1916, Box 31. For mill owners' criticism of city authorities at an earlier stage in the strike, see *PDH*, Feb. 12, March 1, 3, 1919.
116. For a contrasting view see, Michael Ebner, "Strikes and Society: Civil Behavior in Passaic, 1875–1926," *New Jersey History*, 47 (Spring 1979): 7–24.
117. *PDH*, March 27, 1919.
118. Ibid., March 29–April 2, 1919.
119. Ibid., March 31–April 7, 1919.
120. Ibid., March 31, April 3, 1919.
121. For these points, see *New York Call*, April 2, 1919.
122. *PDN*, March 18, 1919.
123. *PDH*, March 28, 1919.
124. Ibid., March 29, 1919.
125. Ibid., April 10, 29, 1919; *PDN*, April 18, 1919; Interview with Mollie Pluhar.
126. *PDH*, April 7, 1919.
127. Saposs Papers, Interview with Matthew Pluhar, Box 21.
128. Interview with Mollie Pluhar.
129. *PDN*, April 7, 1919.

5. Lawrence:
The Battle Renewed

1. Steve Dunwell, *The Run of the Mill* (Boston, 1978), 82–91, 96.
2. *Memoirs of a Corporation—Pacific Mills, 1850–1950* (Boston, 1950); Maurice Dorgan, *History of Lawrence* (Cambridge, 1924), 54.
3. *The Arlington Mills—A Historical and Descriptive Sketch* (Boston, 1891); "The Arlington Mills," *Bulletin of the NAWM* 55 (July 1925): 375–384. For a listing of the largest industrial plants in the United States in 1900, see Daniel Nelson, *Managers and Workers: Origins of the New Factory System in the U.S., 1880–1920* (Madison, Wis., 1975), 7.
4. Edward G. Roddy, *Mills, Mansions and Mergers: The Life of William M. Wood,* (North Andover, Mass., 1982), 33–43, 62–67; "The American Woolen Company," *Fortune* 3 (April 1931): 71–112; Cole, *American Wool Manufacture,* 2:239-241.
5. Records of the NAWM, First and Second Meetings of the Lawrence Conference on Labor Questions, July 24, Nov. 20, 1916, Box 31; Dubofsky, *We Shall Be All*, 247.
6. Dorgan, *History of Lawrence*, 54; *Bulletin of the NAWM*, 49 (July 1919): 227.
7. Massachusetts Consumers' League Papers, Radcliffe College, Schlessinger Library, Cambridge, Mass., Account of Meeting on the Lawrence Strike in the Consumers' League Office, March 8, 1919, Box 25, Folder 416.
8. Berthoff, *British Immigrants in Industrial America*, 38; Alice M. O'Connor, "A Study of the Immigrant Problem in Lawrence, Mass." (Social Workers'

Thesis, 1915), 168–170, Museum of American Textile History; Jean-Claude G. Simon, "Textile Workers, Trade Unions and Politics: Comparative Case Studies, France and the United States 1885–1914" (Ph.D. diss., Tufts University, 1980), 41, 90–109; Cole, *Immigrant City*, 44, 171.

9. O'Connor, "A Study of the Immigrant Problem," 12.

10. In 1920, there were still 4,256 Lawrence residents who had been born in Ireland, many of whom probably came during the last big wave of Irish immigration in the 1880s. See *1920 Census*, 2: 763.

11. Cole, *Immigrant City*, 34–37, 47–49, 81–89.

12. Ibid., 84–88; O'Connor, "A Study of the Immigrant Problem," 183; Berthoff, *British Immigrants in Industrial America*, 38; Rev. Roland D. Sawyer, "The Socialist Situation in Massachusetts," *New Review* 1 (July 25, 1913): 115–118.

13. For the religious background of early Irish immigrants, see Jay Dolan, *The Immigrant Church, New York's Irish and German Catholics* (Baltimore, 1975); for the transition to the church militant, see Donna Merwick, *Boston Priests, 1848–1910: A Study of Social and Intellectual Change* (Cambridge, 1973).

14. Robert H. Lord, John E. Sexton, Edward T. Harrington, *History of the Archdiocese of Boston* (Boston, 1945) 3: 301; *New York Call*, Jan. 16, 1912.

15. *LSA*, June 22, 1917; *Lawrence Sunday-Sun*, March 2, 1919; *LL*, Dec. 12, 1922; Cole, *Immigrant City*, 165; O'Connor, "A Study of the Immigrant Problem," 156.

16. For the French-Canadian migration, see Ralph Dominic Vicero, "Immigration of French Canadians to New England, 1840–1900: A Geographical Analysis," (Ph.D. diss., U. of Wisconsin, 1968). See also *1920 Census*, 2: 952.

17. To the extent this was true in Lawrence, see Cole, *Immigrant City*, 53, 94; for French Canadian participation in the Pulp and Paper Workers Union, see Robert H. Zieger, *Rebuilding the Pulp and Paper Workers Union, 1933–1941* (Knoxville, Tenn., 1984), 107; for the Massachusetts Carpenters Union, see Mark Erlich, *With Our Hands: The Story of Carpenters in Massachusetts* (Philadelphia, 1986), 69–70.

18. Fred Beal, *Proletarian Journey* (1937; rpt. New York, 1971), 29.

19. Hareven's perspective is summarized in Tamara K. Hareven, "Family Time and Industrial Time: Family and Work in a Planned Corporation Town, 1900–1924," *Journal of Urban History* 1 (May 1975), 265–289; see also Hareven, "The Laborers of Manchester, New Hampshire: The Role of Family and Ethnicity in Adjustment to Industrial Life," *Labor History* 16 (Spring 1975), 249–265.

20. Jacques Ducharme, *The Shadows of the Trees: The Story of French Canadians in New England* (New York, 1943); George Theriault, "The Franco-Americans of New England," in Mason Wade, ed. *Canadian-American Dualism: Studies of French-English Relations* (Toronto, 1960), 392–418; O'Connor, "A Study of the Immigrant Problem," 149–150; Lord et al., *History of the Archdiocese of*

Boston, 2: 228–229; Harold J. Abramson, *Ethnic Diversity in Catholic America* (New York, 1973), 133–135.

21. Archives of the Archdiocese of Boston, H. L. Glenard to His Eminence William Cardinal O'Connell, June 10, 1919, St. Anne's File, Folder 53; Richard Abrams, *Conservatism in a Progressive Era; Massachusetts Politics 1900–1912* (Cambridge, 1964), 50–52. See also Ann Sullivan, "Happy Times in Mill City," *Radical America* 15 (July–August 1981): 57–63.

22. U.S. Immigration Commission, Reports of the Immigration Commission, *Representative Community "A"* (Washington, D.C., 1911), 61st Cong., 2nd Sess., 10, part 4, 741–748.

23. Ibid., 772–773.

24. Capraro Papers, Interview with Annie Trina, Box 8; *LET*, March 19, 1919, March 29, 1922.

25. National Archives, RG 65, File #343501, Report of Feri Weiss for May 14, 1917.

26. O'Connor, "A Study of the Immigration Problem," 9–10; U.S. Immigration Commission, *Representative Community "A"*, 747, 770–773; Immigrant City Archives, Lawrence, Mass., Interview with Blanche Davieu; *LET*, Aug. 8, 1917.

27. Robert Todd and Franklin Sanborn, *The Report of the Lawrence Survey* (Lawrence, 1912); O'Connor, "A Study of the Immigrant Problem," 17–24; *Lawrence Telegram* (hereafter cited as *LT*), Jan. 23, 1919; *Boston Herald*, Feb. 23, 1919.

28. For other examples, see John T. Cumbler, *Working Class Community in Industrial America: Work, Leisure and Struggle in Two Industrial Cities, 1880–1930* (Westport, Ct., 1979), chap. 10; James R. Barrett, "Unity and Fragmentation; Class, Race and Ethnicity on Chicago's South Side, 1900–1922," in Dirk Hoerder, ed. *"Struggle a Hard Battle"* (DeKalb, Ill., 1986), 229–253.

29. Theodore Draper, *The Roots of American Communism* (New York, 1957), 43.

30. *Solidarity*, March 18, May 20, Oct. 21, Nov. 18, 1911; Dubofsky, *We Shall Be All*, chap. 10; Justus Ebert, *The Trial of a New Society* (Cleveland, 1913); Ardis Cameron, "Bread and Roses Revisisted: Women's Culture and Working-Class Activisim in the Lawrence Strike of 1912," in Ruth Milkman, ed. *Women, Work and Protest* (Boston, 1985), 42–61.

31. Ebert, *Trial of a New Society*, 59; quoted in Buhle, "Debsian Socialism and the 'New Immigrant' Worker," 280.

32. National Archives, RG 174, Selig Perlman, Preliminary Report of an Investigation of the Relations Between Labor and Capital in the Textile Industry of New England.

33. Dubofsky, *We Shall Be All*, 257.

34. National Archives, RG 174, Perlman, Preliminary Report of an Investigation; *LL*, Oct. 7, 1922.

35. National Archives, RG 65, File #351874, Report of John B. Hanrahan for Nov. 18, 1919.

36. Flynn, *The Rebel Girl*, 146–151; Phillips Russell, "The Second Battle of Lawrence," *International Socialist Review* 13 (November 1912): 417–422; Lord et al., *History of the Archdiocese of Boston*, 1: 569.

37. See, Dubofsky, *We Shall Be All*, 258.

38. U.S. Immigration Commission, *Representative Community "A"*, 669, 745–748; Fenton, *Immigrants and Unions*, 320, 329; *LET*, Feb. 27, March 5, 1912; James Ford, "The Cooperative Franco-Belge of Lawrence," *The Survey*, 27 (April 6, 1912): 68–70; James Ford, *Cooperation in New England: Urban and Rural* (New York, 1913), 39.

39. William Wolkovich, *Bay State "Blue" Laws and Bimba* (Brockton, Mass., 1975), 29–30; Immigrant City Archives, Interview with Olga Veckys; Park, *Immigrant Press and its Control*, 25–27; U.S. Immigration Commission, *Representative Community "A"*, 652.

40. Archives of the Archdiocese of Boston, Rev. A. Jusaitis to His Eminence William H. O'Connell, 7 Oct. 1915, Rev. F. A. Virmauskis to R. J. Haberlin, 3 Nov. 1916, St. Francis File, Folder 17; Father Virmauskis to Haberlin, June 15, 1917, Folder 18; Simas Suziedelis (Rev. Bruzas trans.), *The Story of St. Francis Lithuanian Parish* (Lawrence, 1953).

41. Archives of the Archdiocese of Boston, Fr. Virmauskis to His Eminence the Cardinal, 7 May 1918, St. Francis File, Folder 19.

42. Immigrant City Archives, Interview with Olga Veckys. The Records of the Lithuanian Social Camp Association are in Immigrant City Archives. I am greatly indebted to Jonas Stundza who located these files and who conducted the extremely informative interview with Olga Veckys.

43. *LET*, May 10, 1919; Archives of the Archdiocese of Boston, Fr. Virmauskis to His Eminence the Cardinal, May 7 and Nov. 5, 1918, St. Francis File, Folder 19.

44. For Italians and the 1912 strike see Fenton, *Immigrants and Unions*, 320–366.

45. *LL*, Jan. 29, 1919; *The Lawrence Directory for 1918*, 58; National Archives, RG 65, File #343501, Report of John B. Hanrahan for March 20, 1919.

46. Interview with Tony Fusco, in author's possession; National Archives, RG 65, File #350801, Report of Hanrahan for August 6, 1919.

47. Archives of the Archdiocese of Boston, Reverend Mariano Milanese to His Eminence William Cardinal O'Connell, June 3, 1918, Holy Rosary File, Folder 14; Interview with Fusco; O'Connor, "A Study of the Immigrant Problem," 159; see also Rudolph J. Vecoli, "Prelates and Peasants: Italian Immigrants and the Catholic Church," *Journal of Social History* 2 (Spring 1969), 217–268.

48. National Archives, RG 65, File #343501, Report of Harold Zorian, Dec. 5, 1918; RG 165, File #10110-913, Report of Operative P. A. Kiernan, Jan. 7, 1919. For the origins of Lawrence's Poles, see The Commonwealth of Massachusetts, *The Decennial Census—1915* (Boston, 1918), 319.

49. Records of the Archidocese, (illegible) to His Excellency, the most Reverend

John Bonzano, D.D., Archbishop of Melitine, Apostolic Delegate, Washington, D.C., Feb. 14, 1920, Holy Trinity File, Folder 15. See also Michael Dziadosz to Cardinal O'Connell, Feb. 2, 1919, Folder 14.

50. *The Lawrence Directory for 1918*, 62–63; *LSA*, Sept. 29, 30, 1916; *LL*, Aug. 26, 1922; Cole, *Immigrant City*, 188.

51. National Archives, RG 165, File #10110-406, Report of William West, Oct. 1, 1917, File #10110-913, Report of P. A. Kiernan, Jan. 7, 1919; RG 65, File #343501, Report of Harvey Kartun, Feb. 5, 1919.

52. The strikes can be followed in *LSA*, March 8–June 8, 1916.

53. Ibid., May 13, 19, 22, 1916.

54. The series of events can best be followed in National Archives, RG 65, File #343501, Report of Feri Weiss for May 14, 1917. See also *Daily News Record*, May 18, 22, 23, 1917; *LET*, May 17, 21, 1917. Evidently Lawrence workers did not realize that Rossoni had returned to Italy and had turned against the left. See John P. Diggins, *Mussolini and Fascism: The View from America* (Princeton, 1972), 87.

55. *LL*, Dec. 9, 1922.

56. *LET*, July 9, 1918. See also Saposs Papers, Interview with Thomas McMahon, James Starr and John Golden, Feb. 15, 1919, Box 21.

57. National Archives, RG 2, File #917, Arlington Mills; *LET*, Jan. 7, 1919; *LSA*, Jan. 23, 1919.

58. *LT*, Jan. 21, 1919. In 1912, when the mills had been forced to lower hours from fifty-six to fifty-four in order to comply with the new state law setting this as a maximum workweek for women and children, they made no announcement about wages and workers did not find out about the pay cut until they received their pay envelopes. This then triggered the walkout from the mills. The American Woolen Company issued the circulars in order to prevent a repeat of these events but their language had not been approved by the other mill owners. See Museum of American Textile History, Arthur P. Chickering to Nathaniel Stevens, April 15, 1919, Labor Strike Papers.

59. National Archives, RG 165, File #10110-913, Report of P. A. Kiernan, Jan. 7, 1919; RG 65, File #202600-22 (167030), Report of Harold Zorian for Jan. 15, 1919.

60. *LET*, Jan. 25–Feb. 1, 1919; *LSA*, Feb. 1, 1919.

61. *LT*, Jan. 23, 31, 1919; Records of the NAWM, Executive Committee Meetings, Jan. 14, 17, 1919; John Golden, "Short-Hour Campaign of the Textile Workers," *American Federationist* 26 (March 1919): 247–248.

62. *Daily News Record*, Jan. 31, 1919. The American Woolen Company made this decision as the Massachusetts legislature was about to consider a forty-eight-hour bill for women and child employees and this most likely influenced its decision. The bill itself passed and was signed by Governor Coolidge in April 1919. See *Seventh Annual Report of the Massachusetts Board of Labor and Industries* (Boston, 1920), 15–17.

63. *LSA*, Feb. 4, 1919; *New York Times*, Feb. 4, 1919; *Lawrence Sunday-Sun*, Feb. 9, 1919.

64. *American Wool and Cotton Reporter* 30 (January 30, 1919), 362–363, 366; *LET*, Jan. 4, 1919; *LSA*, Jan. 14, 1919.

65. *Advance*, Dec. 13, 1918; *LSA*, Dec. 24, 1918; John A. Fitch, "Lawrence—A Strike for Wages or for Bolshevism?" *The Survey* 42 (April 5, 1919), 42–46.

66. *Revolutionary Age*, Feb. 8, 1919.

67. *Textile Worker* (Lawrence), April 12, 1919; National Archives, RG 65, File #343501, Report of Nils Johnson, Feb. 11, 1919.

68. Cole, *Immigrant City*, 52–53, 94–95.

69. *LSA*, Feb. 4–12, 1919.

70. *LSA*, June 24, 1916, March 3, 1917; *Boston Herald*, Feb. 28, 1919; Beal, *Proletarian Journey*, 72; National Archives, RG 65, File #343501, Report of Harold Zorian, Feb. 2, 1919.

71. National Archives, RG 65, File #351874, Reports of John B. Hanrahan, March 11, 1919, Jan. 25, 1920; File #343419, Report of Harold Zorian, Jan. 29, 1919; RG 280, Records of the Federal Mediation and Conciliation Service, File #33/2694, H. J. Skeffington to H. L. Kerwin, 14 February 1919.

72. Ibid., File #343501, Reports of Hanrahan, Feb. 4, March 20, 1919; Interview with Angelo Rocco (in author's possession); Harold Rotzel, "The Good Fight of Michael Salerno," *The World Tomorrow* 5 (February 1922), 52–53.

73. National Archives, RG 65, File #343501, Report of Hanrahan, Feb. 7, 1919; File #350801, Report of Hanrahan, Feb. 20, 1919.

74. For Franchesi, see National Archives, RG 174, Perlman, Preliminary Report; *LSA*, July 9, 1918; RG 65, File #350801, Report of Hanrahan, Feb. 6, 1919. For Coco and Misserville, see *Lawrence Directory for 1919*, 165; *Lawrence Directory for 1918*, 58.

75. National Archives, RG 65, File #343501, Report of Hanrahan, March 7, 1919.

76. Ibid., File #344903, Reports of Hanrahan, March 21, April 12, 1919.

77. There were eight women pictured in a photo of fifty-six members of the general strike committee. See *NTW*, April 10, 1920.

78. Capraro Papers, Interview with Annie Trina, Box 8.

79. For Holliday and Adamson, see Ebert, *The Trial of a New Society*, 41. For the IWW membership of all of these leaders, see Immigrant City Archives, IWW Leaders in Lawrence.

80. Nat Hentoff, ed. *The Essays of A. J. Muste* (New York, 1970), 59.

81. See *New Solidarity*, Feb. 15, 1919.

82. Capraro Papers, Cedric Long, Autobiography in Miniature, Box 8; Hentoff, ed. *Essays of Muste*, 55–68; Devere Allen, *Adventurous Americans* (New York, 1932), 106–107; *The Forward*, March–November 1918; National Archives, RG 80, Post Office Department, General File, 1897–1928, General Gilmore to Fred Moore, 30, January 1919.

83. Hentoff, ed. *Essays of Muste*, 58–59; Allen, *Adventurous Americans*, 107–108.

84. *Textile Worker* (Lawrence), April 12, 1919; *NTW*, June 7, 1919; Hentoff, ed. *Essays of Muste*, 64–69.
85. *New York Call*, March 1, 1919; Jerome Davis, "Capitalism on Trial," *The World Tomorrow* 2 (May 1919): 136.
86. Hentoff, ed. *Essays of Muste*, 61; Allen, *Adventurous Americans*, 107–108.
87. *LT*, Feb. 5, 1919.
88. *The Forward* (supplements), February, April, May 1919; *New York Call*, May 11, 1919; *NTW*, May 31, 1919. I would like to thank Daniel Downey for locating these issues of *The Forward*.
89. *LSA*, March 22–24, 1919; *LET*, April 11, 1919; Archives of the Archdiocese of Boston, Waters Report.
90. National Archives, RG 280, File #33/2694, H. J. Skeffington to H. L. Kerwin,14 February 1919.
91. Draper, *The Roots of American Communism*, 131–134; *LT*, Feb. 6, 1919; *LSA*, Feb. 10, 1919; National Archives, RG 65, File #343501, Report of Nils Johnson, Feb. 11, 1919.
92. Emmet Larkin, *James Larkin—Irish Labour Leader—1876–1947* (London, 1965), 234.
93. *Revolutionary Age*, February–May 1919.
94. National Archives, RG 65, File #343501, Report of Harvey Kartun, February 6, 1919.
95. *Lawrence Sunday-Sun*, Feb. 23, 1919; *LET*, March 25, 26, 1919.
96. Ruth Pickering, "The Lawrence Strike," *The Liberator* 2 (May 1919): 36.
97. See statement by Reverend Frank Shipman in *LET*, May 2, 1919.
98. This was the estimate of the *Boston American*, which conducted a thorough analysis of the strike, and it comports with figures compiled by the federal government. For a reprint of the *Boston American* article, see *LSA*, March 19, 1919. See also "Conciliation Work of the Department of Labor, May 16 to June 15, 1919," *Monthly Labor Review* 9 (July 1919): 273–277; *1920 Census*, 9: 656.
99. Massachusetts Consumers' League Papers, An Account of the Meeting on the Lawrence Strike, March 8, 1919, Box 25, Folder 416.
100. Capraro Papers, Interview with Annie Trina, Box 8; *LET*, March 19, 1919; Federal Council of Churches, *Report on the Lawrence Strike*, 8.
101. *LET*, Feb. 3, 17, 20, 24, 27, April 29, 1919; *LSA*, April 2, 1919; *LT*, Feb. 8, 1919; *Lawrence Sunday Sun*, March 2, 1919.
102. Capraro Papers, Victory Bulletin No. 7, Untitled Leaflet, Box 8.
103. Beal, *Proletarian Journey*, 67.
104. Massachusetts Consumers' League Papers, An Account of the Meeting on the Lawrence Strike, March 8, 1919, Box 25, Folder 416.
105. *LT*, Feb. 4, 1919; *LSA*, Feb. 11, 12, 1919.
106. Suzidelis, *The Story of St. Francis Lithuanian Parish*, 144, 158; *LSA*, March 14, 1919; *LET*, June 6, 1919; National Archives, RG 65, File #343501, Report of Hanrahan for Feb. 14, 1919.

107. *LSA*, Nov. 25–27, 1919.
108. Ibid., March 10, 1919; *New York Call*, March 14, 1918.
109. Alexander Trachtenberg, ed. *The American Labor Yearbook, 1919–1920* (New York, 1920), 172. In 1922, Benjamin Legere referred to the 1919 walkout as "almost entirely a strike of foreigners." See *LL*, April 27, 1922.
110. Capraro Papers, Victory Bulletin No. 5, Box 8; *Textile Worker* (Lawrence), April 12, 23, 1919.
111. National Archives, RG 165, File #10110-913, Report Concerning Conditions in the Commonwealth of Massachusetts as of June 10, 1919 by the Intelligence Section of the Adjutant General's Office of the Commonwealth of Massachusetts.
112. *LL*, March–September, 1922; TWUA Papers, American Woolen, Wood and Ayer Mills, Box 10A; Richard Kelly, *Nine Lives for Labor* (New York, 1956), 148.
113. A special report on the Lawrence strike prepared for church officials found that "The great majority of those out on strike do not come within church influence at all." See Records of the Archdiocese of Boston, Waters Report, 9.
114. *LET*, Feb. 11, 12, 1919; *LT*, Feb. 5, March 7, 21, 1919.
115. *Boston American*, Feb. 3, 1919; *LSA*, Feb. 11, 1919; *LET*, Feb. 10, 11, 1919; Federal Council of Churches, *Report on the Lawrence Strike*, 8–9; National Archives, RG 65, File #343501, Report of Hanrahan, Feb. 17, 1919; File #351874, Report of Hanrahan, March 7, 11, 1919.
116. See, e.g., *LSA*, Feb. 6, 21; *LET*, Feb. 7, March 15, 20, April 8, 16, May 15, 1919. For police beatings, see also the special April 1919 edition of *The Forward* entitled "The Police in Lawrence."
117. *LET*, March 26, 1919.
118. For this point, see White, *The Limits of Trade Union Militancy*, 181.
119. Capraro Papers, "Victory Bulletin No. 5," Box 8; *New York Call*, March 14, April 8, May 9, 1919; *Textile Worker* (Lawrence), April 12, 23, 1919; *LET*, Feb. 20, March 5, April 1, May 3, 1919.
120. Hentoff, ed. *Essays of Muste*, 62–64.
121. Most of this material is drawn from an account by Leo Robbins, an ACWA organizer in *NTW*, May 31, 1919. See also, *LET*, March 31, April 1, 12, 18, 23, 24, 30, 1919.
122. *LSA*, Feb. 24, 1919; *LET*, March 3, 1919.
123. Capraro Papers, "To All Textile Workers of America," Box 8.
124. *LET*, April 18, 1919; *Providence Journal*, April 23, 28, 1919. See also TWUA Papers, Bulletin No. 1, Box 674.
125. *LET*, April 18, 1919.
126. Ibid., Feb. 12, March 6, April 7, 1919; *LSA*, April 9, 11, 1919; National Archives, RG 65, File #343501, Report of Harvey Kartun, Feb. 14, 1919.
127. *LET*, May 6–17, 1919; *Lawrence Sunday-Sun*, May 11, 1919; *New York Call*, May 16, 18, 1919; Records of the NAWM, Memorandum May 7, 1919, of

meeting between Winthrop Marvin of the National Association of Wool Manufacturers and a Committee from the Non-English Speaking Business and Professional Men, 1919 Strike folder.

128. *LET,* June 26, July 14, Oct. 26, 1917.

129. National Archives, RG 65, File #343501, Reports of Hanrahan for Feb. 13, March 5, 1919.

130. *LET,* Feb. 4, 28, March 25, 1919. For Calitri's conflict with city authorities, see *LSA,* April 14, 1916.

131. National Archives, RG 65, File #350801, Report of Hanrahan for April 30, 1919.

132. *LET,* May 27, 1919. For Rocco's 1912 role, see Fenton, *Immigrants and Unions,* 332–333.

133. *LET,* March 12, April 9, May 10, 1919; Rudolph Vecoli, "Anthony Capraro and the Lawrence Strike of 1919," in George E. Pozetta, ed. *Pane E. Lavoro: The Italian American Working Class—Proceedings of the American Italian Historical Association, Oct. 27, 28, 1978* (Toronto, 1978), 13–14.

134. National Archives, RG 65, File #343501, Report of Feri Weiss, May 14, 1917; *LSA,* April 9, 1919.

135. *LT,* Feb. 8, 10, 1919; *LET,* March 5, 1919; Museum of American Textile History, Report of Manufacturers Conference, May 1, 1919, 1919 Strike folder. Father Milanese considered it more important the strike be defeated than his parishioners get higher wages and he criticized the mill owners when they finally conceded. See Immigrant City Archives, William M. Wood to Rev. M. Milanese, May 26, 1919 (marked Confidential).

136. Vecoli, "Capraro and the Lawrence Strike of 1919," 14; Records of the Archdiocese of Boston, Waters Report, 3.

137. Records of the Archdiocese of Boston, Waters Report, 13.

138. *Advance,* Feb. 28, 1919; *Daily News Record,* March 5, 1919. It is not clear whether Lawrence workers or the ACWA first proposed the sending of the ACWA representatives.

139. *Advance,* March 28, 1919; *Documentary History of the Amalgamated Clothing Workers of America, 1918–1920* (New York, 1920), 216; Vecoli, "Capraro and the Lawrence Strike of 1919," 11–13. The ACWA's attraction for Italian leftists is discussed further in chap. 6.

140. Capraro Papers, Capraro to Joseph Schlossberg, 19 March 1919, Box 8.

141. *ACWA Documentary History,* 216; *Advance,* March 28, 1919; *Textile Worker* (Lawrence), April 23, 1919; *NTW,* April 10, 1920; *LET,* March 15, 1919. Capraro doubled as a correspondent for the *New York Call* and this paper organized a "New York Relief Committee for the Lawrence Strikers." See *New York Call,* March 23, 30, April 3, 5, 12, 15, 19, May 8, 1919.

142. *New York Call,* March 20, 1919; *LSA,* March 24, 1919.

143. *ACWA Documentary History,* 216; *Advance,* April 11, 1919. The full reason for the ACWA's decision is discussed in chap. 6.

144. National Archives, RG 65, File #361492, Minutes of the First ATWA

Convention; Immigrant City Archives, Report of the Industrial Committee of the YWCA.

145. Montgomery, *Workers' Control in America*, 105–106.

146. Federal Council of Churches, *Report on the Lawrence Strike*, 15.

147. These words were used in the opening sentence of the charter of the independent union. See *LSA*, March 19, 1919.

148. Pickering, "The Lawrence Strike," 36; Capraro Papers, Victory Bulletin No. 5, Box 8; *Textile Worker* (Lawrence), April 12, 1919; Vecoli, "Capraro and the Lawrence Strike of 1919," 21.

149. Federal Council of Churches, *Report on the 1919 Strike*, 15.

150. Arno J. Mayer, *Political Origins of the New Diplomacy, 1917–1918* (1959; rpt. New York 1970), 248; Borkenau, *World Communism*, 100. Many Lithuanian workers in the United States soon enrolled in the Communist party. See Draper, *Roots of American Communism*, 189.

151. National Archives, RG 65, File #343501, Report of Harvey Kartun, Feb. 6, 1919; File #202600, Report of Kartun, Feb. 16, 1919.

152. Capraro Papers, Interviews with Mrs. Bastyani, John Holopich, Mary Glinka and Account of the Lithuanian Mass Meeting, April 4, 1919, Box 8.

153. Davis, "Capitalism on Trial," 136–137.

154. Pickering, "The Lawrence Strike," 35–36.

155. Capraro Papers, Interviews with Fred Telucik and Annie Trina, Box 8.

156. National Archives, RG 65, File #343501, Report of Hanrahan, March 11, 1919. Siimlar resolutions were passed at Lithuanian, Russian, Italian, and Syrian meetings and were in part a protest against the lack of shipping, which meant those who wished to leave could not do so. See *LET*, March 8, 11, April 1, 1919.

157. *Revolutionary Age*, Feb. 15, 1919. For Haywood's comments, see Buhle, "Debsian Socialism and the 'New Immigrant' Worker," 280.

158. National Archives, RG 65, File #343501, Report of Hanrahan, Feb. 4, 1919; File #350801, Report of Hanrahan, Feb. 20, 1919.

159. *LET*, March 26, 27, 31, April 1, 1919.

160. Vecoli, "Capraro and the Lawrence Strike of 1919," 10.

161. *Boston Globe*, March 27, 1919.

162. For the statement by Evans, see National Archives, RG 2, File #2694.

163. Fitch, "Lawrence—A Strike for Wages or for Bolshevism?" 42–46.

164. Records of the NAWM, Executive Committee Meetings, Jan. 29, April 11, 1919.

165. *LET*, April 1, 14, 1919. See also Museum of American Textile History, 1919 Strike Folder.

166. National Archives, RG 65, File #343501, Report of Hanrahan, April 24, 1919.

167. Ibid., File #343501, Report of Hanrahan, March 20, 1919; Vecoli, "Capraro and the Lawrence Strike of 1919," 15–16; Hentoff, ed. *Essays of Muste*,

73–74; Interview with Rocco; *LSA*, May 3, 1919; *Lawrence Sunday-Sun*, May 4, 1919.

168. Hentoff, ed. *Essays of Muste*, 64–65, 70–71; *New York Call*, May 7–11, 23, 1919; *LET*, May 6–8, 1919.

169. Capraro Papers, Evelyn Bramhall to Capraro, 19 May 1919, Box 8; *New York Call*, May 23, 1919; *Advance*, May 16, 1919.

170. *Bulletin of the NAWM*, 49 (April 1919), 186; Records of the NAWM, Conference of Lawrence Manufacturers, May 1, 1919.

171. Cole, *American Wool Manufacture*, 2: 238–239.

172. Museum of American Textile History, Conference of Lawrence Manufacturers, 1919 Strike Folder.

173. Hentoff, ed. *Essays of Muste*, 75–77; *New York Call*, May 20–22, 1919; *LET*, May 20–22, 1919.

6. Establishing an Organization

1. *Advance*, Nov. 22, 1918, March 28, 1919; *Documentary History of the Amalgamated Clothing Workers of America, 1918–1919*, 288–290.

2. *Advance*, Jan. 24, 1919.

3. Ibid, Dec. 13, 1918, Feb. 21, March 28, 1919.

4. *Ibid*, March 28, 1919. See also Josephson, *Sidney Hillman*, 90–100; Leiserson, *Adjusting Immigrants and Industry*, 211–212.

5. For the organization of women clothing workers and their ongoing struggles to gain leadership positions, see Carolyn Daniel McCreesh, *Women in the Campaign to Organize Garment Workers, 1880–1917* (New York, 1983), 198–227; Nancy Schrom Dye, *As Equals and As Sisters: Feminism, the Labor Movement and the Women's Trade Union League of New York* (Columbia, Missouri, 1980), chap. 4.

6. Josephson, *Sidney Hillman*, 110–193.

7. C. Roland Marchand, *The American Peace Movement and Social Reform, 1898–1918* (Princeton, 1972), 317–319; Joseph Rappaport, "Jewish Immigrants and World War I: A Study of American Press Reactions," (Ph.D. diss., Columbia University, 1951), 346–352; Steve Fraser, "Dress Rehearsal for the New Deal: Shop Floor Insurgents, Political Elites, and Industrial Democracy in the Amalgamated Clothing Workers," in Michael M. Frisch and Daniel J. Walkowitz, eds. *Working Class America Essays on Labor, Community and American Society* (Urbana, Ill., 1983), 219–220.

8. For a sympathetic discussion of the ACWA's principles, see Budish and Soule, *The New Unionism in the Clothing Industry*, 270–302; for a critical perspective, see Fraser, "Dress Rehearsal for the New Deal," 212–255.

9. Fenton, *Immigrants and Unions*, 545–546; *Solidarity*, May 20, 1915, April 29, July 8, Aug. 12, 1916, Jan. 27, Feb. 10, 1917.

10. Fenton, *Immigrants and Unions*, 545–546; Montgomery, *Workers' Control in America*, 106; Wolkovich, *Bay State "Blue" Laws and Bimba*, 34–35.

11. *Advance*, Jan. 24, Nov. 14, 1919; Fraser, "Dress Rehearsal for the New Deal," 212–255.

12. *ACWA Documentary History*, 215–217; Hentoff, ed. *Essays of Muste*, 79; *Advance*, May 2, 1919; *NTW*, Aug. 30, 1919.

13. *Advance*, April 18, 1919; *NTW*, April 10, 1920; National Archives, RG 65, File # 361492, Minutes of the First ATWA Convention.

14. I have used the term "intellectual" to describe anyone who had a college education. Though this is not the normal definition for the word, in the context of the labor movement anyone with this level of education did stand out as an intellectual.

15. Capraro Papers, A. J. Muste, "Christianity, The Only Hope of the World," Box 8. For Muste's religious beliefs, see also Jo Ann Ooiman Robinson, *Abraham Went Out: A Biography of A. J. Muste* (Philadelphia, 1981), 15–28. For the Bellancas, see Fenton, *Immigrants and Unions*, 566.

16. *Lawrence Sunday-Sun*, March 9, 1919.

17. Capraro Papers, Handwritten Autobiographical Fragment, Box 2.

18. Ibid, Autobiography in Miniature, Box 8.

19. *LET*, Jan. 26, 1921.

20. National Archives, RG 65, File #25320, Report of H. P. Shaughnessy for July 24, 1918; Capraro Papers, Special April 1920 issue of *The Social Service Bulletin of the Methodist Federation for Social Service* entitled "Christianity and the Labor Movement," Box 8.

21. Norman Thomas Papers, New York Public Library, Evan Thomas to Mother, 4 May 1917, Evan Thomas to Norman Thomas, 14 November 1916, 15 January 1917, 16 May 1918, Box 113; Howard W. Moore, *Plowing My Own Furrow*, (New York, 1985), 106–107.

22. One of Thomas's visitors at Fort Leavenworth described him as "thinner than any human being I had ever seen." See Ella Reeve Bloor, *We Are Many* (New York, 1940), 153.

23. Moore, *Plowing My Own Furrow*, 106–146; Charles Chatfield, *For Peace and Justice, Pacifism in America, 1919–1941* (Knoxville, Tenn., 1971), 63, 78–86; Evan Thomas, "Disciplinary Barracks—The Experience of a Military Prisoner at Fort Leavenworth," *The Survey* 41 (Feb. 1, 1919): 625–629; Evan Thomas, "One of the Worst Tragedies in Life," *The World Tomorrow* 2 (February 1919), 41–42.

24. National Archives, RG 65, File #153964, Reports of R. W. Grimes for March 19, June 8, 9, 1918; Solon de Leon, ed. *The American Labor Who's Who* (New York, 1975), 64. For Dunn's thoughts on labor issues, see Robert W. Dunn, "Towards Industrial Democracy," *The Forward* 2 (Oct. 1918): 106–109; Robert W. Dunn, "Organized Labor in America: The American Federation of Labor," *The Forward* 3 (Jan. 1919): 11–12.

25. Robert W. Dunn, "At Lawrence—Preparing the Workers for a New World," *Young Democracy* 1 (April 15, 1919).

26. Paul Blanshard, *Personal and Controversial* (Boston, 1963), 1–63.

27. *NTW*, March 13, 1920; National Archives, RG 65, File #168799, Robert W. Dunn to Brent Allison, 29 January 1920.

28. Ibid., File #13964; Marchand, *American Peace Movement*, 374–379; Chatfield, *For Peace and Justice*, 62.

29. "Victory at Lawrence," *The World Tomorrow* 2 (June 1919): 164.

30. Walter Rauschenbusch, *Christianity and the Social Crisis* (1907; rpt. New York, 1964), 368.

31. Cedric Long, "Out of Lawrence," *Young Democracy* 1 (July 1, 1919).

32. For a good statement of the ministers' asceticism, see A. J. Muste, "Surfeit and Famine " *The World Tomorrow* 1 (October 1918): 253–255. Rauschenbusch himself had warned those interested in labor problems against being overly concerned with the "stomach question." See Rauschenbusch, *Christianity and Crisis*, 368.

33. Stanley Shapiro, "The Great Reform: Liberals and Labor, 1912–1919," *Labor History* 12 (Summer 1971): 327. The terms in quotation marks are Bruce Laurie's description of antebellum Philadelphia working-class "radicals" but they seem fully applicable to the ACWA and the ministers. See Laurie, *Working People of Philadelphia*, 79.

34. Joseph Schlossberg, *The Workers and Their World* (New York, 1935), 159–202; *Industrial Union News*, May 17, 1919; SLP Papers, Accession, Arnold Peterson to Joseph Schlossberg, Nov. 4, 1916; Schlossberg to Peterson, Nov. 6, 1916, both in Box 9; Suspension and Proposed Reorganization of the Jewish Socialist Labor Federation; Peterson to Englisher, November 11, 1917, both in Box 75, Folder 5; To the National Executive Committee of the Socialist Labor Party, Box 70, Folder 11.

35. SLP Papers, Accession, Russell Palmer to National Secretary, 13 December 1917, Box 70, Folder 11.

36. SLP Papers, Accession, Russell Palmer to NEC, Dec. 13, 1917, Box 70, Folder 11; R. Konetzki to John C. Butterworth, March 13, 1919, Box 77, Folder 4; *Industrial Union News*, March 1919; *Paterson Sunday Chronicle*, Feb. 9, 1919.

37. The seven delegates who can be identified as former WIIU members are H. J. Rubenstein, Russell Palmer, Isidore Friedman, Harry Pechman, Selig Pitkowitz, Bertha Johnson, and Louis Stein. For the WIIU backgrounds of these delegates, see *Industrial Union News*, April 1918; National Archives, RG 165, File #10110–146, Report of Ted Vella to Major Nicholas Biddle, May 8, 1918; *New York Call*, Feb. 3, 1919.

38. The WIIU was often a victim of the SLP's refusal to tolerate dissent from its positions and even Paterson WIIU/SLP member Roman Konetzki, who remained loyal to the national office through all of the turmoil, eventually

resigned from the WIIU and SLP and became an ATWA organizer in Passaic. See *NTW*, March–April 1924.

39. De Leon, ed. *Who's Who in American Labor,* 181, and *Paterson Morning Call,* Oct. 3, 1955; for examples of Palmer's editorials, see *NTW*, Dec. 1922, Oct.–Dec. 1923.

40. National Archives, RG 65, File #118448, Reports of E. T. Drew for April 11, May 3, 1918; *Industrial Union News,* June 1917, Aug. 9, 1919; *NTW*, Jan. 21, Feb. 28, March 13, 1920.

41. Unfortunately, no information is available on the backgrounds of the Passaic staff members.

42. See David Montgomery, *The Fall of The House of Labor* (New York, 1987), 7.

43. Some Communist party leaders eventually solved this dilemma by changing their names. See Harvey Klehr, *The Heydey of American Communism* (New York, 1987), 230–231.

44. Saposs Papers, David Saposs to Bill Leiserson, March 2, 1919, Box 1; Robert W. Dunn and Jack Hardy, *Labor and Textiles* (New York, 1931), 203; Columbia University Oral History Collection, Interview with A. J. Muste; Montgomery, *Workers' Control in America,* 106.

45. *Textile Worker* (Lawrence), April 23, 1919.

47. Some of the delegates for whom only the last name was given cannot be identified by gender. For the delegates at the convention, see National Archives, RG 65, File #361492, Minutes of the First ATWA Convention; for the union's executive board, see *NTW*, Nov. 8, 1919.

47. The word "public" here is used quite deliberately because in neighborhoods there most certainly were women who played instrumental roles in stimulating resistance and organization. For this type of neighborhood activism, see Cameron, "Bread and Roses Revisited," 40–61.

48. For the leadership in the handkerchief strikes, see *PDN*, Feb. 13, March 13, 1919.

49. Theresa Wolfson, *The Woman Worker and the Trade Unions* (New York, 1926), 140.

50. For the participation of women in the ACWA, see McCreesh, *Women in the Campaign to Organize Garment Workers,* 218–228. For the IWW, see Helen Marot, *American Labor Unions* (New York, 1914), 68.

51. In 1919 and 1920, the *New Textile Worker* published only one article on women workers. This dealt with what today would be described as "comparable worth" but the union did not make this a major issue. See *NTW*, July 17, 1920.

52. National Archives, RG 65, File #361492, Minutes of the First ATWA Convention.

53. *ACWA Documentary History, 1918–1920,* 262. See also Hentoff, ed. *Essays of Muste,* 79.

54. *NTW*, July 5, 1919, Aug. 30, 1919, Jan. 31, 1920, Aug. 6, 1921; Lusk Papers, Investigations: Labor Movement, Microfilm copy, Tamiment Library, New

York University, Untitled ATWA leaflet, n.d. reel 3; *Revolutionary Radicalism—Its History, Purposes and Tactics, Being the Report of a Joint Legislative Committee Investigating Seditious Activities Filed April 24, 1920 in the State of New York* (New York, 1920) 1:955.

55. Dunn and Hardy, *Labor and Textiles*, 204; Brooks, "United Textile Workers," 232.

56. *NTW*, Nov. 8, 1919.

57. By 1920, Palmer openly criticized the lack of centralization. See ibid, Aug. 14, Nov. 6, 1920.

58. Ibid, Nov. 8, 22, 1919.

59. *Advance*, Nov. 21, 1919.

60. Clark, *History of Manufactures in the United States*, 2: 321.

61. Anthony Capraro, one of the few persons to visit both cities during the 1919 work stoppages, was struck by the differing tone of the two walkouts. See *New York Call*, March 10, 1919.

62. At the close of the debate, the convention passed a compromise resolution that pledged the ATWA would do "its utmost to further the interests of the Lawrence strike." See National Archives, RG 65, File #361492, Report on Meeting April 12 and 13, 1919.

7. The ATWA in Lawrence

1. Saposs Papers, Digest of Interviews with Trade Union Officials, Box 21. See also *NTW*, May 24, 1919.

2. *NTW*, Jan. 3, March 27, 1920; Capraro Papers, Capraro to Muste, 14 Jan., 1920, Box 2.

3. *NTW*, Sept. 27, 1919.

4. Immigrant City Archives, Report of the Industrial Committee of the YWCA. This document has no date but its context makes it clear that it was written between October and December 1919.

5. For Muste's account of Mach's activities, see Hentoff, ed. *Essays of Muste*, 64–69. Mach was known to Bureau of Investigation agents as Michael Zierhoffer, and he continued to supply information after the strike was over. See National Archives, RG 65, File #361492, report of Hanrahan, Aug. 7, 1919.

6. *NTW*, June 7, Nov. 22, 1919; Capraro Papers, Long to Capraro, 17 June 1919, Box 8; Immigrant City Archives, Report of the Industrial Committee of the YWCA.

7. *Textile Worker* (Lawrence), April 12, 1919; *NTW*, June 7, 28, July 19, Aug. 16, 1919.

8. For the ACWA's interest in cooperatives, see *Advance*, April 15, 1919. The history of working-class cooperatives is a badly neglected topic, but for an

older survey, see Ellis Cowling, *Cooperatives in America—Their Past, Present and Future* (New York, 1938).

9. Capraro Papers, WCU Preamble, Box 4.
10. *NTW,* June 28, 1919, March 27, 1920; Capraro Papers, *Boston Herald,* May 3, 1920, Box 8.
11. *NTW,* Sept. 27, 1920.
12. Ibid., Nov. 22, 1919; *Textile Worker* (Lawrence), April 12, 1919; Capraro Papers, Emsley to Capraro, 20, 30 Oct., 13, 22 Nov., 3, 8 Dec. 1919, 8 June 1920; F. M. Orlando to Capraro, 9 Dec. 1920, Box 8.
13. *NTW,* July 12, 1919, Jan. 17, 1920; National Archives, RG 65, File #351874, Report of Hanrahan, Jan. 25, 1920; *LSA,* Dec. 12, 17, 1919; Capraro Papers, Entertainment for WCU, Box 8.
14. *LSA,* Aug. 12, Nov. 22, 1919; *LET,* Sept. 12, 1919, May 3, 1920; National Archives, RG 65, #361492, Reports of Hanrahan, Sept. 5, 17, 1919.
15. For female participation in these activities, see Capraro Papers, Entertainment for WCU; Emsley to Capraro, Dec. 1919, Box 8.
16. *NTW,* Sept. 27, 1919; See also *LSA,* Jan. 16, 1921.
17. *NTW,* June 7, 1919; Capraro Papers, Long to Capraro, 17 June 1919, Box 8; Immigrant City Archives, Report of the Industrial Committee of the YWCA.
18. *LSA,* July 24–26, Oct. 21, 1919, May 10–11, 1920; *LET,* July 26, Aug. 29, 1919; *NTW,* March 27, May 8, 1920.
19. *NTW,* June 7, Sept. 27, 1919.
20. *LSA,* Oct. 21, 1919.
21. Ibid., Jan. 4, 1921.
22. National Archives, RG 65, File #361492, Reports of Hanrahan June 6, Sept. 5, 1919; Capraro Papers, Rights of the Italian Delegates to the ATWA Convention, Box 8; *NTW,* Sept. 21, 1919.
23. For the problem of convincing recently arrived immigrants to remain in unions, see Saposs Papers, The Problem of Making Trade Unionists Out of the Large Number of Recently Organized Immigrants, Box 21.
24. National Archives, RG 65, File #361492, Report of Hanrahan, July 18, 1919; Capraro to Muste, Oct. 18, 1919, Box 8.
25. *LET,* July 27, Aug. 24, Sept. 9, 1920.
26. *NTW,* Sept. 27, 1919.
27. A. J. Muste, *The Organization of the Textile Industry,* (Katonah, N. Y., 1927), 28–29. See also *LL,* June 15, 1923.
28. Rotzel, "The Good Fight of Michael Salerno," 52–53; *LET,* July 9, 15, Sept. 11, 13, 1920, Jan. 25, 1921. See also Diggins, *Mussolini and Fascism,* 87.
29. *LET,* Sept. 18, Nov. 15, 1920.
30. *A. W. Employees Booster,* 4 (Jan. 1921): 1; *LET,* Jan. 21, 24, 25, 1921; *LSA,* Jan. 21, 24, 1921.
31. National Archives, RG 65, File #361492, Minutes of the first ATWA Convention, Report of Hanrahan, July 16, 1919.

32. *LSA*, Aug. 28, 1919. See also *NTW*, July 19, Oct. 6, 1919.
33. Records of the NAWM, Record of the Meeting of the Lawrence Manufacturers, Nov. 5, 1919. See also *LSA*, Dec. 2, 1919.
34. *LSA*, May 8, 10, 1920; *NTW*, May 22, 1920.
35. For a survey of welfare capitalism, see Stewart D. Brandes, *American Welfare Capitalism* (Chicago, 1976). For the Amoskeag's programs, see Tamara Hareven, *Family Time and Industrial Time* (New York, 1982), chap. 3.
36. Roddy, *Mills, Mansions and Mergers*, 74, 83–112.
37. Ibid., 75–76; Cole, *American Wool Manufacture*, 2: 244–245; *LL*, April 17, 1923; *Bulletin of the NAWM*, 49 (Oct. 1919): 323–327.
38. *A. W. Employees Booster*, 3 (Feb. 1921); 4 (Sept. 1921).
39. *LET*, June 11, July 10, 1920; *LSA*, April 28, 1920.
40. Roddy, *Mills, Mansions and Mergers*, 75; *LET*, July 10, Nov. 2, 1920; *A. W. Employees Bulletin*, 2 (Feb. 5, 1920).
41. William M. Wood, "The Problems of a Manufacturer," *Bulletin of the NAWM*, 50 (April 1920): 247. A sign held by children at one American Woolen Company function said: "This is another one of the benefits we receive from our great benefactor Mr. W. M. Wood". See Roddy, *Mills, Mansions and Mergers*, 76.
42. *LSA*, Dec. 8, 17, 1919.
43. Ibid., Dec. 10, 12, 1919; For the privately expressed resentments of local merchants towards Wood, see Records of the Archdiocese of Boston, Waters Report, 4, 14.
44. *LSA*, Dec. 15, Jan. 3, 1920; Beal, *Proletarian Journey*, 55.
45. *LET*, Dec. 27, 1919, Jan. 5, 1920; *LSA*, Feb. 20, 22, 25, 1920. In 1923, Wood again began to attack the local bourgeoisie when he led a fight against landlords and coal dealers. See *LL*, May 5, Aug. 17, 1923.
46. Museum of American Textile History, Labor Strike Papers, George Kunhardt to Nathaniel Stevens, 4 Nov. 1919.
47. Cole, *American Wool Manufacture*, 2: 245; *LET*, Sept. 3, 1920, Feb. 26, 1921; *LSA*, Dec. 10, 1919, Sept. 4, 28, 1920, April 27, 1921. For the Pacific's employee representation plan, see Robert W. Dunn, *Company Unions*, (New York, 1927), 60–64.
48. Federal Council of Churches, *Report on the Lawrence Strike*, 4; Papers of the NAWM, F. Ernest Johnson to Rev. Samuel McComb, July 29, 1920, Box 88.
49. *NTW*, June 21, Nov. 22, 1919; May 8, 1920; Beal, *Proletarian Journey*, 55.
50. See, e.g., *LL*, Jan. 20, March 17, April 17, May 18, July 6, 1923.
51. *A. W. Employees Booster* 4 (Feb. 1921); Roddy, *Mills, Mansions and Mergers*, 116; *Bulletin of the NAWM* 50 (Oct. 1920): 410.
52. Roddy, *Mills, Mansions and Mergers*, 117–119; "American Woolen Company," *Fortune* 3 (April 1931): 71–112.
53. *LET*, Aug. 21, 1919; *LSA*, Aug. 12, 1919.
54. *NTW*, Nov. 20, 1919; *LET*, Dec. 15, 1919; *LSA*, Dec. 15, 17, 22, 1919.
55. National Archives, RG 65, File #202600–1622, Report of Hanrahan, Nov.

15, 1919, File #351874, Report of Hanrahan, Jan. 25, 1920; *LSA*, Nov. 7, 8, 1919.

56. *LSA*, Jan. 3, 19, 1920; *Lawrence Sunday-Sun*, Jan. 11, 1920; *LET*, Jan. 3, 10, 22, 27, 1920; *NTW*, Jan. 17, 1920. The Palmer raids were deliberately aimed at citizens as well as at aliens since the Bureau of Investigation planned to turn the citizens over to the states for prosecution under various anti-anarchy statutes. See National Archives, RG 65, File #379331, Memorandum from Frank Stone, Dec. 2, 1919.

57. *LSA*, Jan. 6, 1920.

58. Capraro Papers, Muste to Capraro, 15 Jan. 1920, Box 2.

59. National Archives, RG 65, File #351874, Report by Edward B. Chernes, March 23, 1920.

60. Capraro Papers, Capraro to Muste, 14 Jan., 1920, Box 2; National Archives, RG 65, File #351874, Report of Edward B. Chernes, March 23, 1920.

61. Capraro Papers, Capraro to Muste, 14 Jan. 1920, Box 2.

62. *LSA*, Aug. 13, Oct. 3, 6, 1919, March 5, Sept. 13, Oct. 30, 1920; *LT*, Dec. 11, 1920, Jan. 13, 1921; *LET*, Jan. 13, June 15, 1921; *LL*, Nov. 25, 1922; *35th Annual Report of the Statistics of Manufactures for the Year 1920* (Boston, 1921), XIX.

63. The American Woolen Company had received unusually large cancellations of orders after the company's indictment for profiteering (the charges were later dropped) but the Lawrence mills suffered disproportionately from the closings. See *Bulletin of the NAWM* 50 (Oct. 1920): 403–412.

64. *LSA*, July 8, 19, 25, 1920, Jan. 26, 1921; *NTW*, Sept. 11, 1920; *LT*, Dec. 11, 18, 1920, Jan. 6, 1921.

65. *LET*, July 19, 1920. See also ibid., July 17, 1920.

66. Ibid., July 23, 1920.

67. *LSA*, Aug. 1, 1920.

68. *LET*, July 26, 1920. For Carr's campaign, see *LSA*, Nov. 19, 1919.

69. *Lawrence Sunday-Sun*, July 25, 1920; *LT*, Jan. 13, 1921.

70. For bonds between the working class and middle class in the late nineteenth century, see Herbert Gutman, "The Workers Search for Power," in H. Wayne Morgan, ed. *The Gilded Age* (Syracuse, 1963), 31–54.

71. *Lawrence Sunday Sun*, July 25, 1920; *LSA*, Aug. 13, Sept. 11, 1920; *LT*, Nov. 15, 1920; *Bulletin of the NAWM*, 50 (Oct. 1920): 403.

72. The manufacturers had granted a second wage hike of 15 percent on May 31, 1920, just before the cutbacks in employment. See *Bulletin of the NAWM* 51 (Jan. 1921), 136.

73. *LSA*, Dec. 21, 1920; *LT*, Dec. 22, 1920; *Textile Worker* 6 (Dec. 1921), 417.

74. *LSA*, Jan. 10, 16, 1921; *Boston American*, Jan. 17, 1921. See also *LL*, April 27, Oct. 14, 1922.

75. Lusk Papers, Investigations—Labor Movement, Statement of the General Strike Committee, May 22, Reel 4. Written on top of the statement is a note

that reads "written and (illegible) by H. Rotzel but unfortunately not accepted by the committee."

76. *NTW*, Aug. 2, 1919; *LET*, Aug. 21, 1919.
77. Capraro Papers, Capraro to Muste, Oct. 18, 1919, Box 2.
78. *NTW*, Oct. 25, 1919.
79. Capraro Papers, Rotzel to Capraro, Oct. 21, 1919, Box 2.
80. Immigrant City Archives, Report of the Industrial Committee of the YWCA.
81. *NTW*, Nov. 22, 1919.
82. Capraro Papers, Muste to Capraro, 17 Jan. 1920, Box 2. Although the ACWA had rejected the idea of incorporating the textile workers, the national office of the ATWA continued to press for a merger. See *NTW*, Aug. 30, Nov. 8, 1919.
83. Capraro Papers, Emsley to Capraro, Feb. 27, 1920, March 16, 1920, Box 8; Capraro to Muste, March 1, 1920, Box 2.
84. *Solidarity*, Feb. 15, 1913; Snyder, "Women, Wobblies and Workers' Rights," 26–60; Archives of Labor and Urban Affairs, Wayne State University, Matilda Robbins Collection, Matilda Robbins, "My Story," Box 2; National Archives, RG 65, File #363502, Report of R. W. Finch, March 17, 1919.
85. For the OBU, see David J. Bercuson, *Fools and Wise Men: The Rise and Fall of the One Big Union*, (Toronto, 1978); Dutton Savage, *Industrial Unionism in America*, 187–192; National Archives, RG 65, File #125732, "One Big Union", File #143045, Report of Louis Lobel, June 6, 1920.
86. A. Ross McCormick, *Reformers, Rebels and Revolutionaries; The Western Canadian Radical Movement, 1899–1919*, (Toronto, 1977), 158–160; David J. Bercuson, *Confrontation at Winnipeg, Labor, Industrial Relations and the General Strike*, (Montreal, 1974).
87. *New York Sunday Call Magazine*, July 20, 1919; National Archives, RG 165, File #10110–1246, Capt. John Trevor to Director Military Intelligence, May 28, 1919; Benjamin Legere, "The One Big Union in Canada," *Revolutionary Age* (July 1919), 5; National Archives, RG 65, File #363502, Benjamin Legere, "With Force and Violence."
88. *NTW*, Jan. 18, 1921; *LL*, Nov. 25, 1922 (reprint of March 19, 1921 article).
89. Capraro Papers, Emsley to Capraro, June 8, 1920; Capraro to Emsley, 22 June 1920; Mauceri's letter from Lawrence—Translation of letter addressed to Capraro for Muste, June 28, 1920, all Box 8; *LSA*, Aug. 12, 1920; National Archives, RG 65, File #186701–189, Report of M. Robert Valkenburgh, March 22, 1921.
90. Capraro Papers, Verses from the Bible of the Amalgamated Clothing Workers of America, Box 8.
91. *New York Times*, Dec. 26, 1920.
92. For the role of Italian and Franco-Belgian workers in the OBU, see *LL*, April 27, Oct. 14, 1922; Beal, *Proletarian Journey*, 77.

93. *LL,* June 3, 1922.

94. Ibid., July 27, 1923.

95. See ibid., Dec. 16, 1922 for the OBU's critique of the ATWA's activities in the year following the strike.

96. *LT,* Dec. 22, 1920; *LSA,* Dec. 23, 1920.

97. For Legere's efforts in Essex County, see National Archives, RG 65, File #202600–22, Report of M. T. Hart, Jan. 3, 1921; *Salem Evening News,* Jan. 3, 1921.

98. *NTW,* Sept. 25, 1920, Jan. 8, 1921; *New York Times,* Dec. 27, 1920; *Haverhill Evening Gazette,* Dec. 30, 1920.

99. *New York Times,* Dec. 27, 1920; *NTW,* Jan. 8, 1921.

100. For the appeal of ACWA-style unionism for Sicilians, see Donna Gabaccia, "Neither Padrone Slaves nor Primitive Rebels; Sicilians on Two Continents," in Hoerder, ed. *"Struggle a Hard Battle,"* 95–120.

101. *LSA,* Jan. 17, April 14, 1921; National Archives, RG 65, File #202600–22, Report for Jan. 10, 1921.

102. *LL,* April 27, 1922. For the OBU's membership gains, see *Massachusetts Industrial Review,* 8 (June 1922): 19.

103. *LL,* Feb. 10, March 17, June 8, 15, 22, 1923; Beal, *Proletarian Journey,* 76–78.

104. *NTW,* Jan. 8, Feb. 12, 1921; *LL,* Dec. 30, 1922.

8. The ATWA in Passaic

1. *PDN,* April 24, May 17, 1919; *PDH,* April 29, 1919; *NTW,* May 24, 1919.

2. *PDN,* July 24–30, Aug. 22, 23, 25, 1919; *NTW,* June 2, Nov. 22, 1919.

3. Alice Barrows Fernandez, *The Problem of Adult Education in Passaic, New Jersey,* U. S. Bureau of Education Bulletin No. 4 (Washington, D. C., 1920), 19. For the reluctance of Passaic's workers to learn English, see Women's Bureau, *Family Status of Breadwinning Women in Four Cities,* 11–13.

4. Lusk Papers, Investigations—Labor Movement, Report of Robert W. Dunn, Oct. 10, 1919, Reel 3; Papers of the American Civil Liberties Union (hereafter ACLU Papers), Microfilm copy, New York Public Library, Robert W. Dunn to Roger Baldwin, 5 February 1920, vol. 119.

5. National Archives, RG 65, File #361492, "Demands"; Papers of the Amalgamated Clothing and Textile Workers Union, Labor-Management Document Center, Martin P. Catherwood Library of New York State School of Industrial and Labor Relations, Cornell University, Ithaca, N. Y., Muste to Hillman, 26 April 1920. See also, *PDN,* April 27, 30, 1920. I am indebted to Steve Fraser for informing me about the material in the Amalgamated's papers.

6. *PDN,* May 18, 19, 1920; Records of the NAWM, Executive Committee Meeting, May 18, 1920.

7. *PDN,* May 24, 1920.
8. Ibid., June 5, 1920. See also *PDH,* June 1, 1920.
9. *NTW,* June 5, 1920. See also *PDH,* June 1, 1920.
10. *NTW,* July 3, Sept. 11, 25, 1920.
11. National Archives, RG 131, Minutes of the Botany Board of Directors, Aug. 6, 1920, Jan. 7, 1921, Box 49; Shellabarger, "The Shawled Women of Passaic," 467; De Lima, *Night Working Mothers in Textile Mills,* 18; *PDN,* July 7, Sept. 1, Oct. 16, 19, 1920, Feb. 7, 1921.
12. Lusk Papers, Report of Robert W. Dunn, Oct. 10, 1919, Reel 3.
13. *The Jewish Advocate* (Boston), Nov. 14, 21, Dec. 5, 1918, Jan. 23, 1919; Michael R. Marrus, *The Unwanted-European Refugees in the Twentieth Century* (New York, 1985), 63; Oscar Jankowsky, *Jews and Minority Rights, 1898– 1919* (New York, 1933), 358–360; Edward Kantowicz, *Polish-American Politics in Chicago* (Chicago, 1970), 93–94, 117–119; Parot, *Polish-Catholics in Chicago,* 174–175.
14. *PDN,* Dec. 6, 10, 13, 1918.
15. Ibid., May 22, 23, 1919; *PDH,* May 20, 22, 23, 24, 29, June 23, 30, 1919.
16. *PDN,* Dec. 6, 1918, June 27, 1919; *PDH,* May 29, 1919.
17. *PDN,* May 15, 1919; *PDH,* April 25, May 16, June 6, 1919.
18. *PDN,* May 2, 8, 9, 1919.
19. Ibid., Aug. 9, 11, 14, 16, 1920. See also John J. Bukowczyk, "Mary the Messiah: Polish Immigrant Heresy and the Malleable Ideology of the Roman Catholic Church, 1880–1930," *Journal of American Ethnic History* 4 (Spring 1985), 5–32.
20. *PDN,* May 27, 1919. For opposition to Bolshevism during the strike, see ibid., Feb. 22, 26, 27, March 3, 1919.
21. *NTW,* July 5, 1919.
22. Albert Weisbord, *Passaic Reviewed* (San Francisco, 1976), 31–32; *Textile Strike Bulletin* (Passaic), March 22, May 21, June 25, 1926; Mary Heaton Vorse, *The Passaic Textile Strike, 1926–1927* (Passaic, 1927), 6. For efforts by the Passaic local to make use of the German issue, see Capraro Papers, "The Agitator, Injustice," Box 8; *PDH,* May 24, 25, 1920.
23. *PDN,* March 24, Sept. 16, 1919, May 24, 27, 1920; National Archives, RG 65, File #360212, Report of Benjamin Turner, June 7, 1919, Report of K-40, May 27, 1919.
24. For the participation of Hungarian women in the ATWA, see Lusk Papers, Report of Robert W. Dunn, Oct. 10, 1919, Reel 3; National Archives, RG 65, File #384234, Report of Martin Mullen, May 5, 1920; *PDH,* May 3, 1920.
25. This survey found that two-thirds of all Polish women in Passaic for over ten years did not speak English while only one-quarter of all Hungarian women in the country for the same length of time had not learned the language. See Women's Bureau, *Family Status of Breadwinning Women in Four Cities,* 11–13.
26. F. L. Carsten, *Revolution in Central Europe* (Berkeley, 1972), 238–243;

National Archives, RG 65, File # 360212, Report of Benjamin Turner, June 7, 1919; *PDH*, June 12, Aug. 18, 19, 1919; Interview with Deak.

27. Borkenau, *World Communism*, 100–101; Wasyl Halich, *Ukrainians in the U. S.* (1937; rpt. New York, 1970), 7–8, 76; *PDH*, Jan. 3, Feb. 2, 1920; for anti-Polish protest meetings cosponsored by Carpatho-Rusyns, see *PDN*, Dec. 30, 1918, Dec. 9, 22, 1919.

28. *PDN*, June 16, 1921, Feb. 20, 1926; Interview with Deak; Vera Buch Weisbord, *A Radical Life* (Bloomington, Indiana, 1971), 101.

29. *PDH*, April 26, May 5, 1919; *PDN*, July 25, 29, 1919.

30. *PDH*, May 24, 1920.

31. Ibid., May 13, 1919.

32. See, e.g., ibid., May 13, July 29, 1919.

33. Ibid., May 1, 1920. See also *PDH*, April 25, 1919.

34. *PDN*, May 4, 28, 1920.

35. Ibid., July 26–28, 1919, March 5, May 28, 1920; *PDH*, April 16, 17, 26, 1919; National Archives, RG 65, File #361492, Demands.

36. *NTW*, June 11, 1921. See also ibid., Nov. 22, 1919, Jan. 17, Sept. 11, 1920; *PDN*, June 26, 27, 29, 1919; *Textile Strike Bulletin* (Passaic), April 12, 1926.

37. TWUA Papers, Henry Hunt to Thomas McMahon, October 2, 1926, Box 1, File 7A; *PDH*, April 12, 28, May 14, 1919; *PDN*, April 14, 17, 25, 1919, Ebner, "Strikes and Society," 16.

38. *PDN*, June 14, 17, 23, 26, July 26–29, 1919; *PDH*, July 25–29, 1919; National Archives, RG 65, File #360212, Report of Captain of Detectives, Benjamin F. Turner, June 7, 1919.

39. *PDH*, Jan. 3–10, 12, Feb. 2–4, 1920.

40. ACLU Papers, Robert W. Dunn to Roger Baldwin, Jan. 29, 1920, Reel 16; Donald Johnson, *The Challenge to American Freedoms: World War I and the Rise of the American Civil Liberties Union* (Lexington, Ky., 1963), 145–148.

41. *PDN*, March 23, 30, 31, April 2–7 1920; ACLU Papers, ACLU Weekly News Release, April 26, 1920, Reel 20; *NTW*, April 10, 1920; Shellabarger, "The Shawled Women of Passaic," 467.

42. ACLU Papers, Cedric Long to Albert de Silver, 12 May 1920, Reel 20; *PDN*, April 6, 7, June 24, 1920, May 18, 1921.

43. *PDN*, April 10, 21, 1921; William Hand, "America in Passaic," *New Republic* 22 (April 7, 1920): 183; William Hand, "They Must Have Espionage," *New Republic* 22 (April 14, 1920): 277; ACLU Papers, Field Secretary of ACLU to Robert W. Dunn, 17 March 1920, Cedric Long to Albert de Silver, April 23, 1920, Reel 20; Henry F. May, *The End of American Innocence* (Chicago, 1959), 177.

44. ACLU Papers, Cedric Long to Albert de Silver, April 23, 1920, Reel 20.

45. *PDN*, July 5, Nov. 22, Dec. 1, 19, 20, 1919, Jan. 3, 26, 1920.

46. Ibid., Dec., 18–22, 1919; *PDH*, Dec. 18, 19, 1919.

47. *PDH*, March 3–5, 1920. This "benefit" provided an ample opportunity for

spying as in the first two months of the plan's operation, 793 of the mill's 4500 employees had received visits. See ibid., May 3–5, 1920.

48. A full description of the employee representation plan and other welfare programs can be found in *The F and H News* 1 (Jan. 1920). This issue is in Museum of American Textile History and is the only copy of the Forstmann publication that I have located.

49. Dunn, *Company Unions*, 51–56; Mary Heaton Vorse Papers, News Releases, General Relief Committee, July–August 1926, Box 117; *Textile Strike Bulletin* (Passaic), May 28, 1926.

50. National Archives, RG 131, Report of the Botany Board of Directors, Aug. 6, 1920, Box 49. See also RG 131, Report of the Committee on the Welfare of Employees, May 23, 1919, Report of the Botany Board of Directors, Box 49.

51. De Lima, *Night Working Mothers in Textile Mills*, 7; National Archives, RG 131, Report of the Botany Board of Directors, Jan. 7, 21, 1921, Box 49.

52. *PDN*, Oct. 1, 1920. See also, ibid., July 7, Sept. 20, 1920.

53. Ibid., Oct. 18, 1920.

54. Ibid., July 26, 30, 1919.

55. *NTW*, Jan. 17, 1920.

56. The Botany Company believed that its life insurance plan had a "very beneficial effect upon the employees." See National Archives, RG 131, Report of the Botany Board of Directors, July 14, 1919, Box 49.

57. Records of the NAWM, Employment Bureau, conducted by the Industrial Council of Passaic Wool Manufacturers, Report of Paul T. Chernington, March 8, 1921.

58. Mary Heaton Vorse Papers, "Instructions," in News Releases, United Front Committee, March–May 1926, Box 117. For confirmation that these instructions date from 1919, see Vorse Papers, Forstmann vs. United Front Committee, Box 116, which has a statement by John Sherman who was hired in 1919 to be "a clerk, interpreter, and investigator" for the Wool Council.

59. "The Passaic Strike," *The Christian Century* 43 (Aug. 5, 1926): 971; *NTW*, Nov. 22, 1919, Jan. 17, Feb. 28, 1920; *Textile Strike Bulletin* (Passaic), April 12, 1926; *PDN*, Feb. 24, 1920.

60.1 Robert W. Dunn, "F and Hsm in Passaic," *Labor Age* 15 (July 1926): 7–8.

61. *PDH*, July 29, 1919.

62. Dutton Savage, *Industrial Unionism in America*, 259.

63. For an account of the Fernandez controversy, see Siegal, "The Passaic Textile Strike of 1926," 100–105. See also, *PDN*, Feb. 23–25, Sept. 16, 24, Nov. 11, 1920; *NTW*, March 13, 1920.

64. *NTW*, July–Aug. 1924.

65. The ATWA hung on until 1924, but it was finished as a fighting organization after the summer of 1920.

9. The ATWA in Paterson

1. *48th Annual Report of the Silk Association of America* (1919), 81; *PEN*, July 11, 21, Nov. 8, 1919, Jan. 20, 1920; *1920 Census, Manufactures*, 9:219.
2. National Archives, RG 65, File #361492, Carole to A.N.D., Aug. 21, 1919.
3. *Industrial Union News*, Aug. 9, 1919; *New Solidarity*, Aug. 23, 1919; *Rebel Worker*, Sept. 1, 1919.
4. For Hubschmidt and Derrick, see *PEN*, Oct. 23, 1915, Nov. 5, 1919; *PPG*, Nov. 20, 1919; for Harwood, see De Leon, ed. *American Labor Who's Who*, 99; *PEN*, Sept. 13, 1917; for Hendley, see *PEN*, Aug. 8, 30, 1917.
5. For the school and the lecture series, see Tamiment Library, The Paterson ATWA Scrapbook (#20).
6. For the manufacturers' position, see *PPG*, June 27, 1919.
7. *PEN*, July 1, 8, 15, 1919.
8. *Rebel Worker*, Aug. 15, 1919; William Shriver, *A Pioneering Study of the Silkworkers of Paterson* (New York, 1929), 18; Matsui, *History of the Silk Industry*, 43; *PPG*, June 27, 1919; *Paterson Sunday Chronicle*, July 13, 1919; *PEN*, July 26, 1919.
9. *PEN*, Aug. 2–16, 1919; *NTW*, Aug. 16, 1919.
10. *PEN*, Aug. 9, 1919.
11. *NTW*, June 28, July 5, 12, 19, 1919; *PPG*, June 25, 26, July 11, 1919.
12. *NTW*, July 12, 1919.
13. Lusk Papers, Memorandum for Mr. Stevenson from R. W. Finch, n.d., Reel 3. See also *NTW*, July 19, Aug. 2, 1919.
14. *PEN*, Aug. 16–20, 21, 25, Oct. 10, 1919; *NTW*, Aug. 16, Sept. 13, 1919; Elizabeth Glendower Evans Papers, Schlessinger Library, Radcliffe College, "Oppressed Workers Call for Help," Folder 107.
15. *New York Call*, Aug. 17, 1919; *Paterson Morning Call*, Sept. 2, 1919.
16. See, e.g., *PPG*, Aug. 25, Sept. 8, 1919; *PEN*, Aug. 25, 26, Sept. 6, 8, 17, 1919.
17. Cedric Long, "Out of Lawrence," *Young Democracy* 1 (July 1, 1919); Capraro Papers, Capraro to Muste, 10 October 1919, Box 2.
18. "Unions, Strikes and Violence," *The World Tomorrow* 2 (Oct. 1919): 269.
19. *PPG*, Aug. 12, 1919.
20. Norman Thomas, "Organization or Violence," *The Nation* 109 (Oct. 4, 1919): 269.
21. TWUA Papers, Biographical File, Reel 4.
22. *Daily News Record*, July 19, 1919. See also, *NTW*, Dec. 6, 1919; *Textile Worker* 6 (Jan. 1920): 452; *PEN*, Jan. 17, 20, 1920.
23. *NTW*, July 5, 1919.
24. For UTW comments on the "foreign element," see National Archives, RG 2, File #1123, February Hearing, 34; March Hearing 40–41. See also *PEN*, Dec. 20, 1919, Feb. 21, March 1, 1920.

25. For Paterson's Syrian and Armenian population, see *CIR*, 3:2473; Senior Class, *A History of Paterson*, 113.

26. Figures derived from *Davison's Silk Trade* (New York, 1915–1920).

27. Nancy Fogelson, "They Paved the Streets with Silk: Paterson Silk Workers, 1913–1924," *New Jersey History* 97 (Autumn 1979): 140–141; William M. Poz, "Commission Weaving," *American Silk Journal* 38 (December 1919): 55–58; A. K. Baker, "The Growth of Commission Weaving," *American Silk Journal* 40 (July 1920): 73–74. For an interpretation that emphasizes economic rather than cultural factors, see Philip J. McLewin, "Labor Conflict and Technological Change: The Family Shop in Paterson, New Jersey," in Scranton, ed. *Silk City*, 135–158.

28. *CIR*, 3:2573, 2586; *PEN*, March 13, 1919; Interview with Hy Gorinsky, in author's possession. For the analogous situation in the garment industry, see Leibman, *Jews and the Left*, 198–200.

29. See comments of Rabbi Harry Richmond in *American Silk Journal* 39 (July 1920): 44.

30. YIVO Archives, Report from the National Organizations Committee, Oct. 5, 1924, 155.

31. Ibid., Report from the National Organizations Committee, Sept. 10, 1924, 136. This document does not give the exact year in which the chapter was dissolved but it appears to be either 1919 or 1920.

32. See Liebman, *Jews and the Left*, 363.

33. *Rebel Worker*, Aug. 15, Sept. 15, 1919; *New Solidarity*, Aug. 9, Sept. 12, Nov. 8, 22, 1919, Jan. 3, 1920; National Archives, RG 65, File #384195, Special Report in re Anarchistic Propaganda, Feb. 12, 1920. For Blossom, see the brief background sketch in Wisconsin Historical Society, Madison Wis., Frederick Blossom Papers. See also David Kennedy, *Birth Control in America: The Career of Margaret Sanger* (New Haven, Ct., 1970) 88–93.

34. Tamiment Library, *Paterson Textile Worker*, November 1919, in Paterson ATWA scrapbook. This is the only issue of this newspaper that I have located. See also, *Rebel Worker*, Sept. 1, 1919; *New Solidarity*, Sept. 13, 1919, Jan. 1, 1920.

35. See, e.g., *Industrial Union News*, May 3, 1919.

36. Blossom was later accused of being a spy and agent provocateur. These charges do not appear to have had any factual basis and were a further sign of the bitterness that affected many Wobblies in the 1920s. See Blossom Papers, Industrial Workers of the World, Box 4, Folder 9.

37. *PPG*, Feb. 8, 1919; *New Solidarity*, May 8, 1920; *NTW*, Sept. 3, 1921.

38. *Paterson Textile Worker*, Nov. 1919; *NTW*, Dec. 6, 1919; *New Solidarity*, Jan. 3, Feb. 28, 1920; Capraro Papers, Thomas to Capraro, 10 April 1920, Box 8.

39. *New York Times*, Feb. 16, 1920; *PEN*, Feb. 16, 1920.

40. For federal infiltration of the anarchist community, see National Archives, RG 65, File #384195, Special Report in re Anarchistic Propaganda for period

July 16–27, 1919; File #364028, Memorandum for Frank Stone, March 8, 1920.

41. *New Solidarity,* Feb. 28, March 27, 1920. According to one dissident anarchist, Caminata himself was responsible for letting "everybody know that he is the publisher of *La Jacquerie.*" See National Archives, RG 65, File #28943, Letter from Cueno, n.d.

42. Patrick Renshaw, *The Wobblies* (New York, 1967), 175–176. For splits within the Italian radical community, see Nunzio Pernicone, "Carlo Tresca and the Sacco-Vanzetti Case," *Journal of American History* 66 (December 1976): 535–547.

43. *New Solidarity,* Feb. 28, 1920. For the response of Tresca and Giovannitti to these charges, see ibid., March 27, 1920; *New York Call,* March 16, 1920.

44. For the ATWA's expression of these hopes, see *NTW,* June 7, 1919.

45. George N. Berlet, "The 1920 Silk Slump," *The American Silk Journal* 39 (June 1920): 45–46; Robert Paul Volyn, "The Broad Silk Industry in Paterson, New Jersey: A Troubled Industry in Microcosm, 1920 through 1925," (Ph.D. diss., New York University, 1980), 41–42; *49th Annual Report of the Silk Association of America,* 79–80; *PEN,* March 24, April 29, 1920; *Daily News Record,* April 2, 13, May 7, 8, 14.

46. *PEN,* June 5, 1920.

47. *NTW,* July 17, 1920.

48. *PPG,* July 16, 24–27, 1920; *PEN,* July 24–27, 1920; *NTW,* July 31, 1920; Evan Thomas, "Paterson Proves a Moral," *The World Tomorrow* 3 (Sept. 1920): 278–279.

49. *PPG,* July 16, 24, 1920; *PEN,* Aug. 17, 1920.

50. *PEN,* Sept. 24, 25, Oct. 11, 18, 21, 25, 28, Nov. 5, 8, 11, 15, 18, 26, 1920.

51. Ibid., July 7, 1919, Jan. 9, 1921.

52. For Starr's earlier comments, see National Archives, RG 2, Docket #1123, March Hearing, 33; for his later comments, see *PEN,* Jan. 11, April 27, 1921.

53. *PEN,* Aug. 6, Sept. 6, 21, Oct. 7, 1920.

54. Ibid., Jan. 6, 7, 17, 1921; *New York Times,* Jan. 18, 1921.

55. For a sign that this would again emerge as the key issue in Paterson, see "Two Loom System Costs Paterson Millions," *The American Silk Journal* 40 (Nov. 1921): 55–56.

56. See Paterson Public Library, Constitution and By-Laws of the Associated Silk Workers Organized in Paterson, Aug. 5, 1919. See also *New York Call,* Aug. 5, 1919. For the artisanal democracy concept, see Fraser, "Dress Rehearsal for the New Deal," 215–255.

57. *Daily News Record,* July 31, 1919; *NTW,* Aug. 16, 1919.

58. Hat-band weavers are included in references to ribbon weavers in this section.

59. *Daily News Record,* Aug. 7, 1919; *PPG,* Oct. 13, 1919.

60. *PEN,* Sept. 6, 1919.

61. TWUA Papers, Conference of Independent Unions—Minutes, Box 674. So

strong was the ASW's determination to remain free of all outside influences that it did not even wish to participate in this very loose federation.

62. Westerfield serves as a good example of the type of leader the ribbon weavers wanted. In 1894, he had earned respect for his leadership of the shop strikes and in 1913, ribbon weavers turned to him when they rebuked the IWW. It is no surprise then that when the ASW was formed, he was the first person suggested to lead them. See *Paterson Daily Press*, May 18, 1894; *PEN*, Dec. 2, 1913; *PPG*, Aug. 6, 1919.

63. The statement concerning the lack of Jewish participation is based on a listing of over fifty of the ASW's leaders that appears in National Archives, RG 280, File #170/1729, Report of the Labor Group to the General Conference of the Silk Industry, Jan. 18, 1923. See also Weisbord, *Passaic Reviewed*, 12.

64. Paterson Public Library, Constitution and By-Laws of the Associated Silk Workers.

65. For the revolt against the AFL's Boot and Shoe Workers Union, see Thomas Norton, *Trade Union Politics in Massachusetts*, (New York, 1932).

66. Fogelson, "They Paved the Streets with Silk," 142–147; National Archives, RG 280, File #170/1682, William Liller to Hugh Kerwin, 18 March 1922, File #170/1727, The Martyred Workers of Paterson, July 11, 1923.

67. *NTW*, Sept. 3, 1921.

10. Conclusion:
The Locals' Failure

1. My comments here are restricted to Roman Catholic Slovaks and to Galician Poles. Further investigation may demonstrate that Russian Poles, as in Lawrence, and Slovak Lutherans (not present in Passaic) had a different perspective.

2. For the Bishop's Program of Social Reconstruction, see Mel Piehl, *Breaking Bread: The Catholic Worker and the Origin of Catholic Radicalism in America* (Philadelphia, 1982), 37.

3. In many of these groups, women may have remained more attached to the church than men but this aspect goes beyond the purview of this study.

4. Albert Weisbord learned the importance of the local context the hard way since in 1926 he had believed that he could pull Paterson and Lawrence workers out in support of those in Passaic. See *Textile Strike Bulletin* (Passaic), May 28, June 25, 1926; Weisbord, *Passaic Reviewed*, 31.

5. Other factors besides the reliance on local leadership enabled the locals to survive. All of these communities had relatively homogeneous populations and small mills that proved somewhat easier to organize. In addition, none of them had the left sectarian divisions of Paterson or Lawrence. See *NTW*, 1919–1924.

6. Hentoff, ed. *Essays of Muste*, 79–80; Harold Rotzel, "Pacifism in the Labor Field," *The World Tomorrow* 11 (March 1926): 82.
7. Cedric Long, "The Consumer as Revolutionist," *The World Tomorrow* 4 (November 1921): 334–336.
8. *Paterson Textile Worker*, November 1919.
9. Blanshard, *Personal and Controversial*, 65–66; Siegal, "The Passaic Textile Strike of 1926," 149; Hentoff, ed. *Essays of Muste*, 78–83.
10. Capraro Papers, Muste to Capraro, 17 January 1920, Box 2.
11. See Hentoff, ed. *Essays of Muste*, 55–83.
12. George Soule, *The Intellectual and the Union* (New York, 1923).
13. Alice Kimball, "In the Silk," *The World Tomorrow* 6 (January 1923): 50–51. See also Louisa Kimball, "As a Winder Sees It," *The World Tomorrow* 5 (December 1922): 360–361.
14. Martha Glasser, "Paterson 1924: The ACLU and Labor," *New Jersey History* 94 (Winter 1976), 155–172; Shriver, *A Pioneering Study of the Silkworkers of Paterson*, 28.
15. William Z. Foster, "What Ails American Radicalism," *Socialist Review* 10 (April–May 1921): 36–40.
16. Muste, *The Organization of the Textile Industry*, 26–27.

Selected Bibliography

Material in the National Archives, Washington, D.C.

Records of the Department of Justice, Bureau of Investigation, 1908–1922. Record Group (RG) 65.
Records of the Department of Labor. RG 174.
Records of the Federal Mediation and Conciliation Service. RG 280.
Records of the National War Labor Board (World War I). RG 2.
Records of the Alien Property Custodian. RG 131.
Post Office Department. General File, 1897–1928. RG 280.
Records of the War Department. General Staff, Military Intelligence Division, 1917–1941. RG 165.

Other Manuscript Collections

Records of the Amalgamated Clothing and Textile Union. Labor Management Documentation Center, Cornell University, Ithaca, N.Y.
The American Civil Liberties Union Papers. Microfilm Copy. New York Public Library.

Frederick Augustus Blossom Papers. The State Historical Society of Wisconsin, Madison, Wis.

Anthony Capraro Papers. Immigration History Research Center, University of Minnesota, St. Paul, Minn.

Archives of the Diocese of Paterson, Clifton, N.J.

Elizabeth Glendower Evans Papers. Schlessinger Library. Radcliffe College, Cambridge, Mass.

Immigrant City Archives, Lawrence, Mass.

Benjamin Legere Papers. Archives of Labor and Urban Affairs, Wayne State University, Detroit, Mich.

Lusk Papers. Investigations—Labor Movement. Microfilm Copy. Tamiment Institute, New York University, New York, N.Y.

Papers of the Massachusetts Consumers' League. Schlessinger Library, Radcliffe College, Cambridge, Mass.

Museum of American Textile History, North Andover, Mass.

Records of the National Association of Wool Manufacturers.

Scrapbook on Paterson Silkworkers and ATWA (#20). Tamiment Institute, New York, N.Y.

Matilda Robbins Papers. Archives of Labor and Urban History, Wayne State University, Detroit, Mich.

David Saposs Papers. The State Historical Society of Wisconsin, Madison, Wis.

Records of the Socialist Labor Party of America, 1890, 1893–1920, and Socialist Labor Party Papers, 1974 accession. The State Historical Society of Wisconsin, Madison, Wis.

Papers of the Textile Workers Union of America. State Historical Society of Wisconsin, Madison, Wis.

Norman Thomas Papers. New York Public Library, New York, N.Y.

Mary Heaton Vorse Papers. Archives of Labor and Urban Affairs, Wayne State University, Detroit, Mich.

Minutes of the Meetings, National Executive, Workmen's Circle. YIVO Archives, New York, N.Y.

Labor and Radical Newspapers and Magazines

Advance. 1918–1920.
The Forward. 1918–1919.
Industrial Union News. 1912–1919.
Lawrence Labor. 1922–1923.
New Solidarity. 1919–1920.
New Textile Worker. 1919–1924.
New York Call. 1912–1919.
Rebel Worker. 1919–1920.
Revolutionary Age. 1918–1919.

Solidarity. 1913–1917.
Textile Strike Bulletin (Passaic). 1926.
The Textile Worker, 1916, 1918–1926.
The World Tomorrow. 1918–1926.
Young Democracy. 1918–1919.

Local Newspapers

Lawrence Evening Tribune
Lawrence Sun American
Lawrence Telegram
Passaic Daily Herald
Passaic Daily News
Paterson Evening News
Paterson Press Guardian

Business Publications

A. W. Employees Booster, 1919–1924.
The American Silk Journal, 1912–1920.
American Wool and Cotton Reporter, 1917–1918.
Bulletin of the National Association of Wool Manufacturers, 1908–1924.
Daily News Record, 1918–1921.

Secondary Sources

Abramson, Harold J. *Ethnic Diversity in Catholic America.* New York, 1973.
"American Woolen Company." *Fortune* 3 (April 1931): 71–112.
Altarelli, Carlo C. "History and Present Condition of the Italian Colony of Pater-
    son, N.J." Master's Thesis, Columbia University, 1911.
Beal, Fred. *Proletarian Journey.* 1937. Reprint, New York, 1971.
Bercuson, David Jay. *Fools and Wise Men, The Rise and Fall of the One Big Union.*
    Toronto, 1976.
Berthoff, Rowland. *British Immigrants in Industrial America.* Cambridge, Mass.
    1953.
Bing, Alexander. *War Time Strikes and Their Adjustment.* New York, 1921.
Blanshard, Paul. *Personal and Controversial.* Boston, 1971.
Bodnar, John. *Immigration and Industrialization.* Pittsburgh, 1977.
———. *Workers' World.* Baltimore, 1982.
Borkenau, Franz. *World Communism.* Ann Arbor, 1962.
Brody, David. *Steelworkers in America.* 1960. Reprint, New York, 1969.

Selected Bibliography

Brooks, Robert R. R. "The United Textile Workers of America." Ph.D. diss., Yale University, 1935.

Budish, J. M., and Soule, George. *The New Unionism in the Clothing Industry.* 1920. Reprint, New York, 1968.

Buhle, Paul. "Debsian Socialism and the 'New Immigrant' Worker." In *Insights and Parallels,* edited by William O'Neill, 249–303. Minneapolis, 1973.

Bukowczyk, John J. "Mary the Messiah: Polish Immigrant Heresy and the Malleable Ideology of the Roman Catholic Church, 1880–1930." *Journal of American Ethnic History* 4 (Spring 1985): 5–32.

Cameron, Ardis. "Bread and Roses Revisited: Women's Culture and Working-Class Activism in the Lawrence Strike of 1912." In *Women, Work and Protest,* edited by Ruth Milkman, 42–61. Boston, 1985.

Chatfield, Charles. *For Peace and Justice: Pacifism in America, 1914–1940.* Knoxville, Tennessee, 1971.

Cole, Arthur Harrison. *The American Wool Manufacture.* vol. 2. Cambridge, Mass., 1926.

Cole, Donald. *Immigrant City, Lawrence Massachusetts, 1845–1921.* Chapel Hill, N.C., 1963.

Conner, Valerie. *The National War Labor Board.* Chapel Hill, N.C., 1983.

Cumbler, John T. *Working Class Community in Industrial America: Work, Leisure and Struggle in Two Industrial Cities, 1880–1930.* Westport, Conn., 1979.

Davis, Jessie. "My Vacation in a Woolen Mill." *The Survey* 40 (August 10, 1918): 538–541.

DeLeon, Solon. *The American Labor Who's Who.* New York, 1925.

De Lima, Agnes. *Night Working Mothers in Textile Mills—Passaic, New Jersey.* New York, 1920.

Documentary History of the Amalgamated Clothing Workers of America, 1918–1920. New York, 1920.

Draper, Theodore. *The Roots of American Communism.* New York, 1957.

Dubofsky, Melvyn. *We Shall Be All.* Chicago, 1969.

Dunn, Robert W. *Company Unions.* New York, 1927.

Dutton Savage, Marion. *Industrial Unionism in America.* New York, 1922.

Ebert, Justus. *The Trial of a New Society.* Cleveland, 1913.

Ebner, Michael. "Passaic, New Jersey, 1855–1912, City Building in Post Civil War America." Ph.D. diss., University of Virginia, 1974.

———. "The Passaic Strike of 1912 and the Two IWW's." *Labor History* 11 (Fall 1970): 452–466.

———. "Socialism and Progressive Political Reform: The 1911 Change of Government in Passaic." In *Socialism and the Cities,* edited by Bruce Stave, 117–140. Port Washington, N.Y., 1975.

———. "Strikes and Society: Civil Behavior in Passaic, 1875–1926." *New Jersey History* 97 (Spring 1979): 7–24.

Fenton, Edwin. *Immigrants and Unions, A Case Study, Italians and American Labor, 1870–1920.* New York, 1975.

Fitch, John A. "Lawrence—A Strike for Wages or for Bolshevism?" *The Survey* 42 (April 5, 1919): 42–46.

Flynn, Elizabeth Gurley. *The Rebel Girl.* 1955. Reprint, New York, 1986.

Flynn, Elizabeth Gurley. "The Truth about the Paterson Strike." In *Rebel Voices: An IWW Anthology,* edited by Joyce Kornbluh, Ann Arbor, 1964.

Ford, James. "The Cooperative Franco-Belge of Lawrence." *The Survey* 37 (April 6, 1912): 68–70.

Foster, William Z. "What Ails American Radicalism." *Socialist Review* 10 (April–May 1921): 36–40.

Fraser, Steve. "Dress Rehearsal for the New Deal. Shop Floor Insurgents, Political Elites, and Industrial Democracy in the Amalgamated Clothing Workers." In *Working Class America,* edited by Michael Frisch and Daniel J. Walkowitz, 212–255. Urbana, 1983.

Friedlander, Peter. *The Emergence of a UAW Local, 1936–1939, A Study in Class and Culture.* Pittsburgh, 1975.

Gabaccia, Donna. "Neither Padrone Slaves nor Primitive Rebels: Sicilians on Two Continents." In *"Struggle a Hard Battle": Essays on Working-Class Immigrants,* edited by Dirk Hoerder, 95–120. DeKalb, Illinois, 1986.

Greene, Victor. *For God and Country: The Rise of Polish and Lithuanian Ethnic Consciousness in America, 1860–1910.* Madison, Wis., 1975.

———. *The Slavic Community on Strike: Immigrant Labor in Pennsylvania Anthracite.* Notre Dame, Ind., 1968.

Hanko, Arnold. "Passaic, The Passing of an Idyll." *The American Mercury* 20 (June 1930): 228–235.

Hareven, Tamara K. *Family Time and Industrial Time.* New York, 1982.

———. "Family Time and Industrial Time: Family and Work in a Planned Corporation Town, 1900–1924." *Journal of Urban History* (May 1975): 365–389.

———. "The Laborers of Manchester, New Hampshire: The Role of Family and Ethnicity in Adjustment to Industrial Life." *Labor History* 16 (Spring 1975): 249–265.

Hentoff, Nat, ed. *The Essays of A. J. Muste.* New York, 1970.

Hess, Fjeril. *Handkerchief Holiday.* New York, 1942.

Heusser, Albert H. *The History of the Silk Dyeing Industry in the United States.* Paterson, 1927.

Josephson, Matthew. *Sidney Hillman: Statesman of American Labor.* New York, 1952.

Karson, Marc. *American Labor Unions and Politics 1900–1918.* 1958. Reprint, Boston, 1965.

Kelley, Florence. "Wage Earning Women in War Time: The Textile Industry." *Journal of Industrial Hygiene* 1 (October 1919): 261–273.

Kelly, Richard. *Nine Lives for Labor.* New York, 1956.

Kennedy, David M. *Over Here: The First World War and American Society.* New York, 1980.

Kimball, Alice. "In the Silk." *The World Tomorrow* 6 (January 1923): 50–51.

Kimball, Louisa. "As a Winder Sees It." *The World Tomorrow* 5 (December 1922): 360–361.

Kornbluh, Joyce, ed. *Rebel Voices: An IWW Anthology.* Ann Arbor, 1964.

Laurie, Bruce. *Working People of Philadelphia, 1800–1850.* Philadelphia, 1980.

Leinenweber, Charles. "The American Socialist Party and the New Immigrants." *Science and Society* 32 (Winter 1968): 1–25.

———. "Socialists in the Streets: The New York City Socialist Party in Working Class Neighborhoods, 1908–1918." *Science and Society* 41 (Summer 1977): 152–171.

Leiserson, William M. *Adjusting Immigrant and Industry.* 1924. Reprint, New York, 1969.

Liebman, Arthur. *Jews and the Left.* New York, 1979.

Marchand, C. Roland. *The American Peace Movement and Social Reform.* Princeton, 1972.

Matsui, Shichiro. *The History of the Silk Industry in the United States.* New York, 1930.

McCormick, A. Ross. *Reformers, Rebels and Revolutionaries: The Western Canadian Radical Movement 1899–1919.* Toronto, 1977.

McCreesh, Carolyn Daniel. *Women in the Campaign to Organize Garment Workers, 1880–1917.* New York, 1983.

Mendelsohn, Ezra. *Class Struggles in the Pale.* Cambridge, England, 1970.

Merwick, Donna. *Boston Priests, 1848–1910: A Study of Social and Intellectual Change.* Cambridge, Mass., 1973.

Montgomery, David. *The Fall of the House of Labor.* New York, 1987.

———. *Workers' Control in America.* New York, 1979.

Morawska, Ewa. *For Bread with Butter, The Life-Worlds of East Central Europeans in Johnstown, Pennsylvania.* New York, 1985.

Osborne, James D. "Industrialization and the Politics of Disorder: Paterson Silk-workers, 1880–1913." Ph.D. diss., University of Warwick, 1980.

Park, Robert E. *The Immigrant Press and its Control.* New York, 1922.

Parot, Joseph John. *Polish Catholics in Chicago, 1850–1920.* DeKalb, Illinois, 1981.

Pernicone, Nunzio. "Carlo Tresca and the Sacco-Vanzetti Case." *Journal of American History* 66 (December 1979): 535–547.

Peterson, Larry. "The One Big Union in International Perspective: Revolutionary Industrial Unionism, 1900–1925." In *Work, Community and Power: The Experience of Labor in Europe and America, 1900–1925,* edited by James E. Cronin and Carmen Sirianni, 49–87. Philadelphia, 1983.

Pickering, Ruth. "The Lawrence Strike." *The Liberator* 2 (May 1919): 35–36.

Puskas, Juliana. *From Hungary to the United States.* Budapest, 1982.

Quinlan, Patrick L. "The Paterson Strike and After." *New Review* 2 (January 1914): 26–33.

Renshaw, Patrick. *The Wobblies: The Story of Syndicalism in the United States.* Garden City, N.Y., 1968.

Roddy, Edward G. *Mills, Mansions and Mergers: The Life of William M. Wood.* North Andover, Mass., 1982.

Rosenblum, Gerald. *Immigrant Workers: Their Impact on American Labor Radicalism.* New York, 1973.

Russell, Phillips. "The Second Battle of Lawrence." *International Socialist Review* 12 (November 1912): 417–422.

Sanville, Florence L. "Silk Workers in Pennsylvania and New Jersey." *The Survey* 28 (May 18, 1912): 307–312.

Schatz, Ronald W. *The Electrical Workers.* Urbana, Ill., 1983.

Schrom Dye, Nancy. *As Equals and As Sisters: Feminism, Unionism and the Women's Trade Union League of New York.* Columbia, Mo., 1980.

Scranton, Phillip, ed. *Silk City: Studies on the Paterson Silk Industry, 1860–1940.* Newark, N.J., 1985.

Shapiro, Stanley. "The Great Reform: Liberals and Labor, 1917–1919." *Labor History* 12 (Summer 1971): 323–344.

Shellabarger, Eloise. "The Shawled Women of Passaic." *The Survey* 44 (July 3, 1920): 463–468.

Shergold, Peter R. *The "American Standard of Living" in Comparative Perspective, 1889–1913.* Pittsburgh, 1982.

Siegal, Morton. "The Passaic Textile Strike of 1926." Ph.D. diss., Columbia University, 1952.

Simon, Jean-Claude G. "Textile Workers, Trade Unions and Politics: Comparative Case Studies, France and the United States, 1885–1914." Ph.D. diss., Tufts University, 1980.

Singer, I. J. *The Brothers Ashkenazi.* 1936. Reprint, New York, 1980.

Stolarik, M. Mark. "Immigration and Urbanization: The Slovak Experience, 1870–1918." Ph.D. diss., University of Minnesota, 1974.

Sumner, Mary Brown. "Broad Silk Weavers of Paterson." *The Survey* 27 (March 16, 1912): 1932–1935.

Vassady, Béla. "The Homeland Cause as Stimulant to Ethnic Unity; The Hungarian American Response to Károlyi's 1914 Tour." *Journal of American Ethnic History* 2 (Fall 1982): 39–64.

Vecoli, Rudolph J. "Anthony Capraro and the Lawrence Strike of 1919." In *Pane E Lavoro—the Italian American Working Class—Proceedings of the American Italian Historical Association, Cleveland, Ohio, October 27, 28, 1978,* edited by George E. Pozetta, 3–27. Toronto, 1978.

———. *The People of New Jersey.* New York, 1965.

———. "Prelates and Peasants: Italian Immigrants and the Catholic Church." *Journal of Social History* 2 (Spring 1969): 217–268.

Walkowitz, Daniel J. *Worker City, Company Town: Iron and Cotton Worker Protest in Troy and Cohoes, New York, 1855–1884.* Urbana, Ill., 1978.

Wolfson, Theresa. *The Woman Worker and the Trade Unions.* New York, 1926.

Wolkovich, William. *Bay State "Blue" Laws and Bimba.* Brockton, Mass., 1973.

Wood, James E. "History of Labor in the Broad Silk Industry of Paterson, New Jersey, 1872–1940." Ph.D. diss., University of California, 1941.

Index

269

Index